Ambient Intelligence Services in IoT Environments:

Emerging Research and Opportunities

Dmitry Korzun
Petrozavodsk State University (PetrSU), Russia

Ekaterina Balandina
Tampere University of Technology (TUT), Finland

Alexey Kashevnik
St. Petersburg Institute for Informatics and Automation of the Russian Academy of Sciences (SPIIRAS), Russia

Sergey Balandin
FRUCT Oy, Finland

Fabio Viola
University of Bologna, Italy

A volume in the Advances in Wireless Technologies and Telecommunication (AWTT) Book Series

Published in the United States of America by
IGI Global
Engineering Science Reference (an imprint of IGI Global)
701 E. Chocolate Avenue
Hershey PA, USA 17033
Tel: 717-533-8845
Fax: 717-533-8661
E-mail: cust@igi-global.com
Web site: http://www.igi-global.com

Library of Congress Cataloging-in-Publication Data

Names: Korzun, Dmitry, author.
Title: Ambient intelligence services in IoT environments : emerging research and opportunities / by Dmitry Korzun, Ekaterina Balandina, Alexey Kashevnik, Sergey Balandin, and Fabio Viola.
Description: Hershey, PA : Engineering Science Reference, an imprint of IGI Global, [2019] | Includes bibliographical references and index.
Identifiers: LCCN 2019006767| ISBN 9781522589730 (hardcover) | ISBN 9781522596912 (softcover) | ISBN 9781522589747 (ebook)
Subjects: LCSH: Ambient intelligence.
Classification: LCC QA76.9.A48 K67 2019 | DDC 004.01/9--dc23 LC record available at https://lccn.loc.gov/2019006767

This book is published in the IGI Global book series Advances in Wireless Technologies and Telecommunication (AWTT) (ISSN: 2327-3305; eISSN: 2327-3313)

British Cataloguing in Publication Data
A Cataloguing in Publication record for this book is available from the British Library.

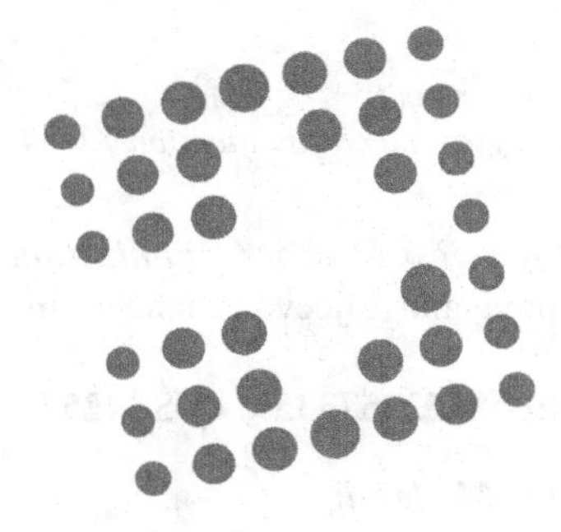

Advances in Wireless Technologies and Telecommunication (AWTT) Book Series

ISSN:2327-3305
EISSN:2327-3313

Editor-in-Chief: Xiaoge Xu, University of Nottingham Ningbo China, China

MISSION

The wireless computing industry is constantly evolving, redesigning the ways in which individuals share information. Wireless technology and telecommunication remain one of the most important technologies in business organizations. The utilization of these technologies has enhanced business efficiency by enabling dynamic resources in all aspects of society.

The **Advances in Wireless Technologies and Telecommunication Book Series** aims to provide researchers and academic communities with quality research on the concepts and developments in the wireless technology fields. Developers, engineers, students, research strategists, and IT managers will find this series useful to gain insight into next generation wireless technologies and telecommunication.

COVERAGE

- Wireless Technologies
- Global Telecommunications
- Telecommunications
- Mobile Web Services
- Radio Communication
- Cellular Networks
- Wireless Sensor Networks
- Broadcasting
- Wireless Broadband
- Digital Communication

The Advances in Wireless Technologies and Telecommunication (AWTT) Book Series (ISSN 2327-3305) is published by IGI Global, 701 E. Chocolate Avenue, Hershey, PA 17033-1240, USA, www.igi-global.com. This series is composed of titles available for purchase individually; each title is edited to be contextually exclusive from any other title within the series. For pricing and ordering information please visit http://www.igi-global.com/book-series/advances-wireless-technologies-telecommunication/73684. Postmaster: Send all address changes to above address.

Titles in this Series

For a list of additional titles in this series, please visit:
https://www.igi-global.com/book-series/advances-wireless-technologies-telecommunication/73684

Handbook of Research on the IoT, Cloud Computing, and Wireless Network Opimization
Surjit Singh (National Institute of Technology Kurukshetra, India) and Rajeev Mohan Sharma (National Institute of Technology Kurukshetra, India)
Engineering Science Reference • ©2019 • 563pp • H/C (ISBN: 9781522573357) • US $425.00

Recent Advances in Satellite Aeronautical Communications Modeling
Andrii Mikhailovich Grekhov (National Aviation University, Ukraine)
Engineering Science Reference • ©2019 • 313pp • H/C (ISBN: 9781522582144) • US $225.00

Strategic Innovations and Interdisciplinary Perspectives in Telecommunications and Networking
Natarajan Meghanathan (Jackson State University, USA)
Information Science Reference • ©2019 • 348pp • H/C (ISBN: 9781522581888) • US $195.00

Next-Generation Wireless Networks Meet Advanced Machine Learning Applications
Ioan-Sorin Comşa (Brunel University London, UK) and Ramona Trestian (Middlesex University, UK)
Information Science Reference • ©2019 • 356pp • H/C (ISBN: 9781522574583) • US $195.00

Paving the Way for 5G Through the Convergence of Wireless Systems
Ramona Trestian (Middlesex University, UK) and Gabriel-Miro Muntean (Dublin City University, Ireland)
Information Science Reference • ©2019 • 350pp • H/C (ISBN: 9781522575702) • US $195.00

Enabling Technologies and Architectures for Next-Generation Networking Capabilities
Mahmoud Elkhodr (Central Queensland University, Australia)
Information Science Reference • ©2019 • 384pp • H/C (ISBN: 9781522560234) • US $195.00

For an entire list of titles in this series, please visit:
https://www.igi-global.com/book-series/advances-wireless-technologies-telecommunication/73684

701 East Chocolate Avenue, Hershey, PA 17033, USA
Tel: 717-533-8845 x100 • Fax: 717-533-8661
E-Mail: cust@igi-global.com • www.igi-global.com

Table of Contents

Foreword

Smartness everywhere at any time drives a major transformation in the surrounding world from Information Age to the Intelligence Age. The new generation of services in the Intelligence Age will be enabled by autonomous communication between intelligent (or smart) devices. Such a device can provide services that are sensitive to people (e.g., user's presence, other person's context and personal needs). Such services can support various aspects of digital assistance for users' needs at work or everyday life. In this perspective, the Internet of Things (IoT) is growing fast into a large industry with the huge potential economic impact expected in near future. The IoT technology evolves to a substrate for resource interconnection and convergence. The users' needs go beyond the existing web-like services, which do not provide satisfactory intelligence level, e.g., personalization, proactive delivery, coupling, and automatic composition when the user tries to solve her/his current tasks.

Ambient Intelligence (AmI) services in IoT environments are an emerging research and development area. The AmI paradigm is going to change the way that technology and services are perceived by the users. The devices become smaller, all time connected, and more integrated into the environment. The technology gradually disappears into the people surroundings until only the user interface remains perceivable by the users. This book considers development of AmI services based on the Smart Spaces approach for IoT. A smart space is deployed in an IoT environment, creating an infrastructure to develop advanced applications that construct and deliver value-added services based on cooperative activity of environment participants, either human or machines.

To illustrate the potential architectural capabilities of the Smart Spaces, the authors show a few examples on Smart-M3 and other smart spaces prototype platforms. The selected platforms create the ontology-based smart spaces, which allow to illustrate shifting of service development process towards development of Web of Things applications and Socio-Cyber-Physical (SCP) systems. Moreover, the provided examples of platform are open source.

The book is primary based on authors' own contributions. Nevertheless, the authors are not just recording their research and vision; they are honouring all the past research and setting out the future. As a result this book forms an original expert view on the emerging generation of digital services that opens AmI opportunities to the users in IoT environments.

Andrei Gurtov
Linkoping University, Sweden
June 2019

Preface

Now the information and communication technology and Internet moves the Information Age to the Intelligence Age. The Intelligence Age needs autonomous communication between intelligent (or smart) devices. Such a device provides services that are sensitive to people (e.g., user's presence, other person's context and personal needs). Services digitally support our tasks during our work or everyday life. In this perspective, the Internet of Things (IoT) is growing fast into a large industry with huge potential economic impact expected in near future. The IoT technology evolves to a substrate for resource interconnection and convergence. The users' needs go beyond the existing web-like services, which do not provide satisfactory intelligence level, e.g., coupling and automatic composition when the user tries to solve her/his current tasks. Ambient Intelligence (AmI) services in IoT environments is an emerging research and development area. AmI is going to change the way that technology and services are perceived by the users: as devices become smaller, more connected, and more integrated into the environment, the technology gradually disappears into the surroundings until only the user interface remains perceivable by users. This book considers development of AmI services based on the smart spaces approach. A smart space is deployed in an IoT environment, creating an infrastructure to develop various applications that construct and deliver value-added services based on cooperative activity of environment participants, either human or machines. Our particular focus is on the Smart-M3 platform, which is now shaping into an open source technology for creating ontology-based smart spaces and its shifting towards development of Web of Things applications and Socio-Cyber-Physical systems.

While many publications in the field of Ambient Intelligence, Internet of Things, Web of Things, Cyber-Physical Systems, Smart Environments, and Smart Services are available, there is no reference book where the latest technological aspects for the application development are systematized. The proposed book is to a large extent based on authors' own contributions as well as diligent survey of existing work in this area. We try to select the most important achievements of the Smart-M3 platform from the open source research and development community.

The main goal of the book is to systemize recent trends and advances for service development with such key technological enablers of modern ICT as AmI, IoT, WoT, and CPS. The considered concepts and models are presented using a reference technology suit for creating smart spaces - the Smart-M3 platform and its evolution towards Web of Things applications and Socio-Cyber-Physical systems. The reference case studies are borrowed from authors' own research and development. The book will be extensively illustrated by examples and case studies to help the understanding as well as include an extensive list of references on recent publications. The material exposition of this book is organized as follows.

Chapter 1 makes introduction providing recent review of methods in AmI, IoT, WoT, and CPS. The chapter shows our roadmap for selected hot research topics in the multi-disciplinary filed.

Chapter 2 reviews several case studies that illustrate opportunities and discuss design details of the smart services development. The chapter provides definition of the key enables of the service smartness, e.g., role of location-awareness, design principles of smart services, etc. Then the discussion on provided definitions and presented enables is supported by presentation of a few use case examples for e-Tourism and e-Healthcare scenarios. Generally, the chapter is targeted to clearly ground the book scope to the real-life use cases.

Chapter 3 introduces advances in fog computing technology for involving various participants - either small or large in capacity, either local or remote - into the service construction. Non-typical computational devices (compared with traditional computers, e.g., laptops, desktops, servers) - such as smartphones, wireless routers, multimedia equipment, and consumer electronics - become aware of information processing in order to construct services essentially based on local resources of the IoT environment.

Chapter 4 discusses the profiling and personalization approach in IoT environments. The section covers topics related to the user profiling that is aimed to keeping information about the user and use it for personalization of the services delivery to him/her. A participant competence profile is aimed to interaction automation between participants for joint service construction.

Ontology-based cauterization method is aimed at grouping users by their interests based on their previous interaction with IoT environment. Such grouping allows to identify new interests of the users and enhance the service delivery process in IoT.

Chapter 5 shows the role of semantic methods in delivering AmI. The smart spaces paradigm applies ontological modeling for representing available IoT resources as shared information. This way, resources are virtualized by local information hubs, which are deployed on existing devices. The virtualization benefits from semantics since relations between resources are also represented, forming a semantic network. In turn, various ranking models can be implemented for information search and knowledge reasoning, e.g., based on such well-known algorithms as PageRank. The structural properties of the semantic network leads to advanced AmI support for constructing proactive services: discovery of certain structures (e.g., cycles) can be interpreted as formation of specific knowledge that initiates service construction and delivery.

Chapter 6 considers semantic interaction issues in IoT environments. Ambient intelligence concept assumes that surrounding devices interact with each other for providing together services to the people. For this purpose, the devices should cooperate and create coalition for joint activities and service provision. Semantic interoperability support allows the devices to understand each other for the services provision. Context model formalize the current situation in the environment and provides possibilities to take it into account for service provision.

Chapter 7 focuses on the evolution of the Smart-M3 platform toward WoS applications, through the adoption of web standards and the definition of proper mechanisms to easily integrate smart devices into web applications. To achieve the result the design of a proper ontology and a control framework is of paramount importance and will be the core of all the practical examples in this chapter.

We expect that the Internet of Things can be seen as one of the most promising technologies for delivering ambient intelligence. This book is primary focus on solutions that use IoT as a technological ground of delivering innovative use cases. Another specifically addressed technology in the book is fog computing technology that allows building solutions involving various module, e.g., small/large in capacity, local/remote in location, etc. As a result, all available computational devices (not only traditional computer systems), e.g., smartphones, wireless routers, multimedia equipment, and consumer electronics, become aware of information processing in order to construct services essentially based on local resources of the IoT environment.

We address issues related to user personification and resources competence modeling in IoT environments. It is important to mention that personification is not limited by UI preferences, but it influence all aspects of UX and even more importantly – it affects the way how information is handled and processed. Here we target to maximum emulate the way humans processing information from own viewpoint and current context. At the same time a critical feature of the automated data processing is in more objective processing data, which allow to avoid traditional problem of human analysis when some important part of the information due to personal dislike are not even processed to analysis phase. The obtained results should be presented to the user in according to his/her preferences from the user profile model. Resource competence profile should store information about the resource competencies and constraints that have to be satisfied to enable these competences. Also, we see a lot of potential in use of semantic methods for Data Mining in Smart Spaces. This is more generic type of solution for enabling AmI, but it is extremely relevant for IoT environments.

A key point of service construction and delivery is support of semantic interaction for Internet of Things (IoT) resources. Semantic interoperability between interacted resources ensures that they can talk to each other. One of the possible approaches to enrich the semantic interoperability is the ontology modeling. The ontology formally represents knowledge as a set of concepts within a domain, using a shared vocabulary to denote the types, properties, and interrelationships of those concepts. Based on the ontology matching techniques, resource ontologies are matched and resources operate in according to this matching. Context is any information that can be used to characterize the situation of an entity. An entity in the considered case is the resource of IoT environment. It is proposed to use the ontologies to describe the context of resource and take this information for task performing. For the service construction it is needed to create the coalitions of resources that can jointly provide the needed service for the user task performing.

Finally, the book discusses an emerging area of solutions based on the Web of Things. The Web of Things (WoT) is a recent research area that addresses the challenges to interoperability posed by the Internet of Things (IoT) through the use of Web Standards. In the book we particularly focus on possible evolution of the Smart Spaces paradigm toward the Web of Things.

Acknowledgment

The scientific content of this book is primarily composed of the research results that have been developed within concurrent activity of the following projects, which are financially supported by the Ministry of Science and Higher Education of the Russian Federation, Russian Science Foundation (RSF), and by the Russian Fund for Basic Research (RFBR). (The projects are listed in chronological order.)

Project no. 16-29-04349 Theoretical and technological foundations for ontology-oriented mobile robots interaction in dynamically formed hybrid coalitions, from RFBR for 2016-2018 (implementing organization: ITMO University).

Project no. 16-29-12866 Theoretical and technological foundations for context-oriented collective interaction of scientific and technological expert networks participants during innovation formation, from RFBR for 2016-2018 (implementing organization: ITMO University).

Project no. 2.5124.2017/8.9 Modeling and Programming Fundamentals of Information-Driven Interaction in Socio-Cyber-Physical Systems for Internet of Things and Big Data, from the basic part of state research assignment for 2017-2019 (implementing organization: PetrSU).

Project no. 18-71-10065 Models and methods for intelligent driver support based on situation in vehicle cabin, from RSF for 2018-2020 (implementing organization: ITMO University).

Project no. 19-07-00670 Ontology-oriented competence management models for intelligent decision support of user groups, from RFBR for 2018-2020 (implementing organization: SPIIRAS).

Project no. 19-07-01027 Semantic methods of smart spaces for ranking resources in mobile edge Internet networks, from RFBR for 2019-2021 (implementation organization: PetrSU).

Project no. 0073-2019-0005 Development of the theoretical and technological foundations for intelligent services, multi-modal interfaces, and infocommunication platforms aimed at human-computer interaction in cyber-physical-social systems, from Russian State Research for 2019-2021 (implementing organization: SPIIRAS).

Chapter 1

Introduction to Ambient Intelligence in Internet of Things Environments and Cyber-Physical Systems

ABSTRACT

This chapter discusses current role and future prospects of ambient intelligence in development of applications for the internet of things environments. The authors provide an introduction to the field of ambient intelligence and specifically discuss what makes it so important to be a core element of cyber-physical systems. The main focus of the chapter is on providing analysis and the reasoning for development of smart spaces and delivering ambient intelligence to internet of things environments. The chapter provides definition and overview of recent trends and advances for service development with all identified key technological enablers of modern info-communication technologies, including data mining, big data analysis, recommendation systems, and so on. The main messages of the chapter are summarized by the conclusion section.

DOI: 10.4018/978-1-5225-8973-0.ch001

INTRODUCTION

The recent trend in service industry is shift of users' interest and preferences towards the context-aware, situational, and personalized services. The Ambient Intelligence defines principles of interworking for all devices that surround the user and so creating proactively-responsive user-friendly environment. Internet of Things (IoT) is a good example of delivering the Ambient Intelligence to the end users. One can find a lot of works on making digital services intelligent and sensitive to the individual needs of the users as illustrated in the papers of (Cook, Augusto, & Jakkula, 2009) and (Evers, Kniewel, Geihs, & Schmidt, 2014). It is important to ensure to provide such services with the critical volume of the reliable data. But only a few services are able to accumulate the required critical mass of data within scope of their routine operations. One of the most classic problems is that data collected in one service is not accessible from another. As a result of the observable lack of mechanisms for information exchange between the services we have a digital ecosystem with high fragmentation of services and data.

Another key challenge is to organize intelligent use of all available information appropriate for the service in a given context of the user. The direct consequence of this challenge is that the service provision chains become lengthy and, in addition to Internet resources, allow to involve a multitude of heterogeneous IoT devices, services, and users localized in the physical surrounding: various embedded and consumer electronics devices as well as personal equipment that accompanies human.

But before diving into details of Ambient Intelligence and surrounding technologies we want to stress attention of the reader on the general history of progress in information and infocommunication technologies (IT and ICT) that we have seen in the last 40 years. Figure 1 illustrates historical evolution of availability of computing power per person.

Only in a few decades our society shifted from high centralization and deficit of computing power and memory, to extreme distribution and availability/ access to the huge volume of computing power and memory at any place. This change in technology availability fuels shift of user expectation on how friendly shall be our environment and much assistance we are expecting from it.

Internet of Things (IoT) is a paradigm that is under active development for the last 10 years and is still among the most referred and desired topic. IoT is targeted to provide seamless support for internetworking of different devices and sensors using Internet. A number of specific platforms have been

Figure 1. Historical evolution and shift on availability of computing power per person

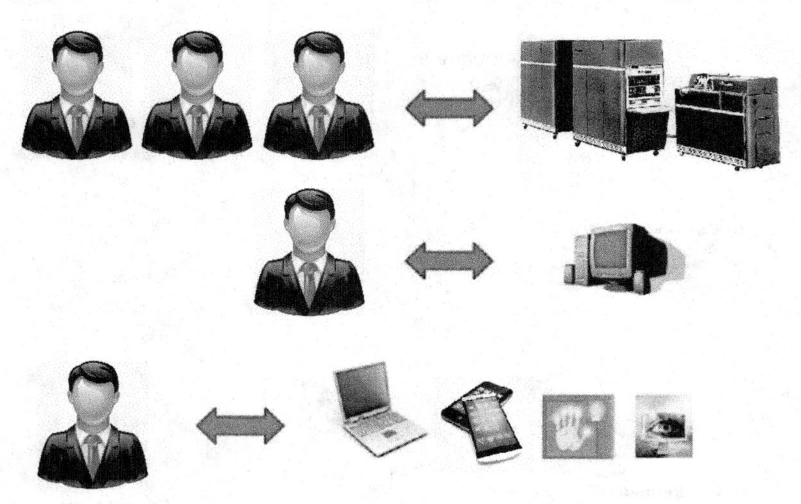

developed to support IoT devices communication, e.g., OpenIoT (Soldatos et al., 2015). The most classic understanding of IoT refers to the connection of physical objects. However, the core of IoT technology is in information interconnection and convergence as discussed in the works of (Atzori, Iera, & Morabito, 2010) and (Wang, Zhu, & Ma, 2013). The IoT work routine is based on continued processing of huge number of data flows, originated by various sources and consumed by multiple applications.

The Ambient Intelligence (AmI) supported by IoT play the key role in development of Intelligent Environments (Augusto, Nakashima, & Aghajan, 2010; Augusto, Callaghan, Cook, Kameas, & Satoh, 2013). Broad deployment of Intelligent Environments will completely change perception of the physical space. The intelligent software agents help to orchestrate all aspects of an environment and so create an interactive holistic functionality that enhances users' experience. The AmI will be one of the key elements of the 4th Industrial Revolution (Trussell, 2018; Winfield et al., 2019).

A simplified but for initial understanding model of human to environment interaction empowered by the Ambient Intelligence services is illustrated by Figure 2. The model puts human into the center of AmI environment. The automatic and accurate tracking of users and their interactions with the environment can be done by an Artificial Intelligence (AI) system. The intelligent agents or robots are used to automate the environment and serve needs of the users.

Figure 2. Human to environment interaction model empowered by Ambient Intelligence

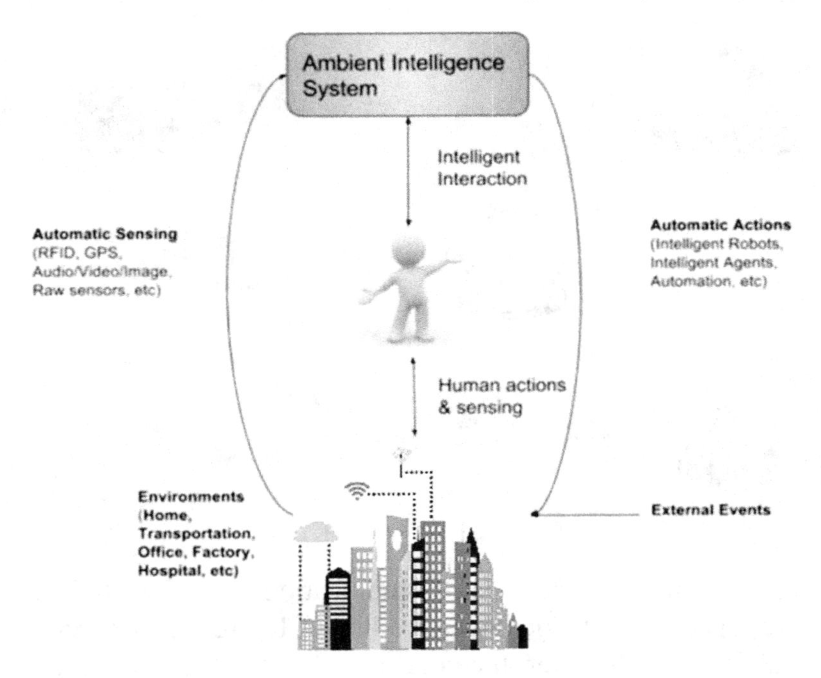

The overall schematic presentation of the AI evolution is illustrated by Figure 3 (Shapiro, Augusto, & Ramos. 2008). We have seen the gradual transformation of AI use scenarios, from applying AI to hardware, e.g., Marvin Minsky and Dean Edmonds' Stochastic Neural Analog Reinforcement Computer, where the neural networks were one of the technologies implemented on the system. The MYCIN expert system is an example for the second phase of computer-center AI use scenario. The American Express's authorizer assistant is an illustration of the 3rd phase of networks-focused AI. The next AI evolution step was related to web, search engines and recommender systems

Figure 3. Ambient Intelligence and evolution of the Artificial Intelligence

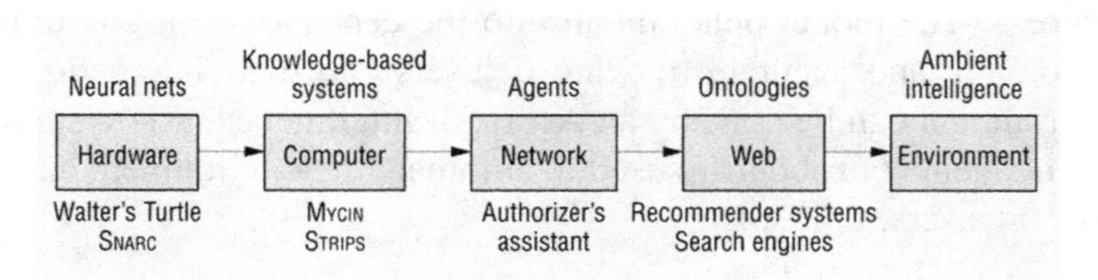

using intelligent agents and ontologies. The Ambient Intelligence is a new application milestone in the evolution of AI.

As was illustrated in (Balandin & Waris, 2009; Smirnov, Kashevnik, Shilov, Boldyrev, Balandin, & Oliver, 2009; Ovaska, Cinotti, & Toninelli, 2012), the smart spaces target to facilitate application development for advanced computing environments, when participating objects acquire and apply knowledge for service construction in order to enhance user experience, quality and reliability of the provided information. The participating objects are represented with a software agent. The latter is an autonomous information processing unit, which is not necessarily attached to a device. Services are constructed by agents interacting on shared information, i.e., the interaction is indirect, in contrast to the communication level provided by the IoT technology.

Ambient Intelligence primarily aims at making IoT environments that support the people inhabiting them (Acampora, Cook, Rashidi, & Vasilakos, 2013). In Cyber-Physical Systems (CPS), the IoT technology enables fusion of real (physical) and virtual (information) worlds (Korzun, Nikolaevskiy, & Gurtov, 2015). Based on data fusion, advanced solutions for service intelligence can be constructed to achieve such properties as service adaptation, personalization, and proactive delivery. Dynamic relation of multi-source data forms a smart space (Korzun, Nikolaevskiy, & Gurtov, 2013). It supports semantics-based analysis of collected data and derived knowledge directly in this space. In particular, the smart space approach allows feeding health services with non-medical data (Korzun, 2017), and enhanced health applications are enabled, which are not based purely on electronic health records (Mandl et al., 2012).

The rest of the chapter is organized as follows. The next section introduces a set of basic definitions and the overall terminology used in the book. The section on delivering AmI is focused on discussing practical aspects and particularly on the role of the IoT environments and the reasoning capabilities provided within scope of the smart spaces paradigm. The section on enabler technologies provides an overview in respect to AmI applications in IoT environments. The section on solutions and recommendations provides a roadmap of the problems and experience studied in this book. Then the section on future research directions shows our view on the interesting open problems and challenges in the AmI and IoT field.

BASIC DEFINITIONS AND TERMINOLOGY

The Ambient Intelligence (AmI) term was introduced by the Palo Alto Ventures team lead by Prof. Elias Zelkha. It defines a set of technologies to bring intelligence to the everyday environments of the users and make those environments sensitive to users' needs and individual preferences. The Ambient intelligence is a generic paradigm enabled by advances in sensors, low energy networking, IoT, pervasive computing, artificial intelligence and creation of advanced service models such as Smart Spaces. The ambient intelligence technologies are based on human-centric computer interaction design, which can be characterized by the following key features:

- Embedded into the environment so that instead of a single assistant device that the user shall carry with him, the whole environment of networked devices take active part in delivery of the personalized services;
- Context awareness - these devices can recognize a user, its individual situational context and correspondingly adjust services;
- High personalization that the system can be tailored to the user needs;
- Transparency (comfortable "invisibility") of the interface, so that a user can interact with the system using natural forms of communications, e.g., by asking questions to the environment rather than typing search query on the mobile phone;
- Be adaptive to user's behavior and reconfigure / change the environment in response to the recognition of the user behavior. For example, to use machine learning to let the environment to learn from experience, extrapolate from current data and expand on their knowledge and capabilities autonomously;
- And be anticipatory, i.e., anticipate user's desires without conscious mediation.

The ambient intelligence paradigm is applied to various types of physical environments, starting from home and work spaces (e.g., office) and to any public spaces and with the time shall cover the whole planet, or at least all areas where people appear on the regular base. A number of various technologies have been created to deliver this new level of experience, starting from smart street lights, to the complex solution that operate smart house, smart city or any topical Smart Space.

Figure 4. High level vision of IoT environment as a system of connected computing devices and resources

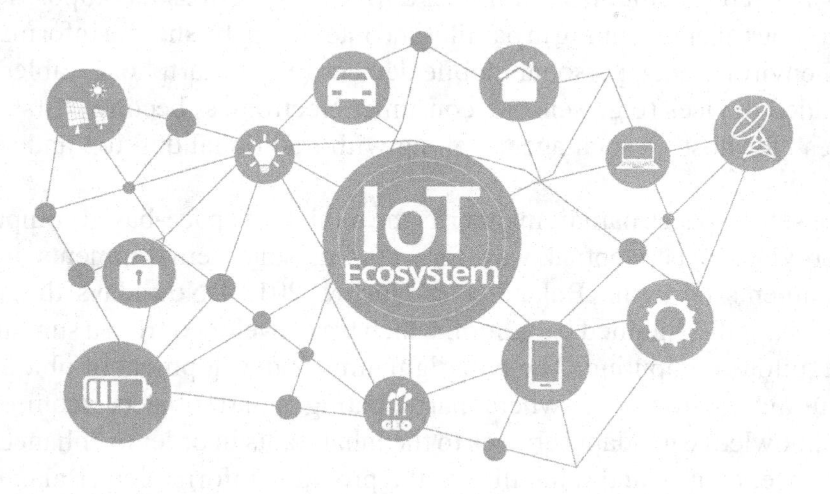

Cook and Das give the following formal definition of Smart Spaces - "Smart Space is able to acquire and apply knowledge about its environment and to adapt to its inhabitants in order to improve their experience in that environment" (Cook & Das, 2004). According to this definition continues interaction of a user with the surrounding environment is assumed, which is targeted in continuous adaptation of services to current needs of the user. This interaction is enabled by:

- **Sensing Functionality:** That gathers information about the space and the user;
- **Adaptation Functionality:** For reacting to the detected changes; and
- **Effecting Functionality:** For changing the surrounding space to benefit the user.

Based on the definition the main focus of Smart Spaces is on user and the core principle of work is to apply space-based computing for delivering enhanced services. This becomes possible thank to sharing common information in a space for joint access.

The basic operational element of smart spaces is smart agent (or smart computational object). Agents can reason knowledge and make decisions using available information and in accordance with the application goals. Multiple parallel processes can cooperate in the space through their agents that publishing/retrieving data into/from the space. This asynchronous publish-based communication model defines a system as a composition of autonomous agents running in parallel and interacting by sharing information. In IoT environments, personal mobile devices (e.g., smartphone, tablet) and embedded devices (e.g., sensors, consumer electronics) become "first-class devices" for hosting such agents, along with traditional desktop and server computers.

The smart spaces paradigm inherits the models of space-based computing and provides a conceptual way for creating smart environments in IoT environments (Korzun, Balandin, & Gurtov, 2013). Nowadays the smart spaces is a self-contained paradigm, which was developed from a sub-stream of ubiquitous computing. The paradigm aims at development of ubiquitous computing environment, where participating smart objects acquire and apply knowledge to adapt services to the inhabitants in order to enhance user experience, quality and reliability of the provided information (Balandin & Waris, 2009). The target is information components of a smart environment and their effective conjunction with communication and decision components. Figure 5 gives a reference layered definition for the smart spaces ecosystem positioning it as an enabler of digitalization and connection between the physical world and the information world.

Figure 5. A reference definition of the smart spaces implementation

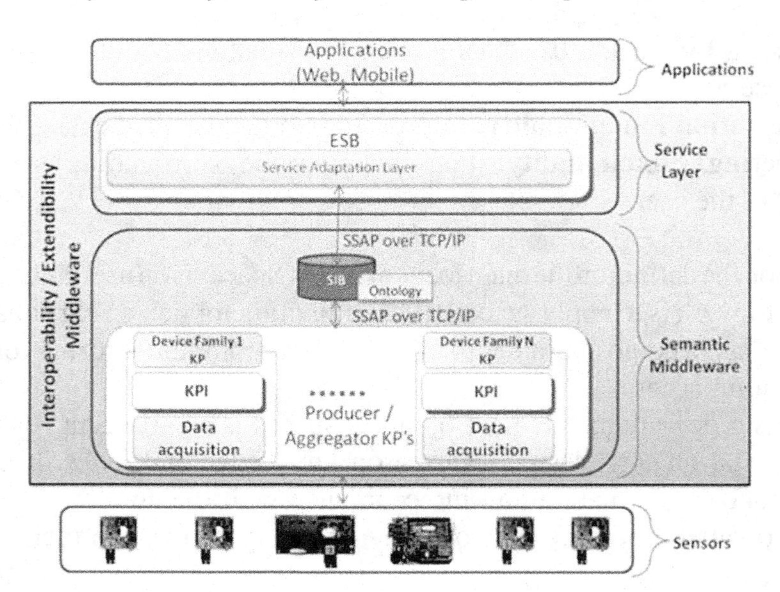

Service construction becomes solving a puzzle over local and global information in the fusion of information and physical worlds. The required intelligence support can be realized using the smart spaces approach (Augusto, Callaghan, Cook, Kameas, & Satoh, 2013), which includes the case of IoT environments (Korzun, Balandin, & Gurtov, 2013; Kiljander et al., 2014; Roffia et al., 2016). Smart spaces follow the vision of ubiquitous computing to establish cooperation of all networked components of the environment in order to effectively serve for users' needs (Balandin & Waris, 2009). The cooperation is based on indirect communication in the form of a shared information space that describes available resources of the environment (Smirnov et al., 2009; Pantsar-Syvaniemi et al., 2012).

The smart space enables information sharing, supporting construction of advanced information services by the participants themselves. Such services are often referred as "smart", emphasizing the new level of service recognition (detection of user needs), construction (automated preprocessing of large data amounts) and perception (derived information provision to the user for decision-making). The key technology layers of the smart spaces are shown in Figure 6.

Following (Smirnov et al., 2009; Ovaska, Cinotti, & Toninelli, 2012) let a shared information space (a smart space) be created; see Figure 7 for illustration. Information services are constructed (and delivered to the users) by agents interacting in this environment by sharing and using the information on available resources. The IoT environment provides hosting for running the agents and network communication means. IoT objects (real things from the physical world or entities from the information world) can be virtualized

Figure 6. Smart spaces technology layers

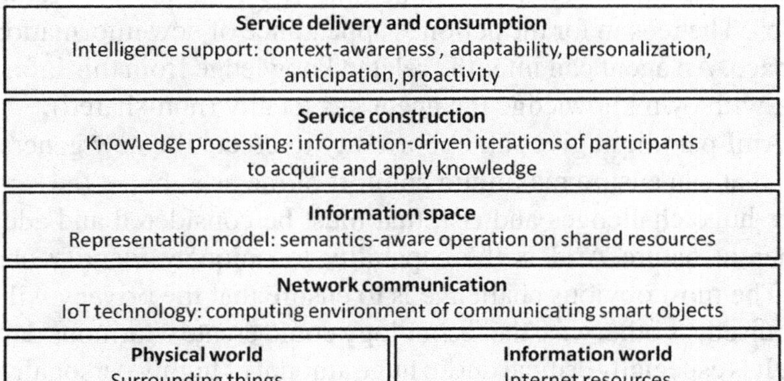

Service delivery and consumption Intelligence support: context-awareness , adaptability, personalization, anticipation, proactivity	
Service construction Knowledge processing: information-driven iterations of participants to acquire and apply knowledge	
Information space Representation model: semantics-aware operation on shared resources	
Network communication IoT technology: computing environment of communicating smart objects	
Physical world Surrounding things	Information world Internet resources

Figure 7. Services constructed in smart space

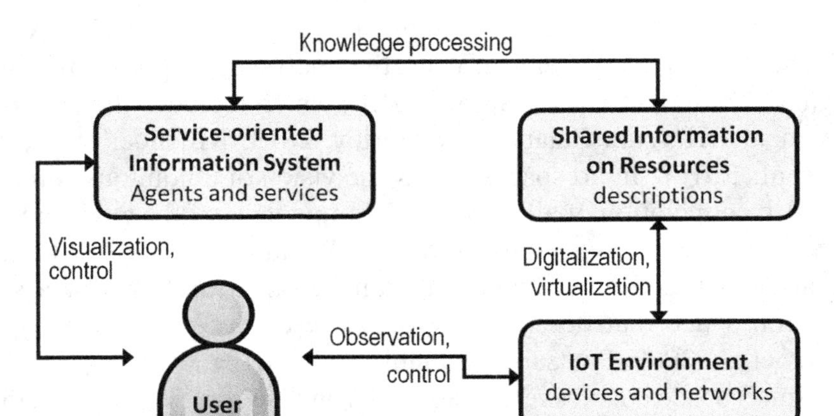

by associated agents and keeping digitalized representations (descriptions) as shared information. Therefore, the smart space connects its agents into a distributed system with "central brain support" for multi-agent interaction and knowledge processing on service construction and delivery.

Service design is made in terms of scenarios with knowledge reasoning acts (Korzun, 2014). Each scenario defines a control flow initiated from the user side (explicit or implicit detection of user needs) and completed at a point where the user perceives a service (something useful for satisfaction of the needs). The perception can be in form of information delivery (typically, in a visual form) to the user (e.g., recommendation) or the user observes some changes in the physical world (e.g., room lighting becomes lower).

A scenario control flow is event-driven, i.e., assuming the behavior "do something if a certain event occurs". This variant can be extended to the information-driven behavior "do something if certain knowledge becomes available". The reason for the action is appearance of new information in the smart space. An agent can infer the related knowledge from this information clarified with own knowledge the agent has locally (non-shared).

The AmI paradigm gives an opportunity to create the new generation of services that can ensure maximum comfort of the user, but at the same time it creates huge challenges and risk that must be considered and addressed. The inherent nature AmI is the capability to uniquely identify and track people. The most obvious challenge is to ensure that the privacy will not be compromised, as otherwise the technology could create enormous damage to the user. It is especially critical due to huge amount of highly personalized data available in the system. When carefully analyzing the key design principles of the Ambient Intelligence paradigm one can notice that there are no features or requirements that directly create privacy thread. But at the same time the high complexity of the systems and its heterogeneity requires from the system designers to pay special attention to the privacy.

Another example of the challenge introduced by the Ambient Intelligence is related to socioeconomics and general freedom of the society. The AmI service infrastructure could enable massive manipulation of people, which even might lead to loss of individual freedom. This is an important and very difficult aspect, as there are no direct measurements that can be applied to the systems to ensure their proper behavior. Moreover, for some industries, e.g., advertising industry, a kind of manipulation is a desirable impact. To address this issue it is critical that the AmI service design will be based on the principle that the individual preferences shall always dominate over group interests and preferences.

In this book, we address a number of other challenges, risks, and related opportunities and design recommendations.

DELIVERING AMBIENT INTELLIGENCE: INTERNET OF THINGS ENVIRONMENT AND REASONING IN SMART SPACES

The smart object is not strictly associated with a particular host device as it is defined for IoT. Moreover, it is less focused on the underlying network communication means. In comparison to the generic definition for multi-agent systems, a smart object can

1. Identify itself as a part of the environment and application,
2. Understand their state,
3. Operate with a certain part of the shared content, and
4. Make over this part own interpretations, decisions, and actions.

The smart object is an autonomous information processing unit. So each smart object is represented as a programmed computational process, which is responsible for a distinguishable portion of the application logic and hosted on one or more devices of the environment. Smart objects are not attached to a particular device, as any available device can host the object. Services are constructed as interaction of smart objects in a shared space. The smart space can be deployed in a cloud or on user's devices that interact with each other and use pertinent services regardless of the physical location. In this book we use the term "agent" instead of "smart object" to emphasize that it is a program executed on some devices.

The Smart Space can be seen as a kind of service cocoon that surrounds the user and relocates together with the user. It is especially important to note that at the same time the user is surrounded by multiple Smart Space cocoons. Each Smart Space has own clearly focused mission. The Smart Spaces can overlap, which in practice means that they include the same services, use same physical devices and share some information.

Smart services paradigm is based on semantics of the collected data. The aim is at support for making intelligent decisions as reaction to recognized meaning of available multi-source data. In particular, services become adaptive to suit best the observed situation and context, provide personalization of operation with users, and allow proactive activation and delivery.

The Semantic Web technologies enable development of the data stores on the Web, building vocabularies, and writing rules for handling data. The key enabler technologies of the Semantic Web are on building, managing and storing linked data. One can say that the Semantic Web is empowered by technologies such as RDF, SPARQL, JSON-LD, OWL and SKOS.

Resource Description Framework (RDF) is a standard model for data interchange on the Web. RDF provides a solution for data merging even if the underlying schemas are different, and supports the time evolution of schemas without requiring changing all the data consumers. RDF allows extending the linking structure of the Web to use URIs for naming the relationship between things as well as the two ends of the link.

SPARQL is a Query Language for RDF that provides directed, labeled graph data format for representing information in the Web. SPARQL language is used to express queries across diverse data sources, when the data is stored natively as RDF or accessed as RDF via middleware. SPARQL provides support for extensible value testing and constraining queries by source RDF graph. It also provides full set of tools for querying required and optional graph patterns with their conjunctions and disjunctions. The result of SPARQL query could be a value set or RDF graph.

JSON-LD is a JSON-based serialization for linked data, with syntax that was designed specifically to easily integrate into deployed systems that already use JSON. Its mission is to provide a way for using linked data to build interoperable Web services in Web-based programming environments and to store linked data in JSON-based storage engines. Basically it is designed to be usable directly as JSON, with no knowledge of RDF. Thanks to full compatibility of JSON-LD with JSON, one can reuse the large number of JSON parsers and libraries available today. Moreover, in addition to basic JSON features, the JSON-LD introduces:

- Universal identifier mechanism for JSON objects using IRIs,
- Way to disambiguate keys shared among different JSON documents by using context for mapping them to IRIs,
- Mechanism in which a JSON object value may refer to a JSON object on a different site on the Web,
- The ability to annotate strings with their language,
- Way to associate data types with values such as date and time,
- Facility to express in a single document one or more directed graphs, such as a social network.

W3C Web Ontology Language (OWL) is a semantic web language that was designed for representing rich and complex knowledge about things, groups of things, and relations between them. The knowledge expressed in OWL can be exploited by computer programs, e.g., to make implicit knowledge explicit, verify consistency of the knowledge, etc. OWL document provide full description of ontologies and they can be published in Web and can refer to or be referred from another OWL document.

Simple Knowledge Organization System (SKOS) - is a data model for sharing and linking knowledge management systems on the Web. Many knowledge organization systems can share similar structure and are used in similar applications. For example, it can apply to thesauri, taxonomies, classification schemes and subject heading systems. SKOS allows capturing this similarity, making it explicit and enabling data and technology sharing across diverse applications. SKOS data model offers a standard, low-cost migration for porting existing knowledge organization systems to the semantic web. Also SKOS provides an intuitive language for developing and sharing new knowledge organization systems. It may be used alone or in combination with formal knowledge representation languages, e.g., OWL.

Semantics methods for knowledge reasoning are based on the description logic that is a decidable subset of the first order predication logic. The overall scheme of knowledge processing and delivery of smart applications by smart spaces is illustrated by Figure 8.

Figure 8. Knowledge processing and service delivery in smart spaces

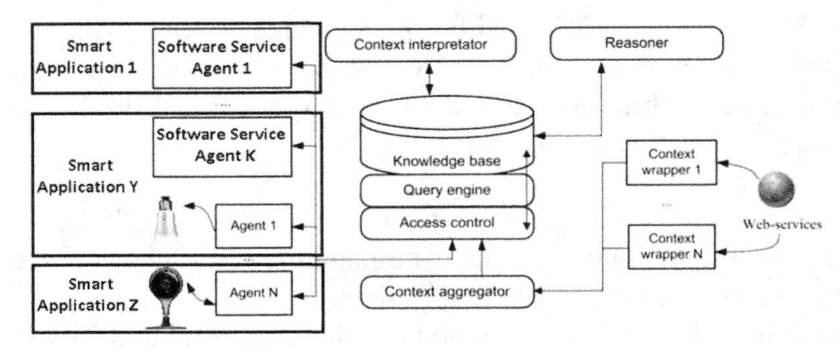

To summarize, the generic model of smart spaces service construction is based on knowledge reasoning and semantic data mining on top of IoT environment as illustrated by Figure 9.

Figure 9. Service construction model for smart space deployed on top of IoT environment

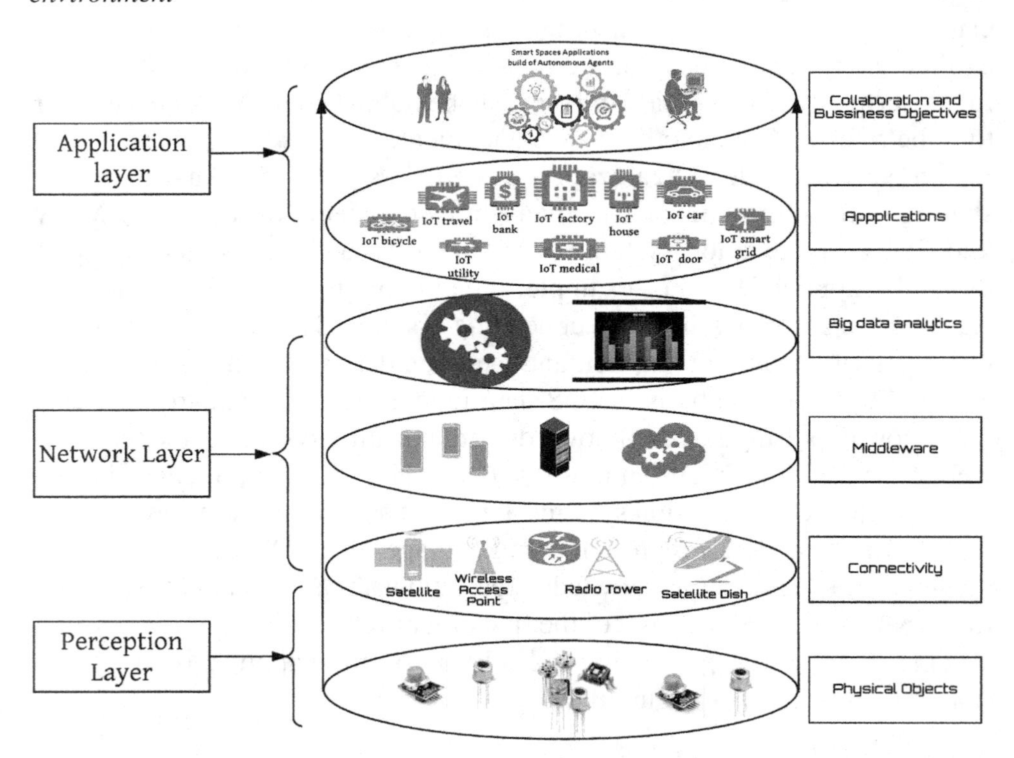

ENABLER TECHNOLOGIES OF AMBIENT INTELLIGENCE

The recent advancement in development of Internet of Things infrastructure and exponential growth of the IoT-enabled devices are the key enablers for development of the Ambient Intelligence services. This is due to the fact that IoT is the main sources of context data and information describing the physical world. Broad deployment of the sensors ecosystems enable continuous monitoring of almost any physical space. Moreover, the Smart Spaces paradigm creates a new type of service ecosystem, which is optimized for mapping and linking the physical world and virtual space. Joint use of Smart Spaces and IoT enables development of services that make proactive actions on the environment conditions in a desired direction, which creates a notion of intelligence. So we get an intelligent environment that allows automating and optimize many tasks that currently rely on overprovision of resources or/and human intervention. As a result, it enables transition from the Internet of Things environment to the Cyber-Physical Systems (CPS). Cyber-Physical System is defined as a mechanism that is controlled or/and monitored by computer-based algorithms and tightly integrated with the Internet. In cyber-physical systems, physical and software components are deeply intertwined, each operating on different spatial and temporal scales, exhibiting multiple and distinct behavioral modalities, and interacting with each other in a lot of ways that change with context. Examples of CPS include smart grid, autonomous automobile systems, medical monitoring, process control systems, robotics systems, and automatic pilot avionics.

An alternative enabler technology is the Web of Things (WoT) paradigm that pivots the concept of Thing Description, an abstraction layer to equalize all the existing devices. The Thing Description of a device (i.e., a thing) is a detailed description of the device's URI, supported actions, events and properties. The Web of Things shall be seen as an overlay built on top of Internet of Things. While IoT silos may exist, the Web of Things could be employed to bridge them providing a standard-compliant interface to the significant resources. Recently we see growth of interest to Web of Things paradigm, as the W3C launch a new working group on it, which includes the top players of the industry, e.g., Samsung, Intel, Google, Panasonic and Fujitsu, etc., which are targeted to transform current general vision of the Web of Things technology into the industrial standards. So it is clear that role of WoT will increase and it shall be studied as an enabler technology for the ambient intelligence environments.

A smart application acquires knowledge about the environment and its users and applies the collected and generated based on reasoning knowledge to improve quality of service, user experience and own efficiency. As explained in the previous sections, the service-oriented IoT-aware application can be developed as a distributed multi-agent system that is hosted on a multitude of devices. This brings us to the definition of the edge-centric computing principle. The edge-centric computing is a distributed computing paradigm that largely or completely based on computations performed on a set distributed device (smart devices or edge devices) as opposed to computations run on a centralized cloud in core network. Alternative approach to bring intelligence and processing closer to the places of data creation is a fog computing. Fog Computing is an architecture that uses collaborative multitude of the user clients and devices located in the user's proximity to carry out major part of processing, storage and communication tasks related to delivery of services to the user. Figure 10 summarize the architectural options on computing

Figure 10. Localization of computations: core (cloud), edge-centric and fog computing

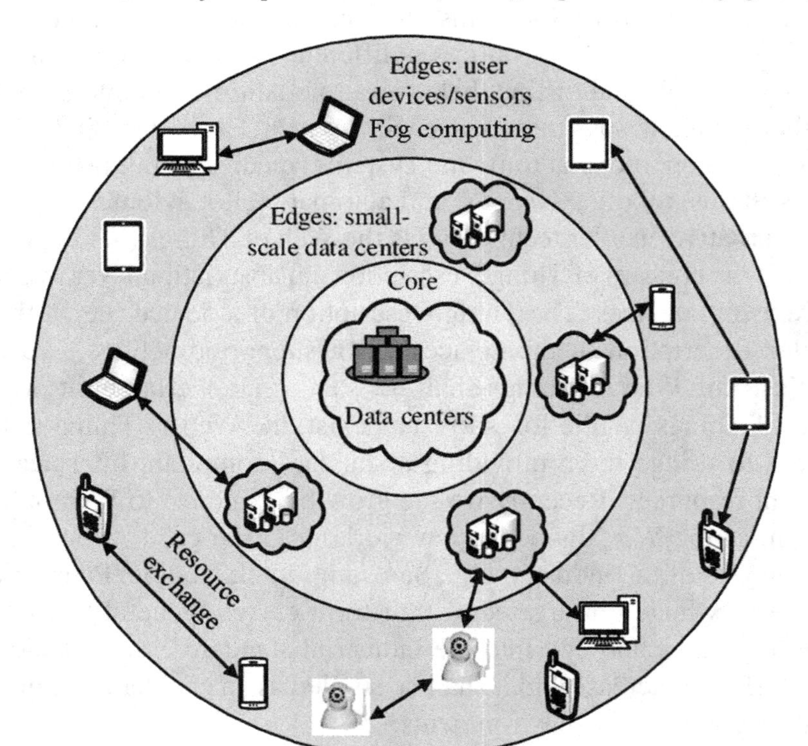

localization that can be applied for implementation of the ambient intelligence environment.

The edge and fog computing appear similar since they both involve bringing intelligence and processing closer to the data originators and consumers. The key difference between them is in definition of the location for intelligence and computing power. The fog environment position intelligence in the local area network, i.e., the data is transmitted from endpoints to a gateway, where it is then transmitted to sources for processing and return transmission. The edge computing places intelligence and processing power in devices, e.g., embedded automation controllers, smartphones, etc. Both computing paradigm are actively used for various use scenarios as the key enablers of ambient intelligence environment.

The next set of the key enabler technologies is related to data mining and big data management (X. Wu, Zhu, G. Wu, & Ding, 2014) and decision making. In particular, AmI is becoming an interesting topic for industrial-level applications of smart (intelligent) environments, e.g., to smart manufacturing and Industrial Internet. Such a digital environment senses people and their actions, machine and materials, physical parameters (and many others). That is, the system can interpret and act on data from sensors in real-time, which is a very challenging property. Example studies on applying AmI can are transportation (Ocalir-Akunal, 2016), healthcare (Tawfik & Anya, 2015), and disaster management (Fersini et al., 2017).

SOLUTIONS AND RECOMMENDATIONS

This book is our attempt to consider and summarize some selected hot research topics in IoT, WoT, and CPS. Accordingly, the roles of subsequent chapters are as follows.

Chapter 2 “Emerging Case Studies of Ambient Intelligence Services” particularly focuses on introduction and provides overview of the emerging case studies around ambient intelligence services. It introduces several case studies that illustrate opportunities and discuss design details of the smart services development. The chapter provides definition of the key enablers of the service smartness, e.g., role of location-awareness, design principles of smart services and so on. Then the discussion on provided definitions and presented enablers is supported by presentation of a few use case examples for e-Tourism and e-Healthcare scenarios. In addition, the chapter discusses general principles of ZeroUI design concept and a role of Virtual and Augmented

Reality in delivering new user experience. Generally, the chapter is targeted to clearly ground the book scope to the real-life use cases and most relevant trends in the industry.

Chapter 3 "Fog Computing Technology for Cooperative Information Processing in Edge-Centric Internet of Things Environments" discusses advances in fog computing technology for involving various participants - either small or large in capacity, either local or remote - into the service construction. The focus of this chapter is on non-typical computational devices such as smartphones, wireless routers, multimedia equipment, and consumer electronics that become aware of information processing in order to construct services essentially based on local resources of the IoT environment.

Chapter 4 "Profiling and Personalization in Internet of Things Environments" considers problems of user personalization and resources competence modeling in the Internet of Things (IoT) environments. Creation of the user profiles and its utilization during the interaction of the user with IoT resources significantly increase the efficiency of such interaction. When the user generates a task to perform by the IoT resources the formal model of this task is expanded by the relevant information in according to user profile model. The obtained results should be presented to the user in according to his/her preferences from the user profile model. Resource competence profile should store information about the resource competencies and constraints that have to be satisfied to enable these competences. In this case resource competence profiles automate their interaction in IoT environment.

Chapter 5 "Semantic Methods for Data Mining in Smart Spaces" shows the role of semantic methods in delivering AmI. The smart spaces paradigm applies ontological modeling for representing available IoT resources as shared information. This way, resources are virtualized by local information hubs, which are deployed on existing devices. The virtualization benefits from semantics since relations between resources are also represented, forming a semantic network. In turn, various ranking models can be implemented for information search and knowledge reasoning, e.g., based on such well-known algorithms as PageRank. The structural properties of the semantic network leads to advanced AmI support for constructing proactive services: discovery of certain structures (e.g., cycles) can be interpreted as formation of specific knowledge that initiates service construction and delivery.

Chapter 6 "Internet of Things Participants Interaction for Service Construction and Delivery" discusses the semantic interaction support for Internet of Things (IoT) resources, which is a key point of the service construction and delivery for the users. Semantic interoperability between interacted resources provides possibilities of their understanding each other. One possible approach to enrich the semantic interoperability is the ontology modeling. Every resource is described by an ontology that formally represents knowledge as a set of concepts within a domain, using a shared vocabulary to denote the types, properties, and interrelationships of those concepts. Based on the ontology matching techniques, resource ontologies are matched and resources operate in according to this matching. Here the context is any information that can be used to characterize the situation of an entity. An entity in the considered case is the resource of IoT environment. It is proposed to use the ontologies to describe the context of resource and take this information for task performing. For the service construction it is needed to create the coalitions of resources that can jointly provide the needed service for the user task performing.

Chapter 7 “Evolution of the Smart Spaces Paradigm toward the Web of Things” presents how the Smart-M3 platform evolved in the direction of supporting web standards (e.g. HTTP and Websockets) to be ready for the Web of Things. The latest step in the Smart-M3 progress is named SEPA (SPARQL Event Processing Architecture). Employing SEPA as a mean for semantic interoperability in the Web of Things means allowing heterogeneous devices to be discovered, accessed and controlled through a set of SPARQL queries, subscriptions and updates according to a given ontology. The chapter discusses ontology for the Web of Things as a demonstration of the real life use case. Using web standards solves the issues of interoperability but poses new challenges with respect to the typical constraints of IoT applications.

FUTURE RESEARCH DIRECTIONS

The book discusses a few examples of use cases of smart services that are under active development, which represent only one part of the complex puzzle that is developed currently and will change the whole landscape of the service industry. More of advanced new breakthrough solutions are expected to appear in the near future.

Profiling and personalization are the emerging trends in modern life. Nowadays, modern information systems track user behavior and adapt their behavior based on this information. IoT environments also should understand the user needs and describe the resource competencies to automate the processes of resources search for task performing. The book identifies and discusses a number of open problems of profiling and personalization in IoT environments, e.g., problem domain ontology construction, cold start, and weighted ontology, and we see that addressing of these problems will be one of the key future research directions.

As the Semantic Web of Things is in its early stages, the new application scenarios may emerge and may require further analysis of the subscriptions processing policies. In particular, one interesting research direction is that of indexing the SPUs to prioritize, e.g., the most frequently or the most recently awakened. Moreover, SPARQL Event Processing Architectures are still built as wrappers on top of existing SPARQL endpoints: a further enhancement of the performance of such architectures could be achieved by a native implementation of the SPARQL Subscribe Protocol in SPARQL endpoints to reduce the computational overhead.

As regards the interface towards the external world, SEPA provides an HTTP server to listen for SPARQL Update and Query requests and a Websocket interface to deal with subscriptions. However, the Internet of Things has seen the proliferation of lightweight protocols for efficient communication also with constrained devices. Therefore, a further analysis to provide a communication interface based on a lightweight protocol can be considered as one of the future works. A preliminary work to start from is C Minor, a semantic context broker with a CoAP interface specifically designed to bring semantics in the Internet of Musical Things. The choice of CoAP is motivated by the simple mapping rules between this protocol and HTTP that would make easy to map the SPARQL 1.1 Protocol on CoAP.

A third future contribution regards instead the security infrastructure. The current SEPA framework allows for a secure communication among clients and brokers, thanks to HTTPS and Secure Websockets. This solution grants security on the communication channel among the involved entities, but is not enough to secure a sub-graph from unauthorized modifications. Every triple in the graph is not bound to a specific owner, so every client authorized to interact with a SEPA is allowed to freely modify the knowledge base. This is why a deeper security layer is one of the priorities of the next releases.

To conclude, a last important future contribution of the SEPA broker will be the support for federated queries that enables the virtual aggregation of multiple smart spaces in a wider ecosystem.

In addition to the above discussed technology-centric directions for future research, it is important to remember about the socioeconomic impacts that broad adoption of AmI will have to various stakeholders. It is clear that AmI will increase productivity of the society as a whole, but it also will affect job functions of many people in the involved industries. That will directly affect the practical rollout of AmI in many areas and demand careful study.

CONCLUSION

The chapter is presenting the background and launching the main discussion addressed by the book. In particular it introduces the Ambient Intelligence in Internet of Things Environments and Cyber-Physical Systems. The chapter makes an introduction to the AmI paradigm and presents its general design principles and underlying technologies. The authors discuss the existing technologies that might play the key role in future development of AmI in IoT Environments. Overall this chapter provides all basic information that the reader needs to help smooth reading for the rest of the book.

ACKNOWLEDGMENT

The primary contributors to this chapter are Sergey Balandin from FRUCT Oy, Finland, Ekaterina Balandina from University of Tampere, Finland, and Dmitry Korzun from Petrozavodsk State University (PetrSU), Russia.

REFERENCES

Acampora, G., Cook, D. J., Rashidi, P., & Vasilakos, A. V. (2013). A survey on ambient intelligence in healthcare. *Proceedings of the IEEE*, *101*(12), 2470–2494. doi:10.1109/JPROC.2013.2262913 PMID:24431472

Atzori, L., Iera, A., & Morabito, G. (2010). The Internet of Things: A survey. *Computer Networks*, *54*(15), 2787–2805. doi:10.1016/j.comnet.2010.05.010

Augusto, J. C., Callaghan, V., Cook, D., Kameas, A., & Satoh, I. (2013). Intelligent Environments: A Manifesto. *Human-centric Computing and Information Sciences*, *3*(1), 1–18. doi:10.1186/2192-1962-3-12

Augusto, J.C., Nakashima, H., & Aghajan, H.K. (2010). Ambient Intelligence and Smart Environments: A State of the Art. *AmI 2010*.

Balandin, S., Bjorksten, M., Hakkila, J., Jekkonen, J., Makela, K., & Roimela, K. (2007). Supporting the notion of seamlessness in personal content management. *2nd IASTED International Conference on Human-Computer Interaction*, 250-256.

Balandin, S., & Waris, H. (2009). Key Properties in the Development of Smart Spaces. *Lecture Notes in Computer Science, 5615*, 3-12.

Bartolini, S., Milosevic, B., D'Elia, A., Farella, E., Benini, L., & Cinotti, T. S. (2012). Reconfigurable natural interaction in smart environments. *Personal and Ubiquitous Computing, 16*(7), 943–956. doi:10.100700779-011-0454-5

Cook, D., Augusto, J., & Jakkula, V. (2009). Ambient intelligence: Technologies, applications, and opportunities. *Pervasive and Mobile Computing, 5*(4), 277–298. doi:10.1016/j.pmcj.2009.04.001

Cook, D., & Das, S. K. (2004). *Smart environments: Technology, protocols and applications*. John Wiley & Sons. doi:10.1002/047168659X

Evers, C., Kniewel, R., Geihs, K., & Schmidt, L. (2014). The user in the loop: Enabling user participation for self-adaptive applications. *Future Generation Computer Systems, 34*, 110–123. doi:10.1016/j.future.2013.12.010

Fersini, E., Messina, E., & Pozzi, F. A. (2017). Earthquake management: A decision support system based on natural language processing. *Journal of Ambient Intelligence and Humanized Computing, 8*(1), 37–45. doi:10.100712652-016-0373-4

Kiljander, J., D'Elia, A., Morandi, F., Hyttinen, P., Takalo-Mattila, J., Ylisaukko-oja, A., ... Cinotti, T. S. (2014). Semantic interoperability architecture for pervasive computing and Internet of Things. *IEEE Access: Practical Innovations, Open Solutions, 2*, 856–874. doi:10.1109/ACCESS.2014.2347992

Korzun, D. (2014). Service formalism and architectural abstractions for smart space applications. *10th Central & Eastern European Software Engineering Conference in Russia, 19*, 1-7.

Korzun, D. (2017). Internet of things meets mobile health systems in smart spaces: An overview. *Internet of Things and Big Data Technologies for Next Generation Healthcare Studies in Big Data., 23*, 111–129. doi:10.1007/978-3-319-49736-5_6

Korzun, D., Balandin S., & Gurtov A. (2013). Deployment of Smart Spaces in Internet of Things: Overview of the Design Challenges. *Lecture Notes in Computer Science, 8121*, 48-59.

Korzun, D., Nikolaevskiy, I., & Gurtov, A. (2015). Service Intelligence and Communication Security for Ambient Assisted Living. *International Journal of Embedded and Real-Time Communication Systems, 6*(1), 76–100. doi:10.4018/IJERTCS.2015010104

Mandl, K. D., Mandel, J. C., Murphy, S. N., Bernstam, E. V., Ramoni, R. L., Kreda, D. A., ... Kohane, I. S. (2012). The SMART platform: Early experience enabling substitutable applications for electronic health records. *Journal of the American Medical Informatics Association, 19*(4), 597–603. doi:10.1136/amiajnl-2011-000622 PMID:22427539

Ocalir-Akunal, E. V. (2016). A Web Based Decision Support System (DSS) for Individuals' Urban Travel Alternatives. In Using Decision Support Systems for Transportation Planning Efficiency (pp. 145-167). Academic Press.

Ovaska, E., Cinotti, T.S., & Toninelli, A. (2012). The design principles and practices of interoperable smart spaces. *Advanced Design Approaches to Emerging Software Systems: Principles, Methodology and Tools*, 18–47.

Pantsar-Syvaniemi, S., Purhonen, A., Ovaska, E., Kuusijarvi, J., & Evesti, A. (2012). Situation-based and self-adaptive applications for the smart environment. *Journal of Ambient Intelligence and Smart Environments, 4*(6), 491–516.

Roffia, L., Morandi, F., Kiljander, J., D'Elia, A., Vergari, F., Viola, F., ... Cinotti, T. S. (2016). A semantic publish-subscribe architecture for the Internet of Things. *IEEE Internet of Things Journal, 99*, 1–23.

Shapiro, D., Augusto, J. C., & Ramos, C. (2008). Ambient Intelligence - the Next Step for Artificial Intelligence. *IEEE Intelligent Systems, 23*(2), 15–18. doi:10.1109/MIS.2008.19

Smirnov, A., Kashevnik, A., Shilov, N., Boldyrev, S., Balandin, S., & Oliver, I. (2009). Context-Aware Smart Space: Reference Model. *International Conference on Advanced Information Networking and Applications Workshops*, 261-265. 10.1109/WAINA.2009.104

Smirnov, A., Kashnevik, A., Shilov, N., Oliver, I., Balandin, S., & Boldyrev, S. (2009). Anonymous agent coordination in smart spaces: State-of-the-art. *Lecture Notes in Computer Science*, *5764*, 42–51. doi:10.1007/978-3-642-04190-7_5

Smirnov, A., Levashova, T., Shilov, N., & Kashevnik, A. (2010). Hybrid Technology for Self-Organization of Resources of Pervasive Environment for Operational Decision Support. *International Journal on Artificial Intelligence Tools, 19*(2), 211–229.

Soldatos, J., Kefalakis, N., Hauswirth, M., Serrano, M., Calbimonte, J.-P., Riahi, M., ... Herzog, R. (2015). OpenIoT: Open Source Internet-of-Things in the Cloud, Interoperability and Open-Source Solutions for the Internet of Things. *LNCS*, *9001*, 13–25.

Tawfik, H., & Anya, O. (2015). Evaluating practice-centered awareness in cross-boundary telehealth decision support systems. *Telematics and Informatics*, *32*(3), 486–503. doi:10.1016/j.tele.2014.11.002

Trussell, H. J. (2018). Why a Special Issue on Machine Ethics. *Proceedings of the IEEE*, *106*(10), 1774–1776. doi:10.1109/JPROC.2018.2868336

Wang, J., Zhu, Q., & Ma, Y. (2013). An agent-based hybrid service delivery for coordinating internet of things and 3rd party service providers. *Journal of Network and Computer Applications*, *36*(6), 1684–1695. doi:10.1016/j.jnca.2013.04.014

Winfield, A. F., Michael, K., Pitt, J., & Evers, V. (2019). Machine Ethics: The Design and Governance of Ethical AI and Autonomous Systems. *Proceedings of the IEEE*, *107*(3), 509–517. doi:10.1109/JPROC.2019.2900622

Wu, X., Zhu, X., Wu, G.-Q., & Ding, W. (2014). Data mining with big data. *IEEE Transactions on Knowledge and Data Engineering*, *26*(1), 97–107. doi:10.1109/TKDE.2013.109

KEY TERMS AND DEFINITIONS

Ambient Intelligence (AmI): Electronic environments that are sensitive and responsive to the presence of a user, which disappear into surroundings until only the user interface remains perceivable by users. The ambient intelligence paradigm builds upon pervasive computing, ubiquitous computing, profiling, context awareness, and human-centric computer interaction design.

Cyber-Physical Systems (CPS): A mechanism that is controlled or/and monitored by computer-based algorithms and tightly integrated with the Internet. In cyber-physical systems, physical and software components are deeply intertwined, each operating on different spatial and temporal scales, exhibiting multiple and distinct behavioral modalities, and interacting with each other in a lot of ways that change with context. Examples of CPS include smart grid, autonomous automobile systems, medical monitoring, process control systems, robotics systems, and automatic pilot avionics.

E-Healthcare (E-Health): A healthcare practice supported by electronic processes and communication.

E-Tourism: The analysis, design, implementation and application of IT and e-commerce solutions in the travel and tourism industry; as well as the analysis of the respective economic processes and market structures and customer relationship management.

Edge Computing: A distributed computing paradigm that largely or completely based on computations performed on a set distributed device (smart devices or edge devices) as opposed to computations run on a centralized cloud in core network.

Fog Computing: An architecture that uses collaborative multitude of the user clients and devices located in the user's proximity to carry out major part of processing, storage and communication tasks related to delivery of services to the user.

Internet of Things (IoT): Is the internetworking of IoT devices that enable these devices to collect and exchange data for a achieving a common goal.

IoT Device: Is a physical device embedded with electronics, software, sensors, actuators, and network connectivity sufficient for collecting and exchanging data with other devices.

Knowledge Corpus: Defines the smart spaces structure that consist of a set of shared resources including data and data processing function, which continuously performs data mining operations for extracting new relevant knowledge and performing routine monitoring functions based on the target functions set by the user or smart space services.

Service Intelligence: Is a measurement of an ability of a service to adopt behavior to the environment without human intervention.

Smart Environment: Is a concept of the physical world that is richly and invisibly interwoven with sensors, actuators, displays, and computational elements, embedded seamlessly in the everyday objects of our lives, and connected through a continuous network.

Smart Space: A set of communicating nodes and information storages, which has embedded logic to acquire and apply knowledge about its environment and adapt to its inhabitants in order to improve their experience in the environment.

Smart-M3: An open-source software platform that aims to provide a smart spaces infrastructure. It combines the ideas of distributed, networked systems and semantic web. The ultimate goal is to enable smart environments and linking of real and virtual worlds.

User Profiles: Contain information about the users.

Web of Things (WoT): The new evolution of the IoT principles that is delivered as an overlay on top of IoT and targeted in adoption of the standards that made the web popular.

Chapter 2
Emerging Case Studies of Ambient Intelligence Services

ABSTRACT

Analysis of currently dominating and emerging use cases provide extremely valuable information for understanding of the key drivers of a technology development. In this chapter, the authors particularly focus on introducing and making an overview of the emerging case studies on top of the ambient intelligence technology. They discuss several case studies that illustrate opportunities and design details for development of highly personalized smart services. The chapter provides definition of the key enablers of the service smartness (e.g., location-awareness, design principles, and restrictions, etc.). The discussion on provided definitions and presented enablers is supported by a few use case examples in the field of e-tourism and e-healthcare. In addition, the chapter introduces the general principles of ZeroUI concept and role of virtual and augmented reality in delivering the new user experience. The chapter is targeted to clearly ground the book scope to the real-life use cases and most relevant trends.

INTRODUCTION

The amount of information is growing in the Internet such that users cannot efficiently manage the existing multitude of resources. The smart services are aiming in intelligent use of all available information in various situations that the user can get as was discussed in the papers by (Balandin & Waris, 2009),

DOI: 10.4018/978-1-5225-8973-0.ch002

(Augusto, Callaghan, Cook, Kameas, & Satoh, 2013) and (Korzun, 2016). This chapter discusses a few examples of the emerging use case developed on top of the ambient intelligence.

As discussed in the previous chapter, the Ambient Intelligence defines principles of interworking for all devices that surround the user and so creating proactively-responsive user-friendly environment. The key for development of the user-friendly environment is in getting as accurate as possible definition of user's context. Taking these observations into account we selected the e-Health and e-Tourism areas as the primary reference cases for the chapter. Both application areas are characterized by access to the most relevant personal context of the user.

In the chapter you can find definition of the key enablers of the service smartness. The analysis part for the presented case studies is targeted to illustrate smart services development process and discuss arising challenges and opportunities. In addition the authors discuss the role of location-awareness, the new trend in UX called ZeroUI and other design principles that can be applied in development of the modern smart services.

The main part of the chapter considers presentation of the selected use case examples of smart services applied for e-Tourism and e-Healthcare use scenarios. The chapter also provides genera discussion on the general principles of ZeroUI concept and the role of Virtual and Augmented Reality in creating a new user experience.

The rest of the Chapter is organized as follows. Section BACKGROUND provides general background, including definitions and discussions of the topic and incorporates views presented in the prior art research on the topic. Section AMBIENT INTELLIGENCE IN E-TOURISM presents an example of ambient intelligence in e-Tourist. Section PROACTIVE SERVICES AS ENABLERS OF THE NEXT REVOLUTION IN DIAGNOSTICS AND HEALTH MANAGEMENT initiates some discussion and presents example of proactive services as enablers of the next revolution in diagnostics and health management. Section IOT BASED SECURE SMART HEALTH CARE provides logical continuation for the e-Health topic by making in-depth analysis of the smart healthcare use cases. Section 6 starts a new independent discussion on the role of zeroUI concept and general role of Virtual and Augmented Realities for delivering new user experience. Section THE ZEROUI CONCEPT discusses solutions and recommendations in dealing with the issues, controversies, or problems presented in the preceding sections. The following section discusses future and emerging trends, and provides insight on the possible future of the discussed use cases. Then we summarize the studied solutions and achieved recommendations.

BACKGROUND

The general principles of Ambient Intelligence (AmI) were introduced 20 years ago and thanks to development of supporting technologies like IoT, now we witness transformation of AmI into a huge industry. Current estimates suggest that by 2020 the number of IoT devices will be over 26 billion units worldwide and the ambient applications will generate more than 8 billion downloads in applications such as personal assistants, social communication, health and fitness, augmented reality and local search applications. Generally AmI transforms the environment into more friendly space where intelligent information processing happens on the edge of the environment and the computational ability is seamlessly injected into all aspects of daily life of the user.

There is a number of properties that can be directly associated with the notion of ambient intelligent service. The first property is an information service, i.e., the service provides the information fragment appropriate to the user in current environment. Then the user (not the service) applies this fragment of information for situational decision-making. As a result, the service provides a kind of informational and analytical support. It is important to stress that there is no strict requirement to apply artificial intelligence (AI) and automated decision making. The service can use AI to remove a part of most boring routine from the user. But the intellectual role of the user shall not be replaced completely. Instead such services shall target to assist the user by using the automated and autonomic computing. The basic challenges of the ambient intelligent services are in organization of efficient information search, construction of the appropriate information fragment, and clear delivery (e.g., visualization) of the constructed information fragments to the user. AmI enables developers to better understand how users want to interact with computers and what they want to get out of such interaction.

When looking in broader perspective, the key characteristics of smart services can be defined as follows:

- Connects and unites objects of the physical and digital worlds into a product;
- Can feature multi-modal interfaces activated through voice or text or touch;
- Enables dealing with any kind of product like with a service with enhanced use scenarios;
- Provides the new degree of freedom for value creation and economic efficiency;
- Facilitates transition from product-centric to customer-centric business model.

To enable the above listed characteristics the AmI smart services should be associated with the following features:

- Aware of the presence of individuals and can recognize individual's identity;
- Aware of contexts and recognize actions, such as gestures or spoken commands;
- Be adapted to the user needs and be flexible to adapt themselves to possible changes of needs and requirements;
- Be able to perform independent tasks and do self-updating;
- Be able to identify failures and act proactively to address them;
- Continuously reduce running costs, optimize themselves and increase productivity;
- Communicate with other services and things.

Delivery of the defined service smartness is supported by the following key enablers:

- Data analytics and data-based intelligence – big data analysis and processing, data mining to support decisions and solutions finding;
- Rise of Ubiquitous Computer Vision in IoT;
- Developments in Intelligent IoT and Fog Computing;
- Service delivery with intensive use of highly interconnected integrated electronics, e.g., sensors, controllers, microprocessors, data storages;
- User-friendly interfaces, seamless interaction with the services and innovative user experience;
- High security and privacy – applying the best mechanisms and tools to ensure security and privacy;

- Smart business models and mindset – customer-centric and value-focused approach in delivering services and applying new types of business models and forms of service delivery.

Another key aspect of the smart service design is ensuring continues availability and mobility of the service. The mobility essentially increases the number of situations which the users can get in. Consequently, such services are acting as a mobile assistant that accompanies the user. The latter follows the style "make everything from my personal mobile device", and the user may have no idea which other devices (surrounding or remote) are involved into the service construction and delivery. The key challenge is making the participation easy and transparent, as well as the service delivery becomes essentially aware of the visualization capabilities of the user's device. Consider an example of user interaction with some physical environment (e.g., IoT-enabled environment). For example, when a user enters to the shopping mall the ambient intelligence services should check what large interaction screens are available, so that when the user is passed by, she/he can take control over the available screens as a temporarily interface for more comfortable interaction with services provided by the shopping mall.

It is also important to mention that the use case scenarios discussed in this Chapter is just a small set of AmI services use cases. Table 1 provides a few more examples and summary description for a few more AmI services use case scenarios.

AMBIENT INTELLIGENCE IN E-TOURISM

People are curious and adventurous from their nature and it is the reason why from the beginning of civilization there is a strong demand to travel, explore and discover. In the last century this demand has experienced major change from privilege of selected people to the mass-market product. Tourism is form of an entertainment that enables individuals to explore the world. But looking carefully to current tourism industry, one can notice that it is based on out dated pattern of what services could be provided.

The traditional mechanisms of heritage transfer from generation to generation nowadays undergo a serious change and experience a great challenge as the digital era unfolds before our own eyes. The digital era prompts developers of content and application to use a new way of delivering information to the consumer. When developing e-Tourism services it is important to remember

Table 1. Examples of AmI services in different problem domains

Problem domain	Description of potential for AmI services
Smart Home assistant	The AmI services enable users to get most benefits out of the living environment. Nowadays one can find a number of services that can be delivered in voice-controlled manner by use of affordable speaker – Echo. For example, the user can set alarm clock, ask to play music, create shopping list, ask for weather forecast, and all these without the hassle of pulling out computers or smartphones. For example, the Alexa platform by Amazon can be used to create such smart home assistant, provide users a more natural way to interact with IoT devices and get new services.
Digital secretary and personal assistant	AmI services can provide intuitive assistance to the user in any daily needs, e.g., book a ride to the airport, keep track of a shopping list, controlling heaters and air conditioners, start playing preferred music, etc. For example, AIsense Inc. created a voice service that transcribes conversations. The service recognizes voices of all participants and prepares a full transcript of the meeting. After meeting it allows deep searches of the materials, pull out main topics, set the conversation threads, and helps to get most of information from any meeting.
In-car assistants and autonomous driving	AmI services provide a broad range of solutions for in-car use, starting from aiding the people drive better and avoid collisions and to entertainment services for passengers. For example, the Distronic Plus system and Infiniti's auto drive mode can fully automate driving process, staying inside the lane, maintaining a distance between the cars in front of them. More recent example is advanced in-car AmI infrastructure provided by Tesla, which allows broad range of services from autonomous driving, including parking and following the owner, and to services like automatic opening door to the garage.
Health care and better life for elderly people	Aging populations, shortage and high cost of health care professionals create demands for Ambient Assisted Living services that target to help seniors prolong independent living. Core idea of this use scenario is to enable remotely monitor and support of seniors by elderly care and health care professionals. For example, Neura Inc. targets to upgrade senior care with ambient apps that learn daily habits and medical needs. Based on collected data the service reminds patients to take medication at the right time and monitor vital signs to check how the medications are working.
Safety at workplace	Ambient Intelligence services have strong potential to reduce the occurrence of accidents in workplaces like construction sites. A large part of accidents are caused by the lack of compliance to safety regulations. AmI services can make continuous "Big brother" monitoring of the environment and the workers and issue immediate alerts when the safety rules are violated.
Management of complicated workflows	AmI services allow complete monitoring and management of multiple short-deadline projects, delivering faster and more accurate communication among networked humans and so creating the competitive edge in workflows management. For example, BellHawk Systems Inc. created planner service that tracks materials, labor and machines in real time and matches them with purchase orders, work orders and shipping orders.
Living and working space security	AmI security services allow transforming simple web cameras into the efficient tool for protecting families and properties. For example, by integrating security camera to the doorbell, allows the homeowners to confront unknown visitors remotely. It is possible to monitor living and working space remotely and get alarm when some motion or any other change is detected.
E-Commerce – personalized experience in unmanned supermarkets	In the last years we see how some e-Commerce giants (e.g., Amazon and Alibaba) start to explore the concept of unmanned supermarkets (e.g., Amazon Go, Tao Cafe). They target to deliver personalized 24/7 shopping experience in physical stores by providing enhanced AmI services, which make shopping experience in the physical environment similar in terms of comfort to the best practices of online shopping.

Figure 1. System scope for e-Tourism services

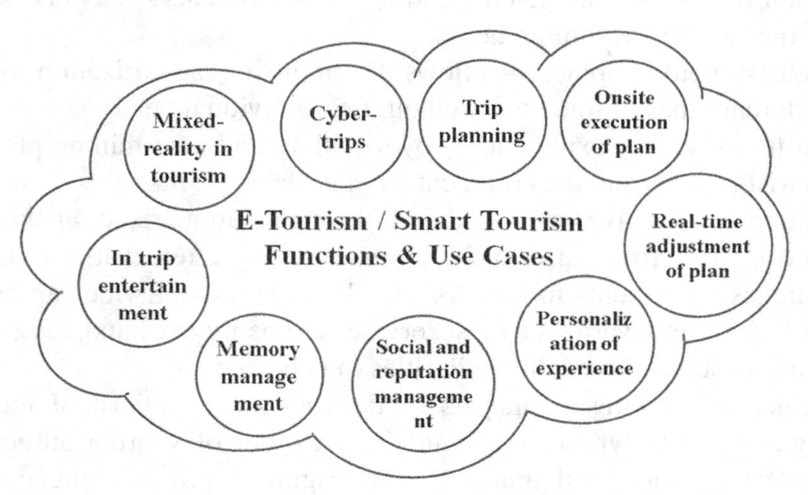

that their mission shouldn't be limited to entertainment of the tourists. These services shall play a key role in preserving and sharing cultural heritage, and soon become a tool to help preserving and developing national identity. This is getting especially crucial in the era of globalization.

The cultural heritage is a type of information that should be accessible for anyone. It should be easy manageable and flexible to be adjustable to needs of any consumer. The best choice is to collect, distribute and preserve such content in the form of open data (OD), which possesses all these values.

It is also important to remember that here authors are talking about large service industry that affects millions of people. As any change it brings new opportunities for those who are ready to them and threats for those who are not ready to the change. Among recent trends one could mention – the service provider does not need physical presence on site; competitive solutions are often delivered by entrepreneurs and SMEs, etc.

In recent years we have seen that role of location-aware services is increasing and the corresponding ecosystem is growing fast and developing in all aspects. Most of mass-market mobile devices have embedded technologies for detecting location. This creates the huge opportunity to develop services and solutions for associating virtual tags with real physical objects and processing user's content in geographical context.

In order to support internal learning mechanisms it is important that e-Tourism services will also continuously collect some relevant data about the tourists. The collected data can be categorized into the following groups:

- Total time spent in a given location – based on check-ins / check-outs in the selected accommodation.
- Tourist demographics – allows to improve categorization of the different types of tourists based on their individual needs.
- Profile of tourist experience – by sampling and data-mining previous tourist records and the comments in the social media.
- Patterns of activities - acquired through summarized analysis of information from all available services, e.g., reservations, tickets purchase, payments for snacks, etc. This analysis provides an overall picture of how various tourist services are being used and can help to cluster tourists based on similarities in behavior.
- Trajectory mining – analysis of the movement pattern of tourists, e.g., preferred type of accommodation, order of visiting attractions, preferred routes and transport, etc. Figure 2 provides the detailed definition of the trajectory mining process (Basiri et al., 2018). Despite originally the process was introduced for indoor short range trajectory monitoring, but its general principles can be applied to trajectory mining at any scale.

Figure 2. The trajectory mining process

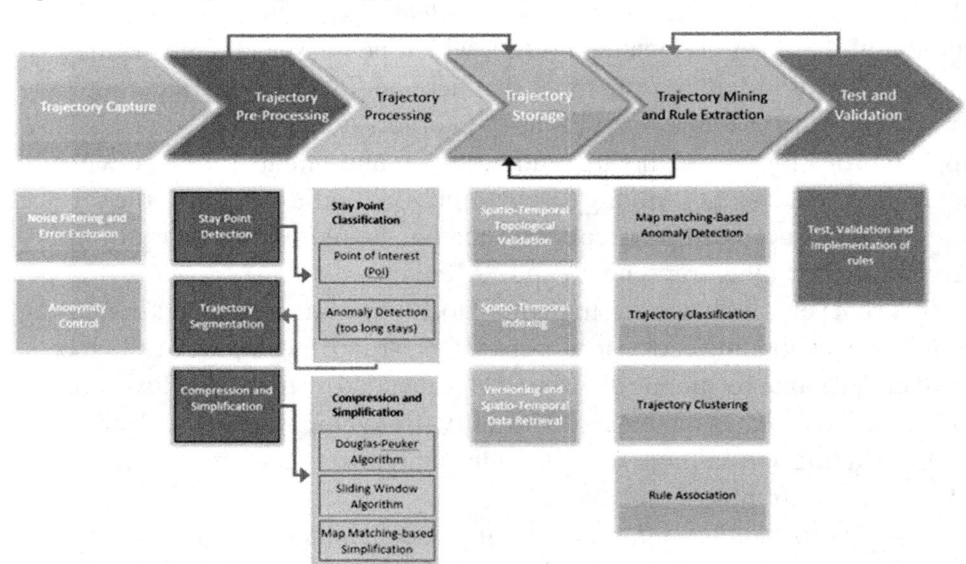

PROACTIVE SERVICES AS ENABLERS OF THE NEXT REVOLUTION IN DIAGNOSTICS AND HEALTH MANAGEMENT

The main problem of current healthcare system is in addressing health issues only after serious, easy observable damage is done. As a result the treatment process gets expensive and not comfortable for the patient. The foreseen next revolution in health management is based on replacement of reactive diagnostics of the health problems by proactive continues monitoring of health condition and early detection and correction of the negative trends. The later description is based on the project Mobile Diagnostics Device (MDD) that already now creates service ecosystem to help mass-users taking good care of own health and monitoring relatives. The project core is a cloud system (MDDCloud) supported by a set of free and commercial applications. The MDDCloud is delivered in B2B and B2B2C models, and the supporting mobile apps are in B2C model. All apps have certain finalized functional and can be used independently or synchronized by the MDDCloud. To enable wider variety of business and research scenarios all apps support user-controlled (manual) and automated synchronization modes.

In manual mode the user oversees collected data and to jointly use multiple apps must follow certain procedure that ensures data consistency. The core functional is available for free use. The commercial apps addressing some specific cases of advanced scenarios, like complex diagnostics on top of multiple parameters. Some apps offer in-app purchases that facilitate work and provide additional services.

In automated scenario the user can link all his apps to the personal account in the MDDCloud. The system takes care of full sync, makes data backup and provides several additional services.

Thanks to highly flexible architecture the MDD project is good for research purposes. Several research projects have been done and currently

Table 2. Pilot AmI services in e-Tourism

Service title	Region	Description and reference
MEGA virtual guide	Sicily, Italy	Parco Archeologico della Valle del Temple in Agrigento, an archaeological area with ancient Greek temples in Agrigento (Pilato, Augello, Santangelo, Gentile, & Gaglio, 2006).
OpenKarelia platform	Karelia region, Finland and Russia	The platform offers a number of AmI services that covers 12 tourist spots in the target region (Balandina, Balandin, Koucheryavy, & Mouromtsev, 2015).

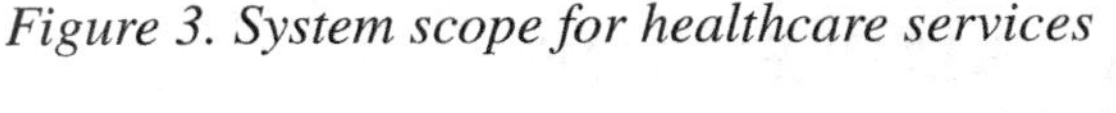

Figure 3. System scope for healthcare services

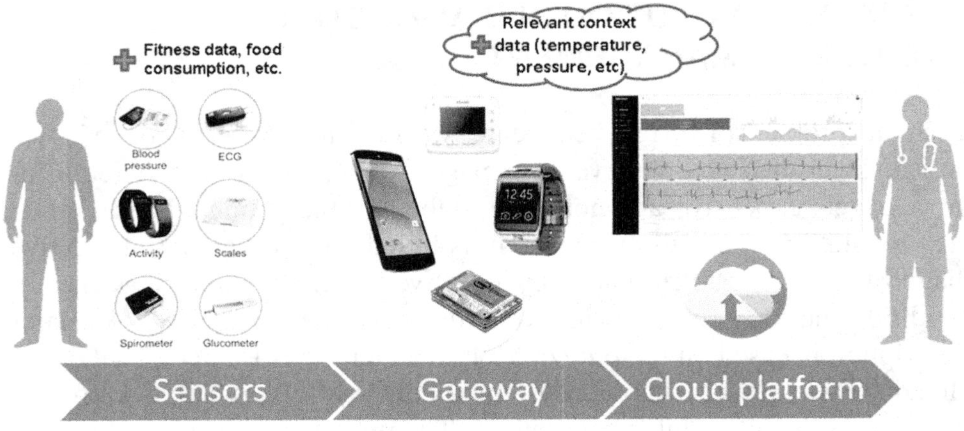

run on top of MDD. The total number of MDD services users exceeds a million. Currently the system gets access to large volume of impersonalized real-life health data. This data is collected thanks to the new program for the users that offer access to a set of new apps and services in exchange to donation of anonymized personal health records. Approximately 15% of the users are interested to join this program. As a result, this program generates sufficient volume of data for deriving statistically reliable results for predictive diagnostics based on common patterns. Based on this data the following set of new advanced free and commercial services that are based on continues analysis of personal health records over time matching them against closest patterns in the database.

The ambient technology offering benefits to patients with mobility challenges. ElliQ is an ambient intelligence app, developed by Intuition Robotics, that adds a personal twist to the smart speaker concept. It's a "social robot" targeted at seniors that stays on top of all their daily activities—keeping them more engaged and behaving more socially than they would likely be on their own. The size of a small lamp with a bobbing head and a touchscreen, ElliQ sits on nightstands or kitchen counters, answering questions and reminding their human companions about what they need to do or get done.

IOT BASED SECURE SMART HEALTH CARE: A DATA ANALYTICS APPROACH

e-Healthcare is a vast ecosystem that includes the personal healthcare, pharmaceutical industry, healthcare insurance, real time health systems, healthcare building facilities, robotics, biosensors, smart beds, smart pills, anything remote and the various healthcare specializations, activities like swift identification and even treatments diseases, that list of Internet of Things applications in healthcare quickly becomes endless.

Internet of Things plays significant role in the transformation of healthcare services. There is even special term - Internet of Healthcare Things (IoHT). The IoHT potential is enormous due to higher demand for remote monitoring of the aging/elderly, creating higher health consciousness among the young population, development of novel implantable/wearable healthcare devices and real-time health care management along with the management of enormous data generated from the devices. Integration of IoT to healthcare produces huge volume of health records to be processed and analyzed. Providing intelligent insights at a right level with significantly reduced downtime and bringing actionable information to the notice of healthcare providers for is major requirement.

In this section we discuss IoHT from the following two standpoints:

1. The big data analytic tools and techniques to be incorporated for the evaluation and prediction of data in Real Time Health care system.
2. Measures that can be incorporated to maintain the security and privacy of the personal/critical data of the patients.

Preliminaries

Healthcare industry is one of the fastest growing industries in the world. Nowadays the healthcare goes through the major internal transformation by changing its perspectives from disease orientation towards patient-oriented service. Healthcare is going through digital transformation that has led to use of smart devices both implantable and wearable, and adoption of electronic medical records and healthcare information systems has led to the generation of high volumes of data. The data associated with the healthcare includes patients' data which consists of the clinical data and the insurance data whereas the non-patient data associated to healthcare comprises of the molecular field data and the socio demographic related data.

The IoT in health care ecosystem allows conversions of medical devices and healthcare services. Healthcare is of two types – curative & preventive. IoT in health care has the capability to connect the medical devices and provide benefit of real time monitoring of the patient. These devices allow connecting and tracking of the individuals and details can be further utilized for research and findings. Major advantage of IoHT is Clinical trials become shorter for pharmaceutical companies, Diagnosis time becomes shorter for patients, Less repetitive visits of the patient to healthcare provider, The insurance providers will be able to ensure compliance with healthcare regulations due to avoidance of unnecessary visits, Companies providing these devices are at greater benefit and their efficiency can be improved across R&D, clinical trials, operations and customer service. IOT in healthcare with big data application can transform the healthcare services and also revolutionaries the pharmacy and other industries in the ecosystem. The overall e-Healthcare ecosystem can be illustrated by Figure 4.

Also the new era of healthcare is based on the five R's i) Right care – availability of timely treatment for the patients and individuals. ii) Right living – active role of individuals in making healthy choices about curative and

Figure 4. Ecosystem of the internet of healthcare things

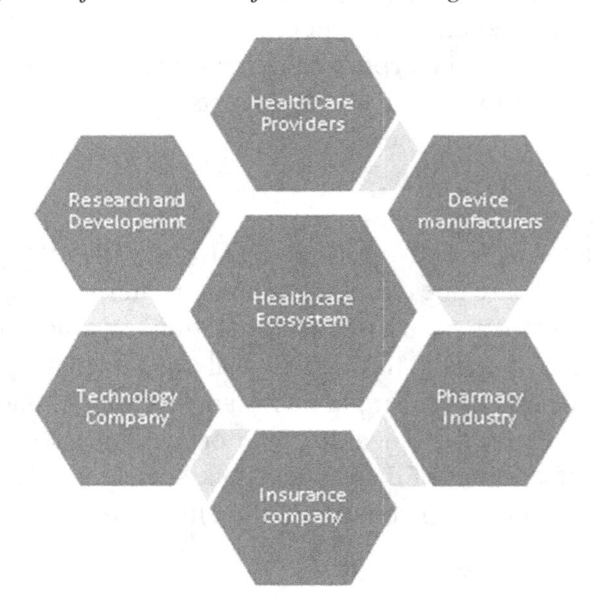

preventive healthcare. iii) Right provider- availability of skilled professionals to treat the patients for best outcomes. iv) Right value- continuously improve the quality of healthcare and eliminate high expenses, v) Right innovation - identify and innovate new approaches and therapies for improved healthcare delivery, as illustrated in Figure 5.

IoT – Big data applications in healthcare can be visualized from the following five perspectives.

Personalized Patient Care: Helps healthcare professionals (HCP) to identify patients eligible for appropriate treatment process as shown in Figure 6.

Another variant is that a healthcare professional is targeted therapy and personalized/precision medicine. The targeted therapy is used specifically in the patients suffering from cancer. This therapy is latest treatment that is able to precisely identify and combat the affected cells. Big data analysis can

Figure 5. Illustration of five R-s principle of the modern healthcare

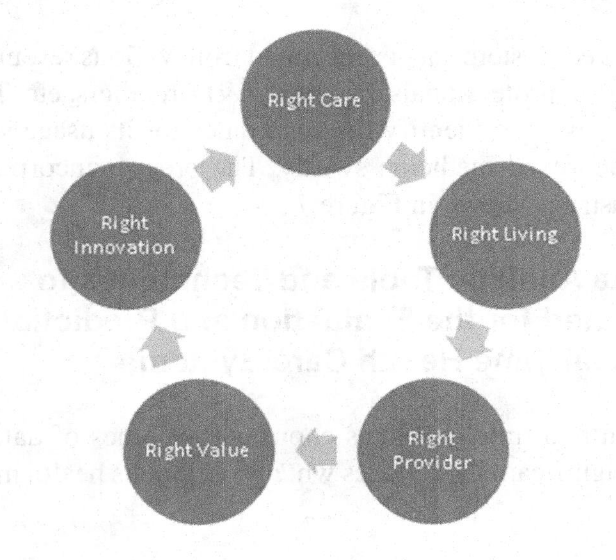

Figure 6. The classic diagnostics disease oriented decision-making chain

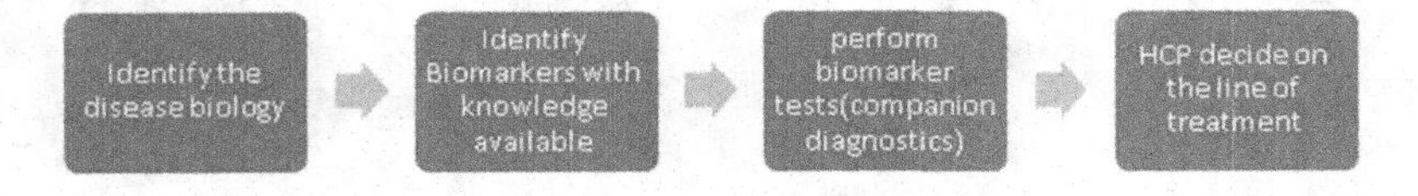

be used to make such critical decisions of identifying the affected cells. On the contrary personalized/precision medicine refers to tailoring the treatment based on the genetic understanding of disease as each individual has unique genetic makeup and to fit in the individual characteristics.

Innovative improvement on society due to information availability has led to the personalized healthcare services. This is for individual users who intend to improve their health. Automatic recommendation system based on the current health status and other various contexts input provided can be provided to the user/ consumer.

Pharmacy Industry: Implications of IoT on the pharmacy industry is major. The advantages in pharmacy industry. I) identify the issue beforehand. Able to fix the device remotely. Able to identify if the device is nearing any malfunction. Able to resupply maintenance items.

Big data is an added advantage to the pharmacy industry for improving the innovation and efficiency of critical trials while designing and developing new tool for use at customer/patients, healthcare professionals, insurers and regulators, etc.

In healthcare ecosystem data is generated from various resources together with the healthcare professionals, patients, R&D, retailers, etc. This data has to be effectively used to identify the candidates for its usage so as to float effective and approved medicine swiftly. The process incorporated in the pharmacy industry is shown in Figure 7.

The Big Data Analytic Tools and Techniques to be Incorporated for the Evaluation and Prediction of Data in Real Time Health Care System

Data sensing in real time generates enormous volumes of data. Real time monitoring is significant in the cases where continuous health monitoring of

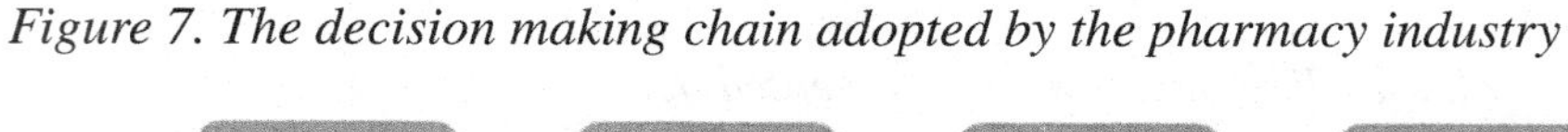

Figure 7. The decision making chain adopted by the pharmacy industry

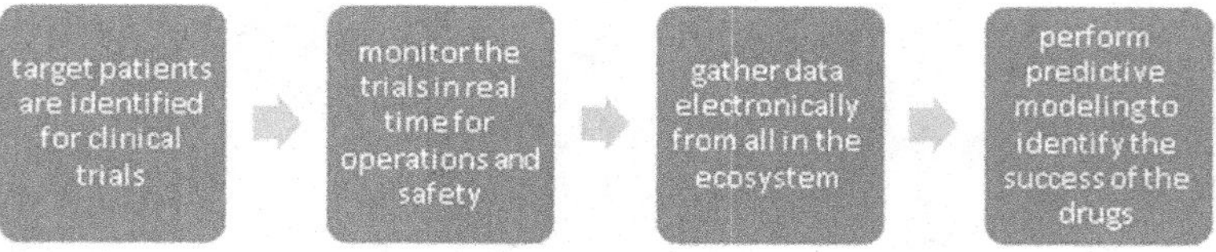

chronic illnesses is required and in cases of lifesaving in emergency situations. Rural and remote areas can be provided round the clock healthcare with IoHT. The IoT – big data framework for monitoring the health consists of the following components: physical sensors, networks for communication, servers for processing of the medical data and clinic terminals. Wireless Body Area Networks (WBANs) are the main source of remote and in-hospital health monitoring and is completely revolutionizing the health care industry and also leading to the evolution of healthcare ecosystem. Nowadays the rapid development of smart phones, sensors, body sensors and wireless communications pave the way for drastic improvement in healthcare innovation, development and monitoring.

In the Wireless Body Area Networks (WBAN) the sensors are implanted in the patient's body or the surrounding environment and these are integrated through controller that periodically collects the data, aggregates and stores into the server. The server acts as an interface between the WBAN and the healthcare professionals. WBANS is configured and managed by PS which includes registration of sensors nodes, initialization, task allocation and specification, setting up secure communication channels between the sensors.

- **Types of Data in IoHT:** A digitized patient's record (Health details) is called as the Electronic Health Record and EHR should be accessible anywhere and anytime. The EHR can be Structured and Unstructured: structured data is prepared by PHC and is well-organized whereas the unstructured data is irregular and vague.
- **Data Processing:** i) Clinical Text Mining: The medical records can be structured, unstructured and may contain textual records. Text mining is the process of extracting high-quality information from the unstructured data. Some of the text mining techniques include sentiment analysis, Categorization, information extraction. Text mining in Electronic Medical Records (EMR) has finer benefits. Clinical text mining is used to discover the unknown disease, greater patient stratification, better targeting of medicines, and unknown side effects of the drugs. The Natural Language Processing (NLP) can be used for information extraction in clinical text mining. Many mining tools are used for analyzing the textual records in health domain. ii) Medical Imaging Data: The unstructured image data includes CT scans and X-rays. One of the systems used to store Medical imaging data is PACS (Picture Archival &Communication Systems). This system is used for storage and retrieval of the images. In medical Retrieval system all the images are stored in biomedical image

database. The image data occupies more space and it is complex. This system is divided into two phases training and testing phase. The feature is extracted by applying various algorithms during the training phase. In testing phase the query result is obtained based on the input query image. iii) Genomic data: Genomic data is a discipline in genetics. It deals with DNA to assemble, structure and sequence the function of genes. All the data's are collected, stored and processed with the help of software. The Genome database (GDB) is the repository of Human Genome. Genome-wide association studies (GWAS) is used to find out the common genetic factors which influence health and disease.

The big data analysis can be used for decision making in health care with the aid of machine learning algorithms. The different approaches of machine learning algorithms and data mining can afford better cure to disease, build up personalized medicines and even prevent disease or epidemics. Traditional Machine Learning Algorithms works on centralized databases. There is necessitate to amend the traditional algorithms or crop up with some common hybrid approaches to manage the large dataset in distributed environment.

Tools and Data analytics platform used in Health care System: The diverse number of tools is used to progress health care data and analytics. This will prop up descriptive, predictive and prescriptive healthcare data analytics.

1. **Advanced Data Visualization (ADV):** ADV can handle various data types. It varies from erstwhile standards bars and line chart. It is trouble–free to use. It supports analysts to explore the data widely. ADV can produce best results and to disclose clinical hidden patterns in the data.
2. **Presto:** Presto is used to analyze enormous amount of data. It is a distributed SQL Query engine. With the help of presto data can be analyzed in few seconds or minutes.
3. **Hive:** The large amount of data can be handled using hive. Unlike presto it is not used for processing and analyzing data quickly. It performs all excel tasks efficiently. Industries use both presto and Hive for preeminent performance. Presto can access data stored on Hive.
4. **Vertica:** It is analogous to Presto. It swathe hefty amount of data including hospitals" data and analytics. It is less expensive as it eliminates costly architecture. It encompasses the feature of scalability. Vertica can improve healthcare by lowering operational costs, accelerating medical reports and analyzing patients" patterns.

5. **Key Performance Indicators (KPI):** It is approach that use electronic medical record data to identify human practice and inventions. KPI can get better quality of medical health care for patients who are vulnerable to hospital conditions. It is used to denote noteworthy indicators to be monitored and corrected.
6. **Online Analytics Processing (OLAP):** OLAP perform statistical calculation in a high speed through multidimensional organized data and amplify data integrity checking, reporting services and quality control. It gives better tracking of medical records and diagnoses. Thus improving health care decision making system.
7. **Online Transaction Processing (OLTP):** It is interrelated to OLAP. It is used to process patient registration, documentation of health records in hospitals, different operations of patients care, and review the results.
8. **The Hadoop Distributed File System (HDFS):** Healthcare data analytics system is enhanced using HDFS. It divides huge amount of data into smaller one. The miniature data is distributed across other systems. It eliminates data redundancy. It is mainly focused on assisting diagnosis, treatment planning, monitoring patient's signs and fraud detections.
9. **Casandra File System (CFS):** CFS is a distributed system similar to HDFS. It is a designated system used to act upon analytic operation with no single point of failure.
10. **Map Reducing System:** Map reducing system handles enormous amount of data. It split the chore into subchore and get together its outputs. It facilitates operational calculations to be performed efficiently. It keeps track on each sever when the chore is being performed. The main advantage of map reducing is high-level of parallelism.
11. **Complex Event Processing (CEP):** CEP is recently used in healthcare sectors. It monitors the different states of patient. Complex event processing relates and link the events to real time. Thus it improves EMR and HER systems.
12. **Text Mining:** In health care systems text mining tools can be an added value for examining clinical records from hospitals. Text mining can recommend treatment plan that can build up a number of standards and protocols. Treatment can be done based on these developed standards.
13. **Cloud Computing:** Cloud computing has greater advantage in health care sector. It offers more flexibility by act in response for the dynamic changes and recent medical updates. It adds a great health care value by

lowering costs, improving the productivity and data analysis, providing better security. It lowers the sprain due to voluminous data.one such example is Phillips Health suite platform.

14. **Mahout:** A mahout is an apache project. It intends to develop applications that can prop up health care data analytics on Hadoop systems.
15. **JAQL:** JAQL is a functional query language used to process huge amount of data. It makes possible parallel processing by translating high level queries into low level ones. JAQL works well with map reducing.
16. AVRO: AVRO make possible data encoding and serialization. It improves data structure by specify data types, meaning and scheme.

Measures that can be incorporated to maintain the security and privacy of the personal/ critical data of the patients

Definition of Privacy

Ensuring privacy requires making sure that individuals maintain the right to control what information is collected about them, who maintains it, who uses it, how it is used, and what purpose it is used for

Definition of Security

Providing security requires preventing access to information or other objects by unauthorized users, as well as protecting against unauthorized alterations or destruction of users' information. The classic definition of security equals it with confidentiality, integrity, and availability, called (by its acronym) the CIA triad.

Security Requirements

The elements of the IoHT are exposed to attacks and threats due to the vulnerability posed by the environment. Any security scheme developed should cater the following requirements.

- Availability. The services offered by the network and the network elements must be available without any interruptions.

- Authentication. Authentication is the basic requirement of any application. The receiver on the other end is able to verify the legitimacy of the sender and the message received.
- Authorization. It ensures that only authorized nodes are involved in a network activity.
- Integrity and freshness. It ensures the message exchanged by the network elements are not modified during transmission. Old and stale messages also create adverse effects on network security. This can be overcome by using timestamps that are appropriately chosen.
- Confidentiality. Concealing of the messages exchanged between the source and destination can be achieved through encryption and decryption.
- Non-repudiation. The sender once it sends a message is unable to deny that it is the sender of the message.
- Fault tolerance. The basic features of the IoHT are still available even in the presence of network or node failures.
- Self-Healing. In case of any failures, the system should be adaptable and continue to function without any interruptions.
- Scalability. The level of security provided by the network should remain the same even when the number of nodes is increased drastically. The addition of new nodes must not disrupt the normal functioning of the IoHT.

Security Threats

There are a lot of threats that can affect WSNs such as insecure radio links and nodes.

- An interruption attack refers to the attacker being able to listen to the incoming communication and prevent the data flow towards the destination.
- An interception attack refers to an attacker being able to listen to the messages exchanged between the source and the destination. The attacker simply listens to the communication between the communicating parties.
- In the modification attack the attacker alters attack the message during transit and the receiver assumes that the message it received is from the sender.

- In the fabrication attack, the attacker creates and transmits a message to the receiver as though the message is from the source node.

Privacy Issues in IoT Applications

Risks of patients' privacy exposure a Personal Health Record (PHR) is "an individual electronic record of health-related information that conforms to the nationally recognized interoperability standards. PHR can be drawn from multiple sources while being managed, shared and controlled by the individual". PHRs are reported to the e-health center directly, and the primary privacy and security issue is to keep the patients' PHRs confidential.

Threats of Cyber-Attacks on Privacy Cyber-attacks can inject false data into a system, causing critical damage in IoT applications. It is fundamental to provide the adequate level of protection against cyber-attacks in in smart home applications for the disabled. However, the resource-constrained nature of many of IoT devices present in a smart home environment do not allow to implement the standard security solutions.

Data Eavesdropping and Data Confidentiality Generally, the health data of patients, including the disabled, are held under the legal obligations of confidentiality, and made available only to the authorized caregivers. It is important to prevent stealing data from storage or eavesdropping on them while they flow over the wireless links. For example, a popular IoT-based disabled glucose monitoring and insulin delivery system utilizes wireless communication links, which are frequently used to launch privacy attacks.

Location privacy Location privacy is concerned with location privacy threats and eavesdropping on a user's location. Location privacy in WSNs, specifically hiding the message sender's location, can be achieved through routing to a randomly selected intermediate node (RRIN). Eavesdropping and tracing of packets can be prevented by the Location Privacy Routing (LPR) protocol, which uniformly distributes the directions of incoming and outgoing traffic at sensor nodes.

Identity Threats and Privacy of Stored Data Loss of a patient's privacy, especially her identity data may result in significant physical, financial, and emotional harm to the patient.

Table 3. IoT-based solutions

Privacy issues	IoT-based solutions
Personal Health Record exposure	Encryption before outsourcing, dividing health system into domains, analyzing whether sensitive data is private
Cyber attacks	Detection methods and system recovery
Data eavesdropping and data confidentiality	Data hiding and cryptographic techniques
Identify threats and privacy of stored data	Pseudonymization of medical data, identify management, anonymity
Location privacy	Security protocols

THE ZEROUI CONCEPT AND ROLE OF VIRTUAL AND AUGMENTED REALITY IN DELIVERING THE NEW USER EXPERIENCE

It is clearly expected that interaction with Ambient Intelligence shall be unobtrusive and seamless, i.e., solutions with the steep learning curve are not acceptable within scope of AmI concept. Traditionally, one of the competing edges for the products was a question on how well a company could adopt the user-friendly design principles in their products. AmI will be a game-changer as the services should work just as a user walk into an AmI environment.

Already now the users of AmI services start learning how to interact with invisible assistants without a device on hand. This is an important mental change which will shape the future AmI environments. The leading companies including Google, Microsoft, Apple and Xiaomi are actively investing in development of own invisible assistants. And the interaction pattern is not limited to voice commands. For example, recently Amazon expanded interaction interface of Alexa platform by camera. As a result the platform got more capabilities to pro-actively serve the users.

This created ground for a paradigm where user's movements, voice, glances, and even thoughts can cause systems to respond by adopting environment to increase comfort of the user. The core idea of the ZeroUI is in breaking dependence of services on traditional graphical UI by replacing it with nature interactions of haptic feedback, context aware, ambient, gestures and voice recognition, even by recognizing conversions that are not directly targeted in transformation of the environment. The most natural enablers of ZeroUI interfaces are voice recognition and natural language processing and analysis of the video stream of user's behavior. Future development of ZeroUI paradigm will be primary connected to further increase of the AI role in such interaction, where AI will take greater responsibility in making decisions for humans. This is very promising approach, but the authors see serious risks in letting AI be in charge on setting life environment, as obvious benefits in the beginning might lead to risk of compromising the freedom of choice and mass manipulations to the whole society. This is an area where each next step forward shall be carefully analyzed and potential negative outcomes and risks must be studied and prevented.

Alternative approach for enhancing the ZeroUI paradigm is by broader adoption of the Augmented and Virtual Reality (AR/VR) technologies. For examples, let's discuss the OdysseusVR – the new Virtual Reality platform that provides Augmented Reality interface for creating the bridge services between the physical and virtual worlds (Bakalin, Nikolaenko, & Balandin, 2017). Thanks to high performance and low resource consumption footprint, the OdysseusVR platform enables new user experience and can be seen as a tool to pilot new principles of ZeroUI interaction. The platform can be used in a single user-mode or support cooperative work of multiple users. Moreover, the OdysseusVR platform design allows using embedded AI engine. The main use scenario for the platform is to enable the user to enhance control of any complex system by using moves of the own body, including eyes. This creates the most natural and easy to use control solution, where the user use movements of the body for shaping VR environment to define desirable changes, simulate outcome and order to transfer changes to the physical world. As a result the Virtual and Augmented Reality allow overcoming restrictions and limitations of the classical human-computer interaction interfaces. The user gets personally adopted cozy UI that provides maximum support of individual style of way of managing what he/she wants to do in physical or virtual words, having maximum freedom of creativity and increasing individual performance. Use of this form of interaction transforms even a routine process into a playful process that is comfortable for the operator. The platform also learns individual patterns and later tries to even more speedup process by suggesting applying recognized patterns. This contributes to development of the individual intelligence as well as cognitive intelligence of the process. The basic version of OdysseusVR platform includes a set of games to illustrate potential of the proposed approach; shows how real could feel the virtual world and help users to learn how to enjoy the new way of interacting with physical and virtual realities. It is also good to mention that OdysseusVR platform environment is a good example of AmI service.

FUTURE RESEARCH DIRECTIONS

Nowadays we are witnessing shaping of the ambient future. The discussed use case scenarios are under active development and we will see a lot of new breakthrough solutions in the near future. Many of already created AmI services offer significant benefits to the users. Further development of AI and other technologies will further boost development of new AmI solutions, which will involve more people in evaluating benefits along with the risks associated with AmI.

In the future AmI will enter to all aspects of human life and become one of the key infrastructures, i.e., something similar to the electricity infrastructure. The IoT infrastructure will be primary used for delivering AmI services like the energy infrastructure. In order to gain people's confidence, AmI will have to place risk management, data security and system reliability as the top priorities for future development.

The list of main open problems and the corresponding areas for future research are summarized by Table 4.

CONCLUSION

It is already 20 years since the Ambient Intelligence concept was introduced for the first time. Nowadays it becomes technically possible to implement many of the elements described and deliver the new services to benefit users. The AmI services have the potential to disrupt business models in many areas. But the technology is still in early stage of the journey. A lot still have to be done to show users the whole potential of AmI services and AmI as a concept still needs to gain the trust of the public. People are starting to already enjoy benefits of AmI services, like discussed for e-Health and e-Tourism applications. In the near future we will be witnesses how these and other AmI use cases will affect all aspects of our daily lives. And to ensure sustainable development it will require a lot of emphasis on accuracy, security, reliability and privacy protection.

This chapter provides an overview of a number of real-life use cases that illustrates potential of ambient intelligence services. In particularly we discuss two hottest areas: the e-Tourist and e-Health. The obtained results clearly illustrate that the ambient intelligence services have much better flexibility

Table 4. Open problems of AmI use cases: e-Tourism and e-Healthcare

Problem title	Target use case	Description
Privacy protection	e-Healthcare, e-Tourism	Privacy is a top concern and topic for further research as Ambient Intelligence becomes more prevalent and powerful. The privacy policies for public and private space shall be explicitly defined and deployed. In order to ensure success of the AmI services the businesses has to be open about the extent of AmI capabilities deployed in their properties and not allow misuse of the power provided by AmI. It is crucial to make transparent to the public that the above principles are fulfilled, which is another large area for future work.
Manipulation and misuse of services	e-Healthcare, e-Tourism	AmI services will have very strong impact on the daily life of the users. The services will be invisible and perceived as a natural part of daily routine, which make them very dangerous tool for manipulation and misuse of users' trust. Here we talk about unprecedented socioeconomic impact potential, so this aspect shall be extremely carefully address in AmI development and be a subject of continues strict control.
Guaranty of failure free solution – no right to mistake	e-Healthcare	Aging of population and demand to maintain longer active independent living lead to dramatic increase of the cost of health care, which already double digit percent of GDP in the developed countries (Sawyer & Cox, 2018). This strongly raises demand for Ambient Assisted Living services for remote monitoring, ensuring optimal treatment and providing support in case of emergency. But to make it widely accepted and used it is absolutely critical to ensure processes that minimize probability of any mistake, especial for fatal mistake by at least two orders of magnitude comparing to the human healthcare professional mistake ratio.
Stable operation of service everywhere	e-Tourism	Specifics of e-Tourism use case suggests that one of the highest demand for services is recorded in the areas with pure or no connectivity. Moreover, in most cases the discussed areas are characterized by low population ratio, which demands to think how AmI infrastructure can be delivered, i.e., more attention shall be given to development of independent localized AmI infrastructure (analogy could be local electricity generators, as a replacement of connection to the electricity infrastructure)

and outperform traditional service solutions, which are currently dominating on the market.

Also the chapter highlights the evolution and current status of research and trends that led to the revolution of healthcare industry through application of Big Data and Internet of Things. These two streams- IoT and Big data analytics have the power to transform the way healthcare and to gain insight on information from data repositories and make apt decisions. IoT requires real time data analysis services which can cope with huge amounts of data which raises new challenge from the Big Data point of view. Issues like security and privacy for IoT and Big data analytics should also be considered which switching over from traditional healthcare to contemporary healthcare.

Applications in healthcare and data analytics have the potential to become more mainstream and accelerate their maturing process. The normal trend of sensor device design is that they have little external security features and hence prone to physical tempering. This increases the vulnerability of the devices and poses tougher security challenge.

Generally, the chapter is targeted to clearly position and ground the book scope to the real-life use cases and most relevant trends in the industry. Thanks to provided examples the more specific in-depth aspects discussed in the book should become clearer for the reader.

ACKNOWLEDGMENT

The primary contributors to this chapter are Ekaterina Balandina from University of Tampere, Finland and Sergey Balandin from FRUCT Oy, Finland. We also used materials kindly provided by Dr. Kiran Kumari Patil (Reva University, India), Prof. Shantala Devi Patil (Reva University, India), and Daniil Bakalin (OdysseusVR).

REFERENCES

Acampora, G., Cook, D., Rashidi, P., & Vasilakos, A. (2013). *A Survey on Ambient Intelligence in Healthcare*. Academic Press.

Augusto, J., Callaghan, V., Cook, D., Kameas, A., & Satoh, I. (2013). Intelligent environments: A manifesto. *Human-centric Computing and Information Sciences, 3*(1), 1–18. doi:10.1186/2192-1962-3-12

Bakalin, D., Nikolaenko, O., & Balandin, S. (2017). *OdysseusVR – Virtual Reality platform with AR support*. Retrieved from http://ovr.fruct.org/

Balandin, S., & Waris, H. (2009). Key Properties in the Development of Smart Spaces. *Lecture Notes in Computer Science, 5615*, 3-12.

Balandina, E., Balandin, S., Koucheryavy, Y., & Mouromtsev, D. (2015). *IoT Use Cases in Healthcare and Tourism*. Academic Press.

Basiri, A., Amirian, P., Winstanley, A., & Moore, T. (2018). Making tourist guidance systems more intelligent, adaptive and personalised using crowd sourced movement data. *Journal of Ambient Intelligence and Humanized Computing*, *9*(2), 413–427. doi:10.100712652-017-0550-0

Borodin, A., Lebedev, N., Vasyliev, A., Zavyalova, Y., & Korzun, D. (2016). An Experimental Study of Personalized Mobile Assistance Service in Healthcare Emergency Situations. *UBICOMM*, *2016*, 178–183.

Korzun, D. (2016). On the smart spaces approach to semantic-driven design of service-oriented information systems. *12th International Baltic Conference on Databases and Information Systems*, 181–195. 10.1007/978-3-319-40180-5_13

Korzun, D., Borodin, A., Timofeev, I., Paramonov, I., & Balandin, S. (2015). *Digital Assistance Services for Emergency Situations in Personalized Mobile Healthcare- Smart Space based Approach*. Academic Press.

Korzun, D., Nikolaevskiy, I., & Gurtov, A. (2015). *Service Intelligence Support for Medical Sensor Networks in Personalized Mobile Health Systems*. Academic Press.

Kulakov, K., Petrina, O., Korzun, D., & Varfolomeev, A. (2016). *Towards an Understanding of Smart Service- The Case Study for Cultural Heritage e-Tourism*. Academic Press.

Laure, D., Medvedev, O., Balandin, S. & Lagutina, K. (2015). *Mobile Apps for Stimulating Healthy Life Walky Doggy Reference Example*. Academic Press.

Petrina, O., Korzun, D., Varfolomeev, A., & Ivanovs, A. (2016). *Smart Spaces Based Construction and Personalization of Recommendation Services for Historical e-Tourism*. Academic Press.

Pilato, G., Augello, A., Santangelo, A., Gentile, A., & Gaglio, S. (2006). An intelligent multimodal site-guide for the Parco Archeologico della Valle del Temple in Agrigento. *First Workshop in Intelligent Technologies for Cultural Heritage Exploitation. European Conference on Artificial Intelligence.*

Sawyer, B., & Cox, C. (2018). How does health spending in the U.S. compare to other countries? *Peterson-Kaiser Health System Tracker*. Retrieved from https://www.healthsystemtracker.org/chart-collection/health-spending-u-s-compare-countries/#item-start

Smirnov, A., Kashevnik, A., Balandin, S., & Laizane, S. (2013). *Intelligent Mobile Tourist Guide*. Academic Press.

Smirnov, A., Kashevnik, A., Ponomarev, A., Shchekotov, M., & Kulakov, K. (2015). *Application for e-Tourism Intelligent Mobile Tourist Guide*. Academic Press.

Smirnov, A., Kashevnik, A., Ponomarev, A., Shilov, N., Shchekotov, M., & Teslya, N. (2013). *Recommendation system for tourist attraction information service*. Academic Press.

Smirnov, A., Kashevnik, A., Ponomarev, A., Teslya, N., Shchekotov, M., & Balandin, S. (2014). *Smart Space-Based Tourist Recommendation System*. Academic Press.

Smirnov, A., Kashevnik, A., Shilov, N., & Ponomarev, A. (2014). Smart Space-Based in-Vehicle Application for e-Tourism: Technological Framework and Implementation for Ford SYNC, Internet of Things, Smart Spaces, and Next Generation Networks and Systems. *LNCS*, *8638*, 52–61.

Smirnov, A., Shilov, N., Kashevnik, A., & Ponomarev, A. (n.d.). Cyber-physical infomobility for tourism application. *International Journal of Information Technology and Management*. Retrieved from http://www.inderscience.com/info/ingeneral/forthcoming.php?jcode=ijitm

Teslya, N., Kashevnik, A., & Pashkin, M. (2013). Context-Based Access Control for Ridesharing Service. *14th Conference of Open Innovations Association FRUCT*. 10.1109/FRUCT.2013.6737958

KEY TERMS AND DEFINITIONS

Augmented Reality (AR): An interactive experience of a real-world environment where the objects that reside in the real-world are "augmented" by computer-generated perceptual information, sometimes across multiple sensory modalities, including visual, auditory, haptic, somatosensory, and olfactory.

E-Healthcare (E-Health): A healthcare practice supported by electronic processes and communication.

E-Tourism: The analysis, design, implementation and application of IT and e-commerce solutions in the travel and tourism industry; as well as the analysis of the respective economic processes and market structures and customer relationship management.

Use Case: Describes how a user uses a system to accomplish a particular goal. The use case is made up of a set of possible sequences of interactions between systems and users in a particular environment and related to a particular goal.

Virtual Reality (VR): An interactive computer-generated experience taking place within a simulated environment that incorporates auditory, visual, and sensory feedback and enables full freedom of operations in the virtual world.

ZeroUI: A paradigm where user's movements, voice, glances, and even thoughts can cause systems to respond by adopting environment to increase comfort of the user.

Chapter 3
Fog Computing Technology for Cooperative Information Processing in Edge-Centric Internet of Things Environments

ABSTRACT

This chapter introduces advances in fog computing technology for involving various participants—either small or large in capacity, either local or remote—into the service construction. Non-typical computational devices (compared with traditional computers, for example, laptops, desktops, servers)—such as smartphones, wireless routers, multimedia equipment, and consumer electronics—become aware of information processing in order to construct services essentially based on local resources of the IoT environment.

INTRODUCTION

Modern digital environments include many networked computational devices representing the Internet edges (Shi, Cao, Zhang, Li, & Xu, 2016). Such devices become "smart objects" experienced by users as real participating entities due to the intelligent activity of software agents running on the devices (Augusto, Callaghan, Cook, Kameas, & Satoh, 2013). The new opportunities

DOI: 10.4018/978-1-5225-8973-0.ch003

are utilized with the emerging concept of Smart Spaces (SmS) (Korzun, 2014) and its underlying network connectivity layer of Internet of Things (IoT) (Kortuem, Kawsar, Sundramoorthy, & Fitton, 2010). In a smart space, its devices are able to discover each others' resources. Many devices in the IoT environment are mobile and heterogeneous in respect to their resources and provided functions (Kamilaris & Pitsillides, 2016), although the number of edge devices can be relatively low compared to IoT environments with large wireless sensor networks.

Edge (or localized) IoT environments become surrounding humans in their everyday lives and work. New applications are deployed using SmS based on fusion of resources from the physical (surrounding reality), information (virtual or cyber space), and social (human activity) worlds (Korzun, Balandin, Kashevnik, Smirnov, & Gurtov, 2017). The semantics of resources are shared using ontological models for representation. The resources become open for service construction performed by involved local and remote participants.

Now IoT leads to appearance of dedicated connection boxes and computational equipment (e.g., embedded in many homes), personal mobile devices (e.g., smartphones and tablets carried by users), and ubiquitous wireless networks (e.g., in many public places). The dependability suffers since the service construction moves from remotes servers to local surroundings—the Internet edge (Korzun, Varfolomeyev, Shabaev, & Kuznetsov, 2018). Some data processing is performed by intermediary devices, i.e., on network data transfer paths to the servers (cloud infrastructure). Furthermore, social computing explicitly involves humans to the computation and decision making loop. This vision is supported with the two emerging IoT-enabled paradigms: Edge-centric computing (Garcia Lopez et al., 2015) and Fog computing (Dastjerdi & Buyya, 2016).

Generally, IoT environments are becoming large, highly dynamic, hyperconnected, and functionally distributed (Korzun, Balandin, & Gurtov 2013). Typically, an IoT environment consists of multiple heterogeneous networks with a large number of networked elements and users' devices. Further evolution of the IoT concept envisions increasing of the number of connections by yet another order of magnitude from currently connected approximately 10 billion "things". This will result in unprecedented challenges in network scalability, resource efficiency, privacy considerations, and overall management of this multitude of "things". The traditional models of networks organization would have serious problems to deal with it, so more and more often some alternative ways to network virtualization are considered (Patouni, Merentitis, Panagiotopoulos, Glentis, & Alonistioti, 2013).

Another key trend that we witness nowadays is a demand for making services be proactive and smarter to increase efficiency of IoT environment use and free more time for the user (Korzun, Balandin, Kashevnik, Smirnov, & Gurtov, 2017). Despite of the elegance and clear advantages, the smart spaces paradigm still has very limited practical use. One of the problems is that its model of virtualization and knowledge sharing is still not so clear for service developers. On the other hand, we can see that these models are very close and even similar to what has been applied for many years in the Peer-to-Peer (P2P) systems area (Korzun & Balandin, 2014).

BACKGROUND

The Smart Spaces concept and IoT technology provide certain concept elements for service construction (Korzun, 2014). They aim at achievement of the following tasks:

1. To semantically integrate resources for SmS participants in the IoT environment,
2. To seamlessly integrate computations on edge devices and remote cloud resources,
3. To involve all many edge devices into the computation,
4. To create an IoT gateway for the variety of edge devices in the IoT environment,
5. To offload computations for rational use of the involved resource-constrained devices.

The problem is organization of interaction of agents and network communication of their devices.

Information Hub

Software agents are primary programmable entities in a smart space application, as Figure 1 shows. They represent data producers and consumers: sensing and actuating equipment, physical objects and humans as well as other representatives from the physical and information worlds. The information is collectively produced and made available using the information hub (i.e., a kind of self-organized knowledge base in the IoT environment). In fact, a hub

Figure 1. Information hub for interacting agents

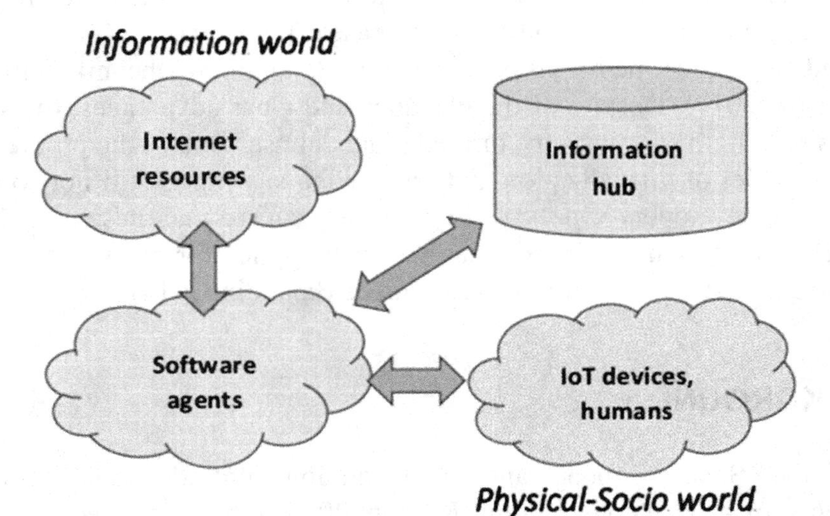

is a server (in particular, semantic information broker) that serves requests in the shared information space from the agents.

The interoperability is defined as the ability for agents to dependably communicate and interact with one another. The network-level interoperability is IoT-supported. Each agent on its device uses an existing network protocol and data structures to communicate with the hub and to exchange data. In the information-level interoperability, the agents interact understanding the shared information.

The semantic methods and models are used (Roffia et al., 2016). In particular, the content representation follows Resource Description Framework (RDF). The elementary unit is a triple, and linked structures (RDF graphs) are created to represent semantic integration in a smart space. The Web Ontology Language (OWL) is used for creating ontologies that describe the structure of shared content (semantic network) and its interpretation. In fact, a semantic network is subject to analysis for inferring new knowledge (Korzun, 2016).

Cloud and Edge-Centric Computing

IoT emergency leads to unprecedented amounts of data that are difficult for processing in the traditional way (Dastjerdi & Buyya, 2016). The cloud computing technology helps by offering on-demand and scalable storage, as well as processing services. The benefit is delegation of complex tasks to the remote computational resources. Processing, storage, and analysis of locally sensed data can be outsourced with the certain security level (e.g., cryptography on transferred data).

This central role of the cloud in the overall infrastructure for connecting Internet edge with global Internet resources in data processing, storage, and analysis is shown in (Esposito, Castiglione, Pop, & Choo, 2017), as Figure 2 shows. Building a data collecting and analyzing network from distributed devices based on clouds presents a series of challenges. Many of them are related to reliable content gathering, unreliable and heterogeneous sources, fast data delivery, real-time scheduling, cross-domain security, and cost efficiency.

The application domain requirements (e.g., industrial equipment fault monitoring, health emergency-response) do not allow the high delay of transferring data to the cloud and back to the application. When data processing is partially performed locally then the network bandwidth is less saturated since less data are sent to the cloud for storage and processing. Many tiny devices (such as IoT sensors) at the Internet edges can perform additional functions beyond sensing. In particular, a device can present a service for nearby users.

Figure 2. IoT-based architecture (many tiny devices at the edge)

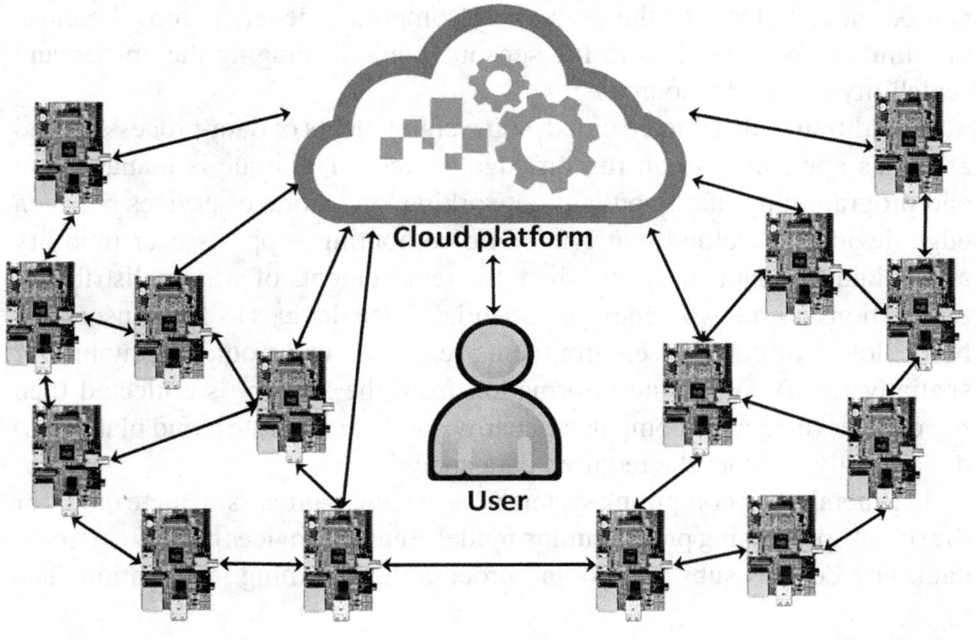

Edge-centric computing aims at using resources of near IoT devices for data storage and processing. As a result, network congestion is decreased as well as analysis and decision making can be implemented directly at the place of data production. However, small edge devices cannot handle multiple IoT applications competing for their limited resources. The contention for local resources increases and the processing latency becomes unsatisfactory high.

When edge resources are connected with cloud computing the application becomes capable to achieve better throughput under high concurrent accesses, mobility support, real-time processing guarantees, and data persistency. In particular, the elastic provisioning and storage capabilities on the cloud platform support scalability, persistency, and reliability requirements. Based on the amount of locally generated data the preliminary processing is adapted to resolve the application requirements.

Fog Computing

It aims at seamless integration of resources at edge devices and cloud platforms along with its own infrastructure (Dastjerdi & Buyya, 2016), as shown in Figure 3. Much IoT data are processed locally by utilizing edge devices near their users and devices in the intermediary networks on the path to the cloud platform (Korzun, Varfolomeyev, Shabaev, & Kuznetsov, 2018). A substantial amount of storage, communication, control, configuration, and management can be moved closer to the users. Fog computing benefits from the close proximity of edge devices to IoT sensors, while leveraging the on-demand scalability of cloud resources.

In addition to distributed cloud, some components of data-processing and analytics applications can run on edge devices. The issue is management and programming of computing, networking, and storage services between edge devices and cloud platforms. Fog computing supports user mobility and ubiquitous data analytics where the requirements of widely distributed applications with low latency are essential. Such devices as IoT sensors can be deployed in different environments (e.g., indoor or outdoor, mobile or spatially fixed). When the information from the sensors is collected then fog devices (e.g., edge computers, nearby gateways, private cloud platforms) dynamically conduct the required data analytics.

In general, a fog computing system uses the sense-process-actuate model or the stream-processing programming model. Sensing devices generates stream data. Fog devices subscribe to and process the incoming information. The

Figure 3. Distributed data processing in a fog-computing environment

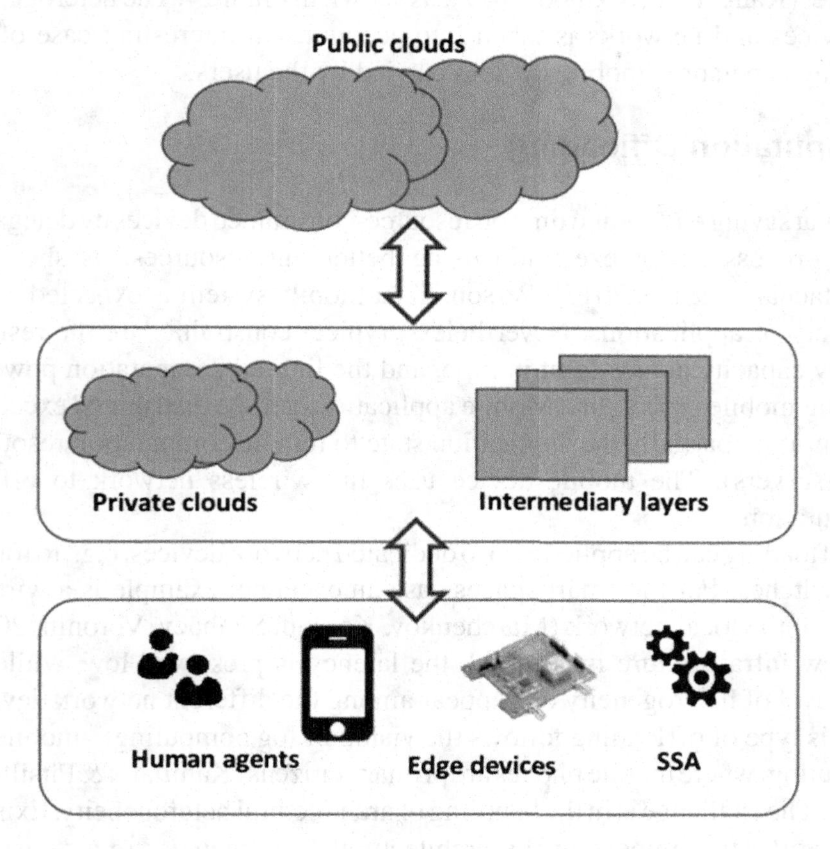

obtained results are then translated into actions and sent to actuators. Edge, intermediate network, and cloud resources needs communication, which is typically uses machine-to-machine (M2M) standards, e.g., Message Queue Telemetry Transport (MQTT) or Constrained Application Protocol (CoAP).

Gateways

Many tiny edge devices need help in communication with other elements of the application. This support is implemented by an IoT gateway. The latter knows several communication protocols for various sensors the gateway can serve. Such a gateway receives data from its sensors and makes the data format conversion to unify the uploaded data formats. That is, IoT gateway bridges various sensing domain networks with public communication networks or

Internet (Kang, Kim, & Choo, 2017), as shown in Figure 4. The heterogeneity of devices and networks is taken into account. An interesting case of IoT gateway is personal mobile devices carried by the users.

Computation Offloading

It aims at saving energy and time on resource-constrained devices by delegating some processing for execution using better-suit resources, as shown in (Bhattacharya & De, 2017). Personalized mobile system is expected to run a variety of applications. Nevertheless, typical constraints are the residual battery capacity at any point in time, and the limited computation power of existing mobile processors. Mobile application can use distributed execution by migrating partially the application state to remote computation resources (e.g., servers). The mobile device uses the wireless network to offload computation.

Offloading can be applied also to dedicated network devices, e.g., to routers and switches. For the smart spaces case an excellent example is a wireless router of the local network (Marchenkov, Korzun, Shabaev, Voronin, 2017). No new infrastructure is required, the latency is preserved low, while the high level of heterogeneity can appear among the different network devices.

This type of offloading follows the vision of fog computing—mobile fog computing, where mobile phones are primary citizens (Kamilaris & Pitsillides, 2016). The challenge is in the handling of architectural heterogeneity. Existing frameworks for supporting the architectural heterogeneity (e.g., openCL) cannot be used by network devices. Development of effective offloading frameworks that properly utilizes mobile fog computing is still an open problem (Korzun, Varfolomeyev, Shabaev, & Kuznetsov, 2018).

Figure 4. General feature of IoT gateway

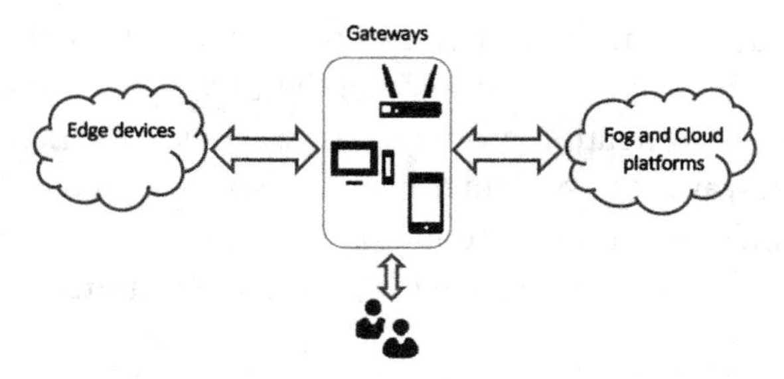

VIRTUALIZATION OF PARTICIPANTS AND THEIR RESOURCES USING SMART SPACES

Let us elaborate on applying information models for virtualization and knowledge sharing in smart spaces deployed in IoT environment. We focused on the traditional approach to modeling P2P networks (Korzun & Gurtov, 2013). Our intention is to see how such models can be adopted for the problems of knowledge virtualization and sharing. As we know it is not a trivial task to make a useful model for the considered problem. In this paper, we are not constructing a finalized ready model that answers most of the questions, rather we are sharing results of study and analysis on how to adopt well-known P2P models for the emerging application area of smart spaces.

In general, the smart spaces paradigm aims at development of ubiquitous computing environment, where participating entities acquire and apply knowledge to adapt services to the inhabitants in order to enhance user experience, quality and reliability of the provided information. A primary operational element is a smart object—an autonomous information processing unit. The term "smart" means (Poslad, 2009) that the object is (i) active, (ii) digital, and (iii) networked. Any smart object (iv) operates to some extent autonomously, (v) is re-configurable, and (vi) has local control of resources it needs to utilize (e.g., energy and data storage). The IoT concept supports this vision on smart objects (Kortuem, Kawsar, Sundramoorthy, & Fitton, 2010). The most common view of IoT refers to the connection of physical objects, while the core of technology is in information interconnection and convergence. Operation of IoT solutions is based on continued processing of huge number of data flows, originated from various sources and consumed by multiple applications.

In contrast to this basic IoT vision, a smart object in the smart space is not necessarily attached to a fixed device, as any available device can host the object. In this regard, the host device can be an Internet server (cloud computing), intermediate network device (fog computing), or edge device (edge-centric computing). This kind of virtualization provides a powerful abstraction for creating complex systems. For instance, the M3 concept for smart spaces employs the term "knowledge processor" (KP) to emphasize the processing responsibility of each object (Korzun, Balandin, Kashevnik, Smirnov, & Gurtov, 2017). Services are constructed as interactions of smart objects in this shared space. The deployment flexibility is very high. For example, the smart space can be deployed using a cloud or on user's devices that interact with each other and use pertinent services regardless of the physical location.

A smart space makes it possible to mash-up and integrate information between a wide spectrum of applications and domains spanning from embedded domains to the Web. Information from physical world (objects and devices in the physical environment) becomes easily available for participants in the shared smart space. The latter also is a hub linking the information to other services and solutions in the Internet. Therefore, smart spaces open embedded data kept in many surrounding devices to use by applications for creating local services in various physical places (Kiljander, Ylisaukko-oja, Takalo-Mattila, Etelapera, & Soininen, 2012).

The multitude of participants (humans, machines, processes) obviously leads to the interoperability problem. The M3 concept provides the following conceptual solution (Ovaska, Cinotti, & Toninelli, 2012) where a smart space is defined as a digital entity where the relevant real-world information (i.e., information about the physical environment, the objects therein located, and the recent situation) is stored in an interoperable, machine understandable format, kept up to date and made available to unanticipated and authorized situation dependent applications. This definition supports three interoperability levels.

1. At the bottom, the communication level provides techniques for transmitting data between devices. It enables the device and network world to exchange bits.
2. At the middle, the service level provides technologies for devices to share services in the smart space. It enables the service world to use the services across device boundaries.
3. At the top, the information level allows the information to be understood similarly in all the smart objects. It equips the information world with the interoperability means to make the same meaning of information for different participants.

The notion of semantics is subject to various definitions, e.g., see (Aiello et al., 2008). Since a smart space aims at encompassing (directly or indirectly) all information pieces the application system needs for service operation, we can characterize semantics as follows. Semantics is a relationship or mapping established between such information pieces. This definition also covers the case when relations are established implicitly, due to relating elements of the information structure. For instance, in ontology terms, such implicit relations appear between concepts (classes).

A characteristic property of any smart space is information sharing with knowledge self-generation from the collected content. Ideally, all data a service needs should be accessed via its smart space: either the data are directly stored in the smart space or they are accessed indirectly by a kept reference. The property leads to many concurrent and low coordinated contributions, and we can consider information content of a smart space a large dynamic collection I of disparate knowledge fragments.

No careful design of a single comprehensive ontology or a database schema in advance is possible to represent finely tuned structure of the content. The corpus-based representation principle is used instead (Halevy & Madhavan, 2003). Smart space content I is structured dynamically, in ad-hoc manner. For its participants, the smart space provides search query interfaces to reason knowledge over I and its instant structure.

Based on the ontological modeling approach, we can consider I consisting of information objects and semantic relations among them (Palviainen & Katasonov, 2011). Its basic structure is defined by problem domain and activity ontologies (classes, relations, restrictions), e.g., using OWL. Factual objects in I are represented as instances (OWL individuals) of ontology classes and their object properties represent semantic relations between objects. As a result, a kind of semantic network is formed in the smart space (Korzun, 2016).

The P2P approach can be applied for modeling the virtualization of objects in the smart space and the derived knowledge representation (Korzun & Balandin, 2014). Any object i in I is treated a peer. Each i keeps some data (values of data properties) and has links to some other objects j (object properties). Therefore, a P2P network G_I is formed on top of I. Contributions from smart space participants (insert, update, delete) change the network of objects, similarly as it happens in P2P due to peers churn and neighbors selection. We shall also use the terms a node and a link when referring an element in G_I and its relation.

This P2P model extends the notion of ontology graph (interrelated classes and instances of them) to a dynamic self-organized system. The following model properties clarify this extension.

Virtualization

Objects in G_I are self-contained pieces of information. It can be effectively described using OWL in terms of individuals and classes. Each object provides a digital representation of a real thing (sensor, phone, person, etc.) or of an artificial entity (event, service, process, etc.). This property suits well the IoT concept as well as its evolution to Internet of Everything (Patouni, Merentitis, Panagiotopoulos, Glentis, & Alonistioti, 2013). Participants (agents) and information objects become equal nodes. From the point of view of applications, all essential system components become observed on "one stage" (with all semantic relations) and manipulated by changing their information representation (digital).

Hierarchy

The decomposition principle from ontological modeling allows defining semantic hierarchies of concepts, e.g., hierarchy of classes of an ontology. Objects in G_I becomes connected with hierarchical semantic links, as it happens in hierarchical P2P systems. In particular, this idea was applied by Matuszewski and Balandin (Matuszewski & Balandin, 2007) for P2P-like structuring personal information about a person and groups of persons.

Emergent Semantics

There can be non-hierarchical semantic relations in G_I. They reflect the recent state of the dynamic system. For instance, relation "friendship" connects two persons or relation "is reading" appears between a person and a book. Object originals are autonomic and they constantly evolve. The representation of relations between them is also subject to frequent changes. Even global information is highly evolutionary: changes on the object's origin side (not in the representation in I) influence the semantics. That is, if an object corresponds to a database then updating its content can change the object's relations to others. This type of dynamic semantics consolidation from the local semantics held by participating objects follows the emergent semantics approach for knowledge management (Aiello et al., 2008). The property corresponds to the P2P network topology maintenance problem.

Composition

The granularity level of objects provides an additional degree of freedom. One can consider a group of objects in I as a node in G_I a self-contained element with own semantic relations. For instance, a group of persons forms a team or a service is constructed as a chain of simpler services. From the P2P point of view, the composition property is similar to peer clustering and aggregation, including superpeer-based P2P systems.

Data Integration

A smart space can be considered a virtual data integration system (Bertossi & Bravo, 2005) for multiple sources. Some objects in I represent external data sources (e.g., databases) and the means to access data (or even reason knowledge over these data) from the sources. This property is conceptually close to hybrid P2P architectures and P2P-based search problem, including semantic-aware P2P systems.

Based on this P2P model we can translate some well-known P2P problems for use in smart spaces.

1. Nodes heterogeneity. Objects in I are of different concepts (even incomparable) of the application problem domain. It provides basic restrictions on node linkage in G_I. For instance, some nodes cannot be connected with a direct link or cannot be clustered together, similarly as it happens in structured P2P networks. The same restrictions exist in practical deployments of P2P systems due to the Internet Protocol (IP) level reachability factors (e.g., a NAT prevents establishing a direct IP connection between two P2P nodes).
2. Neighbor selection. Every knowledge fragment should serve the system goals. It means that any object of I relates some other objects to form local semantics (over the data attributes the object has). When an object has many relations the knowledge becomes less concretized, thus, similarly to the P2P case, a node in G_I preferably keeps a moderate number of direct links. In P2P networks, a node has short-range and long-range links: the former is for nearby nodes, the latter allows jumping to distant area of the network. A short-range link in G_I describes a kind of persistent or system-wide knowledge. Similarly, emergent semantics provide long-range links for G_I, representing less stable knowledge relations.

3. Network topology maintenance. Objects can apply certain system-level rules when selecting neighbors, as it happens in structured P2P networks. The aim is at maintaining knowledge representation that allows efficient knowledge reasoning over I based on some existing technologies of Semantic Web (e.g., SPARQL). To some extent, the maintenance can also preserve the consistency of collected knowledge.
4. Routing. Knowledge reasoning over I is reduced to traversal in G_I, when semantic relations between objects allows interpreting and then forming derivate knowledge. Knowledge can be defined as a connected subgraph in G_I (i.e., following the semantic network model approach). In particular, such a subgraph consists of a node and some paths starting from this node. Routing algorithms provide a way to construct such graphs. An object (node in G_I) acts as a client when it needs knowledge, a server when it completes knowledge reasoning, and a router when it forwards the construction to subsequent objects for additional knowledge.

In summary, the model allows considering content *I* as interacting objects, which are active entities (make actions) on one hand and are subject to information changes (actions consequence) on the other hand. Result of interaction is derived knowledge in a graph-based form. This fact allows us to describe formally the conceptual processes of service construction and delivery.

Let us consider how the P2P model supports the structural description of virtualization and knowledge sharing in smart spaces. As a result, service construction can be formulated in terms of flows of information changes, which is convenient for the use in service design.

Given a starting object *s* in *I* and its initial change. Let *D(s)* be a graph routable from *s* in G_I. Construction of a service corresponds to a routing path $s \rightarrow^* d$, as it is schematically depicted in Figure 5 using thick arrows. Injection of the change starts the service, analogous to a P2P node starting a lookup query. The sequence of changes flows in G_I. Note that parallel paths are possible. Any point when an agent reads an object can be considered a final step of the service construction since the agent consumes an outcome.

Figure 5. Service construction as P2P route

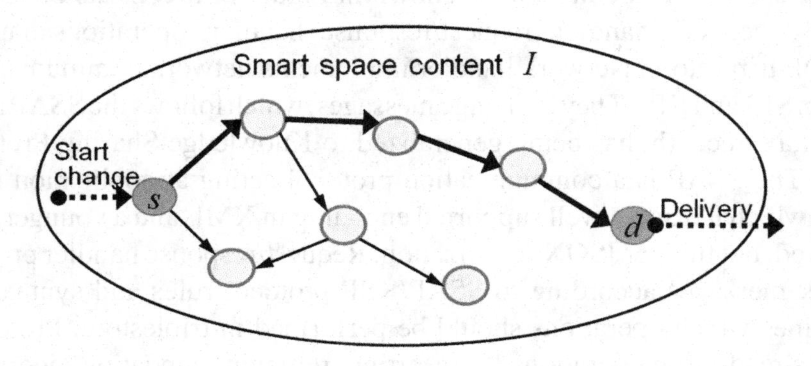

DEPLOYMENT OF COMPUTING ENTITIES ON APPROPRIATE SURROUNDING DEVICES

The M3 architecture defines two principal software components and an interaction protocol for them (Honkola, Laine, Brown, & Tyrkko, 2010): the semantic information broker (SIB), the Knowledge Processors (KPs), and the Smart Space Access Protocol (SSAP). Each SIB manages and shares a knowledge base (KB) with all the smart space participants. The KB is semantic, in the form of a RDF triplestore. Starting from 2008, when the first SIB prototype was produced, several SIB implementations have been appeared optimized for a specific purpose like portability and performance.

Let us examine the following SIB implementations (Viola et al., 2016), which include the five open source projects: Piglet-based SIB, its optimized descendant RedSIB, OSGi SIB for Java-based systems, pySIB for embedded and resources constrained devices with Python, and CuteSIB for Qt crossplatform device family. From a functional point of view, SIB implements an information hub forming a logical rendezvous and information-level interoperability infrastructure on the top of an RDF triple-store (or a SPARQL endpoint). Each SIB acts as an access point to a shared KB that describes the overall information state and context of the environment. The information representation is semantic, based on an oriented labeled graph, i.e., following the Semantic Web concept. The basic SIB role is to manage the read&write accesses to this graph. Advanced access operations are possible, including such persistent queries as subscription: a subscription notification mechanism to improve the reactivity and the band usage where the subscribe-notify paradigm is applicable.

The generic SIB architecture is shown in Figure 6. It consists of several modules: network handler, request/response handler, operations handler and RDF triplestore. Network handler implements network communication between SIB and KPs. They exchange messages, which follows the SSAP rules and syntax, recently has being generalized to Knowledge Sharing Protocol (KSP). The SSAP is a communication protocol acting at application level and for which it exists a well supported encoding in XML and a younger, less supported, but thinner JSON serialization. Request/response handler process network messages according to SSAP/KSP protocol rules and syntax and determines which operations should be performed in triplestore. Protocols provides read-write operations for inserting, removing, updating, querying, and (un)subscribing. The set of operations can be extended with advanced SPARQL queries and persistent operations. Operations are performed in operation handlers using a particular triplestore library to manage information in the RDF triplestore.

Each KP is a software agent and a participant to the Smart-M3 based scenario. The way in which such an application scenario evolves and its intelligence is provided, is the cooperative knowledge processing over the shared data and context, which is a much powerful approach with respect to an autonomous participation in the IoT environment.

Figure 6. The architecture of general SIB

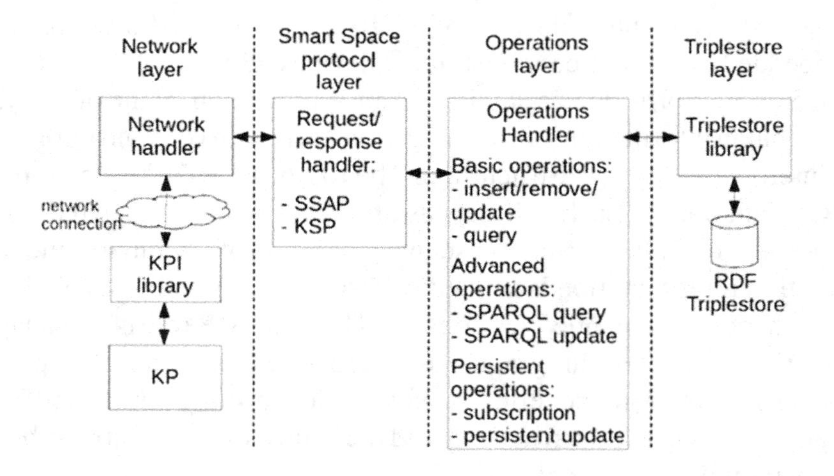

The Piglet-Based SIB

This implementation has been first released in 2009. It was used by the FRUCT community in such application development projects as SmartConference (http://fruct.org/sc), SmartScribo (http://fruct.org/smartscribo), and Ridesharing (http://fruct.org/ridesharing).

The piglet-based SIB architecture is shown in Figure 7. SIB consists of two main parts: the SIB daemon (sibd application written in C language with Glib library) and network handlers. SIB daemon handles the information access, operations processing and the storage of the RDF Graph. Network handlers maintain network communication with KPs. The Piglet SIB supports two communication technologies: TCP/IP and Nota implemented as a separate application (sib-tcp and sib-nota respectively). They are connected to the SIB daemon over D-Bus.

The architecture offered the opportunity to add new interfaces by implementing the corresponding daemons and connecting them to the D-Bus. The principles guiding the design of Smart-M3 are simplicity, extensibility and being agnostic to the used communication mechanisms.

The simplicity ensures scalability for small devices and for large number of users, while the extensibility makes it possible to tailor the implementation easily to uses where the standard functionality is not sufficient. Furthermore, by not dictating a specific communication mechanism, the Piglet SIB should be easy to deployed on top of many existing infrastructures.

Figure 7. The piglet-based SIB architecture

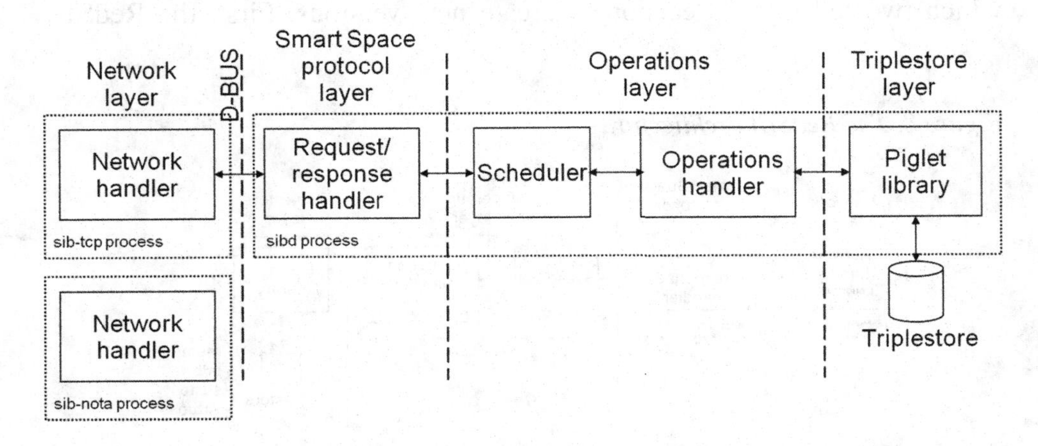

The layer runs in a single thread which schedules and executes the requests from the threads handling the SSAP operations. The communication between the SSAP operations threads is handled by using asynchronous queues. The triple operations layer is currently implemented by using Piglet RDF store. The triple operations layer is not tied to any specific RDF store, and any RDF store supporting the basic operations of read, write and delete may be substituted in the place of Piglet. However, changing the RDF store will require changing the code in the graph operations layer to adapt to the concrete interface provided by the new RDF store.

RedSIB

A direct descendant of the Piglet SIB implementation. They share the same architectural design and the code is essentially inherited. RedSIB was built upon the experiences gained in the early Smart-M3 applications. The goal was to solve the most relevant issues the application developers detected as well as improving the performance and avoiding criticalities. Feedbacks of the Smart-M3 community were used to improve the SIB adding more functionalities.

At a high level of the abstraction, the RedSIB architecture (Figure 8) is the same of the piglet-based SIB implementation with one RDF store and two main daemons communicating through D-Bus: the monolithic SIB daemon (redsibd application) and the TCP one (sib-tcp application).

The RedSIB has been applied in many domains like maintenance, telemedicine, and computer-human interaction to name a few (Korzun, Balandin, Kashevnik, Smirnov, & Gurtov, 2017). The efforts performed by the research community during the years revealed also some limits among which two led to the decision to create new versions. First, the RedSIB

Figure 8. The RedSIB architecture

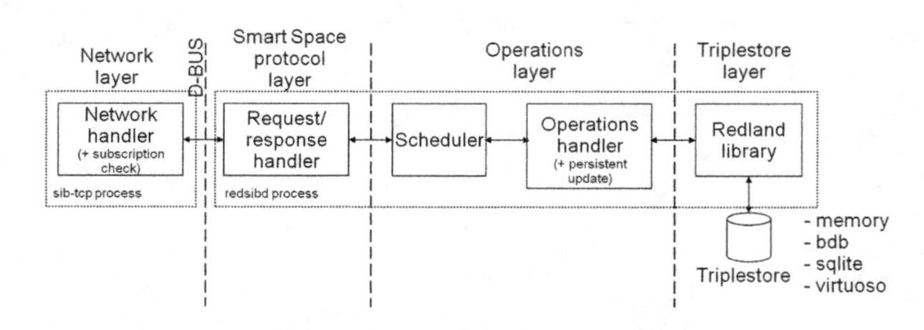

implementation is still bound to the D-Bus, an interprocess communication daemon. The D-Bus daemon limits performances for certain specific tasks. Second, the RedSIB implementation has a monolithic architecture, which requests huge efforts to the developers when new features are needed.

Being a result of the Semantic Web concept applied to IoT, which is still an experimental topic of the research scenario, many features and setups are to be implemented, deployed and prototyped and this conflicts with the monolithic approach of the code. Much efforts are still needed to optimize the subscription management or to include access control mechanisms. The features to be added and tested are in a queue that the community cannot dispose due to the lack of modularity. One issue is the lack of portability and extensibility, which leads to the need for many different modular version optimized for different target architectures. The described needs and the proliferation of SIB versions are not unexpected because in the overall vision the integration point is the SSAP protocol which remains unchanged. Therefore, coherently with the IoT concept, multi-SIB architectures with different SIB versions running on heterogeneous devices are possible and welcomed.

OSGi SIB

OSGi SIB was created and is currently maintained by the University of Bologna and Eurotech. The focus of the OSGi SIB developers is on the IoT and M2M industrial domains. The main strength of the OSGi SIB is its portability: the Java programming language and the OSGi framework grant the ability to run on different operating systems. The development of the OSGi SIB led to the creation of a specific Android version of the Semantic Information Broker, suitable for mobile devices. With respect to the other implementations of the SIB, the OSGi SIB introduces a new primitive called Persistent Update (PU): it consists of a SPARQL 1.1 update executed once when the command is issued to the SIB and then acting persistently on the data-store until it is deactivated. Together with the Python lightweight implementation, the OSGi SIB is the only one providing support for the JSON encoding of the SSAP protocol which grants bandwidth usage ranging from the 60% to the 90% of the current XML encoding (still in its early stage). The OSGi SIB also provides support for persistent storage thanks to TDB module of the Jena libraries. The OSGi SIB is implemented as OSGi Java application and is made of several interacting modules – bundles registered to the OSGi framework.

TCP Bundle is responsible for managing the network connection with KPs. It receives messages from KPs and manages a queue of the requests to be satisfied. Protocol bundle parses each message received from the TCP bundle in order to build an internal representation of the request. Scheduler bundle binds an identifier to each request processed by the Protocol bundle and sends request on processing. Operation bundles process each request with help of Jena library and provide a reply. Persistent operations bundle is responsible for the management of every active Persistent Update operation.

pySIB

Developed by ARCES department of the University of Bologna, pySIB is a lightweight SIB implementation designed to run mainly on embedded devices and System on Chips (SoCs). The implementation is written in Python and relying on the Python bindings of the RDFlib, pySIB results easy to install and run. pySIB, despite being in its earliest stable releases, shows good performance both in updating the knowledge base and retrieving data from it.

The modular architecture of pySIB makes it easy for the developers to extend it by adding new features or replacing existing modules with different ones (e.g. to support a different SSAP parser).

The Network handler module constitutes the interface between the SIB and the external world. Every message received from the outside (currently over TCP) is forwarded to the Protocol handler that builds an internal dictionary representation of the SSAP message. The current implementation supports by default the JSON encoded version of the SSAP protocol. Security manager checks access rights on the requested operation and then passes approved operations to Operation handler.

Operation handler performs the actions required by the KP on the RDF store, then sends back a dictionary to the Protocol handler which transform it into a reply message. The Network handler module sends the reply packet to the KP. As triplestore pySIB uses RDFlib library which maintains in-memory volatile triplestore which is fast but not persistent. Due to the modular architecture and to the simplicity of Python, pySIB is also used for educational matters into the Interoperability of Embedded Systems course of the University of Bologna where Smart-M3 has a central role.

CuteSIB

The implementation is developed and maintained by Petrozavodsk State University (PetrSU). CuteSIB is a reengineered version of RedSIB. The implementation is based on the Qt framework in order to support a wide spectrum of Qt-based IoT devices. A modular SIB design supports such important properties as extensibility, dependability, and portability.

The first distinctive property is elimination of D-Bus. One reason is that D-Bus is used only in Unix-based systems, thus preventing the use of SIB in other operating systems (e.g., Windows). Another reason is that D-Bus does not effectively support transfer of big amounts of data. Operation becomes unstable when transferring fast data streams of triples. As a result of the D-Bus elimination, the interprocess communication has simpler structure.

SIB communication modules for various network protocols (e.g., TCP or UDP) become plug-ins. They can be loaded/unloaded from the main SIB program as dynamic libraries. When higher portability is needed, such plug-ins can be integrated to SIB using static compilation. In this case, SIB does not load external libraries and is used as monolith application with the customizable set of network protocols. This feature targets SIB portability, taking into account devices with operating systems that have limited or no support of dynamic libraries.

The second distinctive property is the plug-ins based architecture in order to achieve higher extensibility due to the modular approach, see Figure 9.

The architecture allows inclusion/exclusion of certain modules in compilation phase or in runtime. The feature affords to customize the SIB functionality for given host device and IoT environment. Network layer is implemented as a pool of access points, each is an external module for SIB.

Figure 9. The plug-ins based CuteSIB architecture

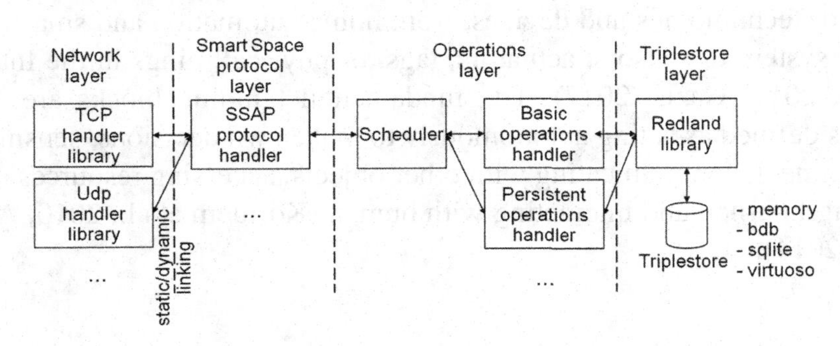

Protocol manager interacts with a specific access point and performs request parsing and response generation. Access protocol (such as SSAP or KSP) is implemented as a separate module, which parses request messages and creates response messages. In particular, it becomes possible to implement SPARQL over HTTP to access SIB as a common SPARQL access point. Scheduler module controls processing of CuteSIB commands with KPs requests/responses and internal notifications (to control runtime of other modules).

The scheduler delegates each command to an appropriate operation handler. Three command handlers can be distinguished: basic operation handler (for insert, remove, update, and query operations), persistent operations handler contains persistent operations (such as subscription), and SPARQL handler for advanced search queries. Persistent operations are always stored on the SIB side (continuous in time) and a response is generated whenever a specified event occurs.

SOFTWARE AGENTS INFRASTRUCTURE FOR INTERACTION SUPPORT IN IOT ENVIRONMENT

IoT provides diverse networked environments for deploying smart spaces (Korzun et al., 2013). A smart space supports a shared view on available resources in the IoT environment and creates semantics for the use of these resources in cooperative construction of services by multiple devices. In this section, we consider the deployment problem of smart spaces in respect to the opportunities of emerging IoT, Web, and semantics technologies. To solve the deployment problem, smart spaces middleware can be developed for installing in a particular IoT environment. Based on the presented study of existing technologies, we systemize the requirements to smart spaces middleware.

The IoT concept enables the capability of connecting and integrating a wide range of technologies and devices, from home automation and smart cities to any system of sensors, actuators, tags, or physical things in the Internet (Chen, 2017; Gazis, 2017). The fundamental building blocks are smart objects defined as acting autonomously to make own decisions, sensing the environment, communicating with other objects, accessing resources of the existing Internet, and interacting with human (Kortuem et al., 2010; Atzori et al., 2014).

The next IoT evolution step is connecting smart objects and the Web, leading to the so-called Web of Things (WoT) (Guinard et al., 2011; Heuer et al., 2015). The interactions are enabled through the definition of application programming interfaces over HTTP protocol based on Web Services following the RESTful architecture. Accordingly, the services and information provided by the objects can be incorporated in the Web. As a result, IoT smart objects can use the same language as other resources on the Web. One can easily integrate physical devices (things) with web pages (information world) allowing web users and services to experience the physical world and act on its data and services.

The Semantic Web of Things (SWoT) further advances the Web technologies and WoT concept with the Semantic Web technologies (Jara et al., 2014). The technologies are focused on enabling wide scale integration and interoperability (Gyrard et al., 2015). Global share and re-use of smart objects enable provision of semantic services based on interlinked meaning of the involved resources and processes. One of the challenges to move towards the SWoT is to define common semantic descriptions (ontologies) that allow data to be universally and understandable. SWoT ensures an extension to the IoT allowing integration of both the physical and information worlds.

Examples of services for IoT environments can be found in (Kortuem et al., 2010; Atzori et al., 2014; Korzun et al., 2017). Smart spaces are used in various problem domains such as collaborative work (Marchenkov et al., 2017; Korzun et al., 2014b), mobile healthcare (Zavyalova et al., 2017; Korzun et al., 2015), digital museums and cultural heritage (Smirnov et al., 2014; Korzun et al., 2016). In general, smart spaces middleware provide support for interaction and integration of various devices, software components, and information resources within a common goal for service construction and delivery (Galov et al., 2015; Viola et al., 2016; Roffia et al. 2018). The support is implemented as a separate layer on the top of IoT (the network communication layer).

There are many variants of IoT middleware that implement the network communication layer, e.g., see (Bandyopadhyay et al., 2011; Razzaque et al., 2016; Ngu et al., 2017). Such IoT middleware can be considered from the semantic-oriented viewpoint (among many other viewpoints), reflecting the observable growth of using the semantic methods in the IoT. In this case, IoT middleware become an appropriate base for deploying smart spaces (in some IoT environments), i.e., can be transformed to smart spaces middleware.

The existing semantic-oriented IoT middleware solutions can be divided into the following groups based on their design approaches (Razzaque et al., 2016; Bonte et al., 2017): event-based, service-oriented, VM-based, agent-based, tuple-spaces, database-oriented, application-specific, and data-driven. Typically, mixed approaches are used in existing middleware implementations. In particular, the database-oriented and agent-based approaches can be combined to support indirect communication of agents with each other. In contrast to the direct communication, when an agent has to discover another agent and explicitly connect to exchange data or commands, the indirect communication uses the shared view model (e.g., blackboard) implemented in some database (e.g., local device storage, nearby storage in the IoT environment, cloud storage).

Commercial IoT middleware follow the three main centralized design approaches to deploying smart spaces (Derhamy et al., 2015): 1) one cloud for all, 2) local cloud, and 3) local cloud with shared global functionality. The first approach is suitable for organizing the cooperation of many distributed devices. The approach is provided by IBM, Microsoft, and Intel, since a large number of software and hardware resources are required to maintain the cloud environment. The second approach deploys a local shared storage for devices in a physical spatial-restricted area. The third approach is a combination of the previous ones. Decentralized design approaches are also possible, e.g., based on peer-to-peer methods (Meshkova et al., 2008).

Based on the semantic-oriented properties of existing IoT middleware, we conclude that smart spaces middleware should provide data integration, easy knowledge exchange, and intelligent reasoning over the shared information as well as interoperability and integration within a heterogeneous IoT environment of ubiquitously interconnected objects and systems. This kind of requirements to smart spaces middleware can be classified onto three groups: 1) functional requirements, 2) non-functional requirements, and 3) application development requirements. The summary view is then shown in Figure 10.

SOLUTIONS AND RECOMMENDATIONS

As solutions and recommendations let us systemize the properties that a particular smart spaces middleware can have. Middleware development uses this requirements system to map particular properties to generic-form requirements. The system also serves as a basis for determining to which extend an existing IoT middleware can be used as smart spaces middleware.

Figure 10. Smart spaces middleware requirements

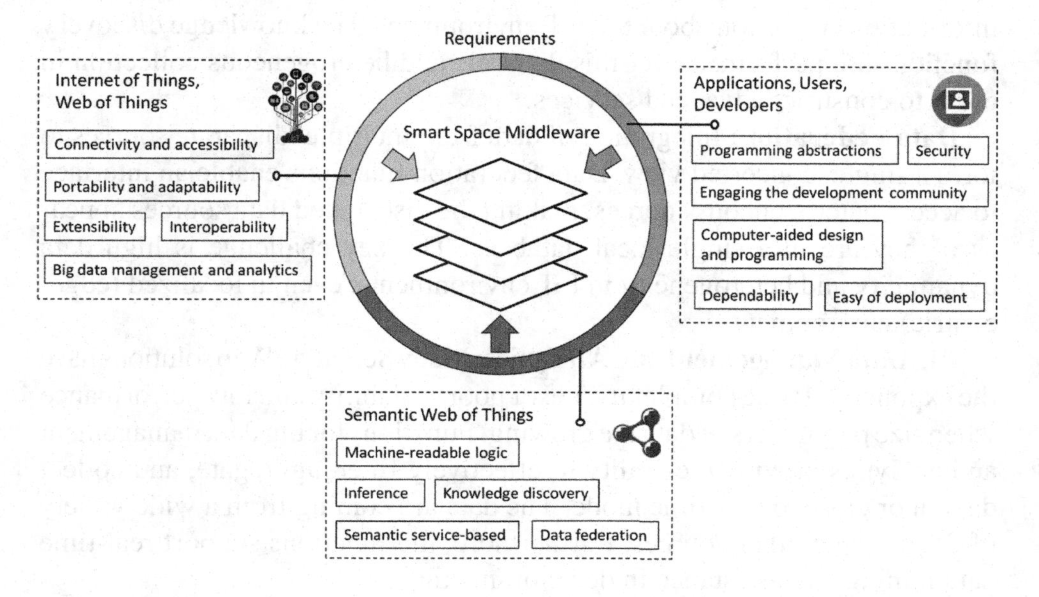

Functional requirements cover the functions provided by smart spaces middleware. The requirements are related to the Semantic Web standards and technologies and their software implementation constraints. Straightforward transfer of global-scale Semantic Web solutions for localized (edge-centric) IoT environments with resource-constrained devices is inappropriate for practical use. The functional requirements reflect such constraints in smart spaces middleware as follows.

Machine-Readable Logic: Smart space middleware follows the W3C standard for encoding semantics of stored data as class and property axioms of some description logic in RDF/XML, which is machine-readable. The encoding functions use OWL built upon RDF, RDF Schema, and XML Schema. The machine-readable logic provides a logical system specifying instances, their relationships (properties or predicates), and the sets (classes) to which instances or relations belong.

Inference: Semantic inference supports discovering new relationships based on the stored semantics and deduction rules. The inference functions use the graph-oriented RDF properties, reducing the problem to connectivity analysis among the basic facts.

Knowledge Discovery: In general, knowledge discovery is defined as "the nontrivial extraction of implicit, unknown, and potentially useful information from the data" (Kalarani & Uma, 2010). This process is the key component of enhanced information retrieval in semantic databases. A smart space is an information collection about the IoT environment. The knowledge discovery functions are performed over this dynamic and heterogeneous collection in order to construct advanced services.

Data Federation: Integration of data from multiple, disparate sources to form a single, concerted view. Data federation functions enable an interface to access heterogeneous sources, making the distributed data sources appear as if they are in a single local database. The key challenge is high data dynamicity and heterogeneity in IoT environments, even in localized (edge-centric) environments.

Big Data Management and Analytics: Many Semantic Web solutions have the exponential time complexity, i.e. of poor scalability and low performance when size parameters of data are growing. Functions for big data management and analytics provide the ability to effectively filter, aggregate, and collect data in or close to real-time mode. The data are coming from a wide variety of devices and other sources. Furthermore, the functions support real-time data mining and assistance in decision-making.

Non-functional requirements describe constraints on the smart spaces middleware as a whole system or for a particular function. The non-functional requirements are mainly inherited from the corresponding requirements for IoT middleware.

Extensibility: Middleware architecture is composite, e.g., based on plug-ins or modules. This property offers high extensibility when new functions are added. The composite architecture supports inclusion/exclusion of certain plug-ins or modules in compilation time or in runtime. In particular, the middleware functionality can be customized for a given IoT environment and other prerequisites.

Connectivity and Accessibility: The property of ubiquitous computing, when the middleware keeps regular connectivity for any participant to access appropriate resources in the IoT environment. Moreover, the middleware supports participants with ability to discover resources and each other.

Dependability: Smart space middleware should remain operational during an application process, even in the presence of failures. The dependability of a middleware helps in achieving application dependability. Every component in a middleware should be dependable to achieve overall dependability, which includes devices, communication, technologies, data, and implementation of middleware layers.

Interoperability: Middleware should support simultaneous operation of heterogeneous applications (each constructs services) when information is exchanged between applications and their services. The semantic interoperability means transparent and easy information exchange even if the set of participants is dynamically changed (e.g., new devices join the IoT environment). To enable the semantic interoperability, smart spaces middleware can use ontologies to represent shared data such that the information is interpreted similarly by any participant.

Security: A security mechanism is needed to ensure the three key concepts: integrity, confidentiality and availability. Use of context-awareness may disclose some personal-like information (e.g., phone number, home address, current location). In order to preserve the owner's privacy, the smart spaces middleware support organizing, controlling, and delimiting the access to information shared in the smart space.

Portability and Adaptability: The requirement is important specially due to the expansion of various computing devices (PC, tablets, smartphones, routers, etc.), including Linux and Windows based systems, as well as embedded systems. Such devices are used to host some middleware components. The middleware should provide certain independence level from network protocol, programming language, and operating system. The adaptability supports evolution of hosted middleware component in respect to changes in the IoT environment.

Easy of Deployment: Middleware architecture, which defines the components hosted on various devices, should support easy elaboration, evolution, and understanding by third-party developers. The multi-device components deployment is not oriented to expert knowledge. A common user can deploy the components, with no complicated installation and setup procedures.

Engaging the Development Community: Community engaging is important since no single company or developer can create and support all smart space middleware components. The new functionality can be implemented by third-party developers and preferably as open source.

The use of smart spaces middleware for application development needs appropriate programming models and software development tools On the one hand, the ever-growing number of smart spaces applications impose requirements on simplifying the application development and software maintenance. On the other hand, the Semantic Web technologies impose unified standards for application development.

Programming Abstractions: Providing an API for application developers is an important requirement for any smart space middleware. The required support is implemented as high-level programming interfaces for application developers. The programming abstraction (e.g., the publish/subscribe model) and the interface type that defines the style of the programming need to be considered when defining an API.

Semantic Service-Based System: The Semantic Web introduced the concept of semantic web services, which can be used in smart spaces. A smart space application aims at constructing services with uniquely described semantics, accessible through the Internet, and suitable for automated discovery, composition, and proactive initiation.

Computer-Aided Design and Programming: Smart spaces middleware should provide application development approaches with heavy developer involvement and extensive use of tools of computer-aided design and computer-aided programming that support application prototyping. Computer-aided design tools are being used to automate the work of creating and maintaining the various ontological and graphic representations of smart space application systems design. Computer-aided programming tools are being used to simplify the task of programming of smart space applications providing an integrated developed environment and automated program-code generation tools.

FUTURE RESEARCH DIRECTIONS

Problem "Concept Model of Multi-Layer Smart Space Infrastructure"

The software infrastructure of smart space middleware is responsible for the organization of the processes of constructing and delivering services in the application systems. It is deployed in computing environments including the host devices, network equipment, and system software, which provide operation and network communication. In order to describe software infrastructure of smart space middleware the four layers were defined: middleware base, middleware infrastructure, application systems infrastructure, and physical and information worlds

Problem "Semantic Services Model Based on Ontologies"

The use of semantic services within the M3 smart spaces paradigm changes the principle of designing services for the application systems, and also gives the design process and such systems a number of advantages. The design of semantic services in this case is performed on the basis of a general unified ontology that defines not only the service interface in terms of the data being transferred and the return values, but also the purpose of the service, the process of its construction and delivery. Due to such a uniform design method, the services of various smart space applications are endowed with the ability to interact with each other regardless of the problem domain and the environment in which the intellectual space deployments. Providing network interaction of the computing environments of smart spaces, it is possible to achieve the integration of both the spaces themselves and their applications to solve joint tasks based on semantic services.

Problem "Computer-Aided Design and Programming Tools"

The ever-growing number of smart space applications and the direction of the paradigm to create ubiquitous computing environments impose an additional requirement on a middleware related to simplifying the application development and maintain process. In order to meet this requirement traditional methodologies for applications design and development are being replaced with methodologies that promote approaches with heavy developer involvement and extensive use of tools of computer-aided design (CAD) and computer-aided programming (CAP) that support application prototyping.

CONCLUSION

This chapter introduced the way how smart spaces can be realized based on fog computing in IoT environments. We studied the use of multi-agent systems, where agents run on various IoT devices and interact each with others. Agents supports transformation of cloud computing to fog computing, and even to edge-centric computing. All participants become virtualized (as information entities and processes) in a shared information space. All resources of all devices and services thus can be effectively utilized.

ACKNOWLEDGMENT

The primary contributors to this chapter are Dmitry Korzun from Petrozavodsk State University (PetrSU), Russia and Fabio Viola from ARCES (University of Bologna), Italy. We also used materials kindly provided by Francesco Antoniazzi (ARCES, University of Bologna, Italy) and by Sergey Marchenkov (PetrSU, Russia).

REFERENCES

Aiello, C., Catarci, T., Ceravolo, P., Damiani, E., Scannapieco, M., & Viviani, M. (2008). Emergent semantics in distributed knowledge management. In Evolution of the Web in Artificial Intelligence Environments (pp. 201-220). Springer-Verlag. doi:10.1007/978-3-540-79140-9_9

Augusto, J. C., Callaghan, V., Cook, D., Kameas, A., & Satoh, I. (2013). Intelligent Environments: A Manifesto. *Human-centric Computing and Information Sciences*, *3*(1), 1–18. doi:10.1186/2192-1962-3-12

Bertossi, L., & Bravo, L. (2005). Consistent query answers in virtual data integration systems. In Inconsistency Tolerance (pp. 42-83). Springer-Verlag. doi:10.1007/978-3-540-30597-2_3

Bhattacharya, A., & De, P. (2017). A survey of adaptation techniques in computation offloading. *Journal of Network and Computer Applications*, *78*(C), 97–115. doi:10.1016/j.jnca.2016.10.023

Dastjerdi, A. V., & Buyya, R. (2016). Fog computing: Helping the Internet of Things realize its potential. *Computer*, *49*(8), 112–116. doi:10.1109/MC.2016.245

Esposito, C., Castiglione, A., Pop, F., & Choo, K. K. R. (2017). Challenges of connecting edge and cloud computing: A security and forensic perspective. *IEEE Cloud Computing*, *4*(2), 13–17. doi:10.1109/MCC.2017.30

Garcia Lopez, P., Montresor, A., Epema, D., Datta, A., Higashino, T., Iamnitchi, A., ... Riviere, E. (2015). Edge-centric computing: Vision and challenges. *Computer Communication Review*, *45*(5), 37–42. doi:10.1145/2831347.2831354

Halevy, A. Y., & Madhavan, J. (2003). Corpus-based knowledge representation. In *Proceeding of the 18th International Joint Conference on Artificial Intelligence (IJCAI'03)* (pp. 1567-1572). Morgan Kaufmann Publishers.

Honkola, J., Laine, H., Brown, R., & Tyrkko, O. (2010). Smart-M3 information sharing platform. In *Proceeding of IEEE Symposium on Computers and Communications (ISCC'10)* (pp. 1041–1046). IEEE Computer Society. 10.1109/ISCC.2010.5546642

Kamilaris, A., & Pitsillides, A. (2016). Mobile phone computing and the internet of things: A survey. *IEEE Internet of Things Journal*, *3*(6), 885–898. doi:10.1109/JIOT.2016.2600569

Kang, B., Kim, D., & Choo, H. (2017). Internet of everything: A large-scale autonomic IoT gateway. *IEEE Transactions on Multi-Scale Computing Systems*, *3*(3), 206–214. doi:10.1109/TMSCS.2017.2705683

Kiljander, J., Ylisaukko-oja, A., Takalo-Mattila, J., Etelapera, M., & Soininen, J.-P. (2012). Enabling semantic technology empowered smart spaces. *Journal of Computer Networks and Communications*, *2012*, 1–14. doi:10.1155/2012/845762

Kortuem, G., Kawsar, F., Sundramoorthy, V., & Fitton, D. (2010). Smart objects as building blocks for the Internet of Things. *IEEE Internet Computing*, *14*(1), 44–51. doi:10.1109/MIC.2009.143

Korzun, D. (2014). Service formalism and architectural abstractions for smart space applications. In *Proceeding of 10th Central & Eastern European Software Engineering Conference in Russia* (pp.19:1–19:7). ACM. 10.1145/2687233.2687253

Korzun, D. (2016). On the smart spaces approach to semantic-driven design of service-oriented information systems. In *Proceedings of 12th International Baltic Conference on Databases and Information Systems (DB&IS)* (pp. 181-195). Academic Press. 10.1007/978-3-319-40180-5_13

Korzun, D., & Balandin, S. (2014). A Peer-to-Peer Model for Virtualization and Knowledge Sharing in Smart Spaces. In *Proceedings of the 8th International Conference on Mobile Ubiquitous Computing, Systems, Services and Technologies (UBICOMM 2014)* (pp. 87-92). IARIA.

Korzun, D., Balandin, S., & Gurtov, A. (2013). Lecture Notes in Computer Science: Vol. 8121. *Deployment of Smart Spaces in Internet of Things: Overview of the Design Challenges*. Springer.

Korzun, D., Balandin, S., Kashevnik, A., Smirnov, A., & Gurtov, A. (2017). Smart spaces-based application development: M3 architecture, design principles, use cases, and evaluation. *International Journal of Embedded and Real-Time Communication Systems*, *8*(2), 66–100. doi:10.4018/IJERTCS.2017070104

Korzun, D., & Gurtov, A. (2013). *Structured Peer-to-Peer Systems: Fundamentals of Hierarchical Organization, Routing, Scaling, and Security*. Springer. doi:10.1007/978-1-4614-5483-0

Korzun, D., Varfolomeyev, A., Shabaev, A., & Kuznetsov, V. (2018). On dependability of smart applications within edge-centric and fog computing paradigms. In *Proceedings of 2018 IEEE 9th International Conference on Dependable Systems, Services and Technologies (DESSERT)* (pp. 502-507). IEEE. 10.1109/DESSERT.2018.8409185

Marchenkov, S., Korzun, D., Shabaev, A., & Voronin, A. (2017). On Applicability of Wireless Routers, to Deployment of Smart Spaces in Internet of Things Environments. In Intelligent Data Acquisition and Advanced Computing Systems: Technology and Applications (IDAACS) (Vol. 2, pp. 1000-1005). IEEE. doi:10.1109/IDAACS.2017.8095237

Matuszewski, M., & Balandin, S. (2007). Peer-to-peer knowledge sharing in the mobile environment. In *Proceedings of the 5th International Conference on Creating, Connecting and Collaborating Through Computing (C5 '07)* (pp. 76–83). IEEE Computer Society. 10.1109/C5.2007.24

Ovaska, E., Cinotti, T.S., & Toninelli, A. (2012). The design principles and practices of interoperable smart spaces. *Advanced Design Approaches to Emerging Software Systems: Principles, Methodology and Tools*, 18–47.

Palviainen, M., & Katasonov, A. (2011). Model and ontology-based development of smart space applications. In *Pervasive Computing and Communications Design and Deployment* (pp. 126–148). Technologies, Trends, and Applications. doi:10.4018/978-1-60960-611-4.ch006

Patouni, E., Merentitis, A., Panagiotopoulos, P., Glentis, A., & Alonistioti, N. (2013). Network virtualisation trends: Virtually anything is possible by connecting the unconnected. In Proceedings of 2013 IEEE Software Defined Networks for Future Networks and Services (SDN4NFS) (pp. 1-7). IEEE.

Poslad, S. (2009). *Ubiquitous Computing: Smart Devices, Environments and Interactions.* John Wiley & Sons. doi:10.1002/9780470779446

Roffia, L., Morandi, F., Kiljander, J., D'Elia, A., Vergari, F., Viola, F., ... Cinotti, T. S. (2016). A Semantic Publish-Subscribe Architecture for the Internet of Things. *IEEE Internet of Things Journal*, *3*(6), 1274–1296. doi:10.1109/JIOT.2016.2587380

Shi, W., Cao, J., Zhang, Q., Li, Y., & Xu, L. (2016). Edge computing: Vision and challenges. *IEEE Internet of Things Journal*, *3*(5), 637–646. doi:10.1109/JIOT.2016.2579198

Viola, F., D'Elia, A., Korzun, D., Galov, I., Kashevnik, A., & Balandin, S. (2016). The M3 Architecture for Smart Spaces Overview of Semantic Information Broker Implementations. In *Proceedings of the 19th Conference of Open Innovations Association FRUCT* (pp. 264-272). IEEE. 10.23919/FRUCT.2016.7892210

KEY TERMS AND DEFINITIONS

Agent: A software module that represents simplest version of node in the smart space. An agent can reason knowledge and make decisions using this information and in accordance with the application goals.

Fog Computing: An architecture that uses collaborative multitude of the user clients and devices located in the user's proximity to carry out major part of processing, storage and communication tasks related to delivery of services to the user.

Internet of Things (IoT): The internetworking of physical entities represented by devices that enable these entities to collect and exchange data for a achieving a common goal.

Smart Space: A set of communicating nodes and information storages, which has embedded logic to acquire and apply knowledge about its environment and adapt to its inhabitants in order to improve their experience in the environment.

Smart-M3: An open-source software platform that aims to provide a smart spaces infrastructure. It combines the ideas of distributed, networked systems and semantic web. The ultimate goal is to enable smart environments and linking of real and virtual worlds.

Chapter 4
Profiling and Personalization in Internet of Things Environments

ABSTRACT

The chapter considers problems of user personalization and resources competence modeling in the internet of things (IoT) environments. Creation of the user profiles and its utilization during the interaction of the user with IoT resources significantly increase the efficiency of such interaction. When the user generates a task to perform by the IoT resources, the formal model of this task is expanded by the relevant information in accordance with the user profile model. The obtained results should be presented to the user in accordance to his/her preferences from the user profile model. Resource competence profile should store information about the resource competencies and constraints that have to be satisfied to enable these competences. In this case, resource competence profiles automate their interaction in IoT environments.

DOI: 10.4018/978-1-5225-8973-0.ch004

INTRODUCTION

Latest information systems become more and more smart. The systems are aimed at user behavior accumulation, his/her preferences recognition, and adapt their behavior (Horgan, 2018; Zhang & Sundar, 2019). In the Internet of Things environments profiling and personalization plays essential role (Lu, Papagiannidis, & Alamanos, 2018). Such systems aim to connect different devices and services (resources) at any time and any place, giving rise to innovative new applications and services. In this case, it is needed to consider as user profiles that are aimed at accumulated his/her competencies and preferences to use this information during the interaction with another resources as well as resource competence profile that should store information about the resource competencies and constraints that have to be satisfied to enable these competences.

Profiling and personalization in IoT environment are an ability of such environment to filter the content and change it in according to user preferences accumulated in user profile. For acquisition of this preferences to the user profile IoT environment should contain the special service that keeps the history of interaction with user and analyze it. Grouping of the users by preferences provides possibilities to identify users with similar interests and provides the information that is interested for one user to another users in the group based on the context situation. For automation of the interaction between different resources the competence profile of a resource is proposed. This profile keeps information about possibilities of the resource and constraints that have to be satisfied to utilize these possibilities.

In scope of the chapter the information model of the user profile is proposed. This model describes the user interacting with Internet of Things resources. The profile includes the following main sections: "personal information", "user context", "competences", "preferences", and the "interaction history". Analysis of existing user profile models showed that the "personal information" section is basic for a user profile and is used for the most systems that support profiling components for storing personal and contact user information. A distinctive feature of the developed user profile model is the accumulation of information about the user context, his/her competencies, preferences, and interaction history as well as the description of this information in an ontologically oriented form. The "user context" section includes information about the user, which changes depending on the current situation. The "user competence" section includes a set of knowledge and skills with defined proficiency level and taking into account the context for application of this knowledge or skill. The section "user preferences" includes information about tasks, methods, settings for presenting results, as well as groups of users formed by preferences. In this case, it is proposed to divide the preferences into explicit and implicit ones. Explicit preferences are indicated by the user, while implicit ones are detected automatically. The "interaction history" section is used to store the user activities for further analysis. The section is used for offline analysis of user actions, splitting users into groups and updating user preferences.

For the proposed information model of the resource profile the following sections were defined: section "basic information", "competences and constraints", "resource context", and "historical information". The main task of description a resource profile is to formalize the tasks that this resource can perform, and the constraints that have to be met in order for this resource can perform the tasks.

The section "basic information" is essential for a software resource profile and is used in most systems that support profiling components for storing resource descriptions. The section includes a textual description of the software resource in natural language. The section "competences and constraints" includes a set of knowledge and tasks that a given software resource can perform with an assessment of the level of knowledge and taking into account the context in which this knowledge and tasks can be applied, as well as the constraints that have to be met for use this software resource to obtain the above knowledge or perform tasks. This section is described in an ontological-oriented form. The section "resource context" includes actual information about the resource that is changed by time. The section "historical information" includes the history of the interaction of a software resource with IoT environment. This section contains information about the competencies and constraints of a resource, the current situation and the ontological model of the task at the time it is completed by the resource, as well as information about the success of the task execution by the software resource.

The chapter is structured as follows. Background section presents broad definitions and discussions of the topic and incorporate views of others. The section user profile modeling for personalization of the user interaction with Internet of Things environment discuss the user profile model in details. The section resource competence profile modeling for automation its interaction with other resources propose the competence profile model that describes the resource. The section ontology-based clusterization method for grouping users by their interests presents a method for grouping users or resources based on their behavior in the system. Solutions and recommendations section discuss solutions and recommendations in dealing with the issues, controversies, or problems presented in the preceding section. The section future research directions discuss the future work in the area of personalization. Conclusion summarize the chapter.

BACKGROUND

Authors of the paper (Amoretti, Belli, Zanichelli, 2017) propose a system for building user profiles and implementing context-oriented information filtering for recommendation generation to users that search the information. According to the authors, the main components of a personalized system are: (1) the classification of the content that the system provides to the user; (2) user profile; (3) filtering of the content that most closely matches the user's profile. The authors proposed a hybrid user profiling strategy. In scope of this strategy the user is described not only by his/her behavior, but also by the behavior of other users who are similar to him/her. To identify similar users, the authors propose to use preference profiles and demographic profiles of users and perform clustering. The clustering is implemented based on the K-Means clustering algorithm. The obtained user groups determine the behavior profile of each user, based on the user's interaction. A demographic profile is a set of personal user data (for example, age, gender, type of activity), which are entered at the stage of user registration in the system. Profile preferences based on feedback from the user. In this case, the profile is based on the ratings of users who rate the sights proposed by the system. The authors have developed a mobile application that recommends attractions to users based on the proposed theoretical studies.

According to (Kaneko, Kishita & Umeda, 2018), the user profiling technique includes: (1) behavior modeling based on user interaction with the system and evaluation of user actions in the future based on analysis of past actions; (2) interest modeling, which consists in defining a function for calculating the degree of interest to the user of a new information, product or service; (3) intention modeling that aimed at finding the real goals of the user, in accordance with which he/she began to interact with the system.

Authors of the work (You, Bhatia, Luo, 2016) propose a three-level, and then extend it to a multi-level user profile model for personalized search. The model is based on the integration of tags and ratings of objects, which are used to build a user profile. In the three-levels model the authors single out interesting, annoying, and ordinary user objects. Moreover, objects rated by the user with a high rating are interesting for the user. By annoying objects authors are defined the objects rated by a user with low rating. Under the usual objects, the authors understand the objects rated by the user average rating. Based on this separation, the authors proposed a three-level user profile model. For a multilevel model, the authors suggest using not three characteristics of objects, but n.

An approach to personalizing services for mobile users using the concept of pervasive computing is presented in (Xiong et al., 2016). The approach involves the use of semantic technologies for modeling users and the implementation of the logical inference of knowledge based on ontologies for the purpose of personalization. The authors note that pervasive computing systems are designed in such a way that the relevant contextual information is used to adapt to the user's characteristics and behavior at the current time. The authors present a service-oriented distributed architecture that uses semantic web technologies for the purposes of user modeling and logical inference of knowledge for personalization, implementing the concept of "help on demand". According to the authors, the approach to personalization includes various types of entities in the subject domain: the user, his environment, the current situation and services, as well as interactions and interconnections between these entities. The process of user ontological modeling is defined by the authors as the following sequence of steps: (1) analysis of the characteristics and needs of the user in a context-oriented environment; (2) the establishment of relationships between the basic entities of the subject area; (3) the definition of basic concepts that can model and represent these entities, as well as the definition of properties that can be used to describe these concepts; (4) classification of concepts and properties into a hierarchical structure; (5) use of ontology development tools for coding these concepts and interconnections, as well as their presentation in a formal ontological language.

A personalized service for user's smartphone is presented in (Skillen et al., 2014). The service collects information from the sensors of the smartphone, generates a user profile, finds users of similar interest and recommends the services that are interesting to the user to the user. The service collects information such as: location, payment for goods and services using a smartphone, as well as applications that are often used by the user. At the same time, the location information does not violate the user's privacy, as the service collects location information, but not the time at which the user was at this location. The service collects only information about how much time the user has been in one place or another and the places where the user has been in a long time can be considered interesting to him.

Author of the paper (Delic, 2016) presents a recommender system for the interaction of various companies based on a model of predictions based on fuzzy logic. The author uses data from the Yelp service, which provides information about the ratings of various companies estimated by customers. The presented recommender system allows to search for companies that can meet the needs of the same users. For example, car refueling can be located near the supermarket, as it is often convenient for drivers to fill the car and buy products.

Author of the paper (Tsai, 2016) presented an automated method for observing, recording, and then analyzing the ways of moving users through museums and the time the user spent at each point on his/her path. The author notes that the user's modeling technology in this context allows to model the user's interests based on feedback from him/her and generate recommendations for interesting sights based on the interests of the user. The author investigated four basic models for personifying recommendations of sights to users. Two collaborative ones: collaborative filtering based on the nearest neighbor method and filtering based on spatial processes. And two content-based models: content-based filtering and least-mean squares filtering. In this paper it is noted that the approaches based on the content allow us to estimate the time for viewing unvisited sights by comparing the characteristics of these sights with those already visited, for which the time of the visit is known. Collaborative models are based on the accumulation of a database of ratings related to the viewing of attractions by various users, and using this base to estimate the rating of an individual attraction for a particular user.

Authors of the paper (Lepri et al., 2016) propose an approach, implementation, and evaluation of a personalized service for hotel users. By personalization, the authors understand the possibility of providing products and services to the end user, depending on his needs. The process of personalization according to the authors includes two subprocesses: learning and matching. Training is a subprocess of data retrieval by an organization about a user by interacting with it in one way or another. Interaction can be either direct - polling the user to see whether he is satisfied or not satisfied, or indirect, including an analysis of user behavior. A subprocess mapping is a mapping of user preferences and company offerings or modification of various components of a service based on user preferences. The authors have developed a service HtlCo system, which was tested on archival data, including about one hundred thousand bookings of hotels in the period 2010-2014 years.

A methodology for building a profile of user interests based on user actions in a social network is proposed in (Wei, Meng, & Arunkumar, 2018). This methodology is focused on the description of user preferences along with levels of interest in these preferences. In the presented methodology, the following two strategies were used to build a profile: tag clustering based on the concept of a semantic link between two tags in the real world and using the network of users' friends in social networks.

USER PROFILE MODELING FOR PERSONALIZATION OF THE USER INTERACTION WITH INTERNET OF THINGS ENVIRONMENT

An information model of the user profile is proposed in the section. The model describes the profile of a person interacting with IoT resources. The profile includes the following main sections: "personal information", "user context", "competencies", "preferences", and "interaction history". An analysis of existing user profile models shown that the section "personal information" is the base for the user profile and is usually used in most systems that support profiling components for storing personal and contact information about the user. A distinctive feature of the developed profile model is the accumulation of information about the user's context, his/her competencies, preferences, and interaction history with the IoT environment. Thus, the section "context" includes information about the user that is changed based on the current situation. The section "competencies" includes a set of knowledge, skills, and communicative abilities relevant to the user with an assessment of the professional level and taking into account the context where the competence can be applied. The section "preferences" includes information about tasks and methods used for solving these tasks, results representation options, and groups of similar users formed by the IoT environment. At the same time, it is suggested to divide preferences into explicit and implicit ones. Explicit preferences are indicated by the user himself, while the implicit preferences are automatically detected by IoT environment. The section "interaction history" is used to store information about the interaction of the user with the IoT environment. The section serves for offline analysis of user actions, splitting users into groups and updating user preferences.

The developed information model of the user profile is presented in Figure 1. The "personal information" section includes the following information about the user: name, family name, gender, birthdate, languages, phone number, e-Mail, website, and occupation. This information is basic for the user profile and is used in most systems that is supported the profiling components.

The "user context" section contains the following information about the user: role, access level, group, hardware used to access the IoT environment, location, time zone, status, and rating calculated for the user based on information of his/her task performing. The attribute "role" defines a type of tasks the user can perform. The attribute "access level" differentiates rights of the user in IoT environment that specifies the information and knowledge that the user can utilize. The attribute "group" is used to specify a list of groups the user belongs to; the specification is based on his/her preferences and competencies. The attribute "hardware" contains information about the device the user use to interact with the IoT environment. This information is important to form the restrictions for interaction with the user regarding

Figure 1. Information model of user profile

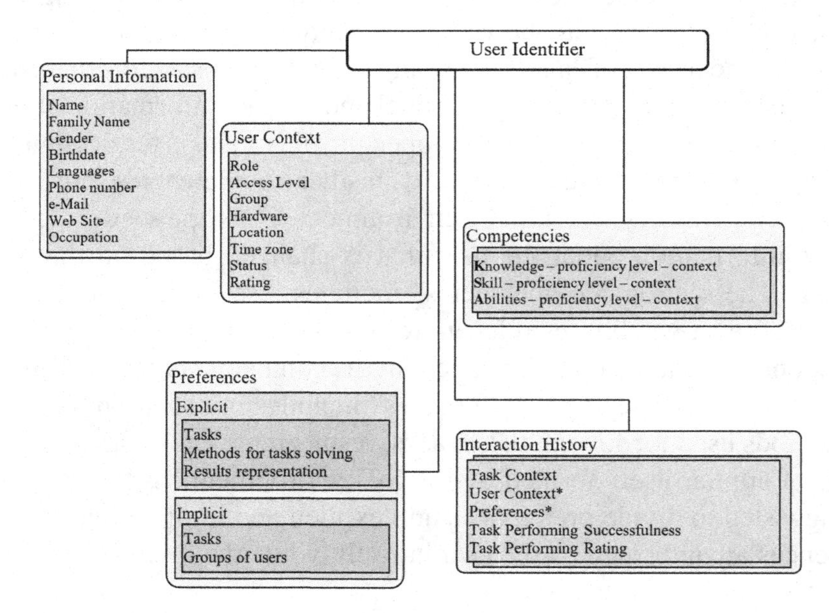

the amount of information provided to him/her and the modalities used for representation. The attribute "location" contains information about the region where the user is currently located and can be used for providing him/her location-based services. The attribute "time zone" reflects the user's time information and is used to determine is the user can be engaged for the task performing at the moment or not. The attribute "status" indicates the availability of a user at the moment to participate in the task performing or not. The attribute rating determines the weighted rating calculated for the user by all performed tasks that characterized the user capabilities.

The "competences" section contains information about the user's knowledge, skills, and abilities (KSA model described in (Reh, 2018) associated with proficiency levels and contexts where these skills can be applied. Formalization of competencies allows automatically select users who has competencies to solve various tasks. Competences are supposed to be assigned to users manually by selecting skills from the ontology and linking to it a level of knowledge characterized by a numerical value.

The "preferences" section includes information on user-preferred tasks for execution, methods for solving these tasks, options for presenting results, as well as groups of users. This section is divided into two subsections: "explicit preferences" and "implicit preferences". Explicit preferences the user specifies manually while the implicit preferences are detected by the system automatically. For the "explicit preferences" subsection, the user selects tasks from ontology that he/she is interested to perform, choose methods that he/she usually utilize for task perfprming, and options for presenting results (text, table, picture, audio recording, video recording, and etc.). The "implicit preferences" subsection is filled in automatically by the system based on the history of working of the user with IoT environment. This subsection includes the tasks detected by the system and information about the user groups determined based on clusterization technique.

The "interaction history" section is used to store information about the user behavior in IoT environment. In this section, the formalized description of the task, the context of the user, his/her preferences at the time of task performing are preserved as well as task performing successfulness and rating estimation. This section serves for offline analysis of user actions and updates in the automatic mode of the subsection implicit preferences from the "preferences" section. The user enters part of the information in the profile manually while the part is filled in automatically by the system during its operation. When this subsection "implicit preferences" is filled by the system during the analysis of the interaction history during the offline phase of work.

RESOURCE COMPETENCE PROFILE MODELING FOR AUTOMATION ITS INTERACTION WITH OTHER RESOURCES

Internet of Things environments require the effective management of applications and resources interacting with each other (Piccoli, Lui, Grün, 2017). Resource profiles help to improve the efficiency of such management by automating the searching process of resources for the required task. The following resource profile model has been developed (see Figure 2).

In scope of the model the following sections have been defined for resource profile model: "basic information", "competencies and constraints", "resource context", and "historical information". The "basic information" section is a usual section. It includes a text-based description of the software resource in natural language. The "competencies and constraints" section includes a set of knowledge that describe tasks the resource can perform with an assessment of the level of possession and taking into account the context situation. This section is described in an ontology-oriented form using the competence ontology. The competence ontology includes all possible competencies and constraints that can be used in IoT environment. The section includes the following attributes: "basic competencies", "extended competencies", and "constraints". Basic competencies are the competencies that resource

Figure 2. Information model of resource profile

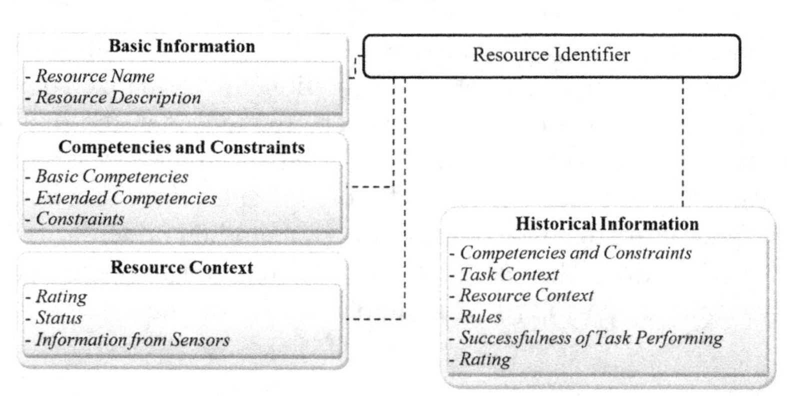

is used to perform the required tasks. The extended competencies are the competencies that are used by the resource to perform the optional tasks. Constraints specify the requirements that have to be satisfied to utilize the resource competencies.

The "resource context" section is storing information about a software resource that reflects its current state. This section includes the following attributes: rating, status, and information from sensors. The rating is calculated dynamically based on the evaluations of other members of IoT environment as follows:

$$R = \frac{\sum_{i=1}^{n}\left(r_i \cdot c\right)}{m},$$

where R is the rating of the resource, n is the total amount of resources, r_i is the current resource rating set by member i, c is the coefficient determining whether the current context of the resource corresponds to the context at the time of member evaluation i (if yes $i = 1$, if not, $i = 0$), and m - the number of estimates of the current resource made with a similar context. The attribute "status" determines whether a given resource can currently be used to participate in solving a task or not. The attribute "information from sensors" reflects the values of variables or information from sensors (in case a software resource controls a physical object) that describe the current status of the resource.

The section "historical information" includes the history of the interaction of the resource with the IoT environment. This section contains the following attributes: "competences and constraints", "task context", "resource context", "rules", "successfulness of task performing", and "rating". The "competences and constraints" attribute is a dump of the "competencies and constraints" section described at the time of the task performing. The attribute "task context" describe the formal task description in ontological form. The attribute "resource context" describes, in ontological form, the current situation in which the resource is located and contains all the information that can be used to describe this situation (Dey, Salber, Abowd, 2001). The attribute "rules" specifies knowledge that have been used to perform the task by the resource. The attribute "successfulness of task performing" describes the estimation is the resource has performed the task successfully or not. The attribute "rating" describes the quantitative characteristics of how well the resource performed the task. The section "historical information" is used by the Internet of Things environment in offline mode to identify new knowledge about the resource and to update the section "competences and constraints", as well as the section "resource context".

ONTOLOGY-BASED CLUSTERIZATION METHOD FOR GROUPING USERS BY THEIR INTERESTS

The proposed clusterization method is based on ontologies aimed at problem domain knowledge representation. The ontology describes common entities: objects, resources, processes, and etc. of the IoT environment, and relationships between them. Knowledge within the approach is represented in a declarative way. It is proposed to use object-oriented constraint networks for the knowledge representation that simplifies domain formalization since most of objects and relationships between them can be described in terms of constraints. According to the formalism of object-oriented constraint networks, ontology is represented by a set of classes; a set of class attributes; a set of attribute domains; and a set of constraints.

$$O = \left(C, A, D, C\right),$$

where C is a set of *entities* or *object classes* ("*classes*"). A is a set of class attributes ("*attributes*"), D is a set of attribute domains ("*domains*"). C is a set of *constraints* (like taxonomical, hierarchical, and etc.).

The goal of user clusterization is forming the groups of users with similar interests. User profiles contain history of interaction between users and the IoT environment. They contain the tasks that have been implemented for users and smart space ontology that has been stored for the moment of task execution completion. For different users and different tasks different ontologies are stored. Based on these ontologies the clusterisation is implemented that is aimed to determine similarity between users. After that users with high degree of similarity are joined to groups. The clustering algorithm has been proposed for these purposes.

Let us consider the method of ontology-based clusterization on the example of determining group of users in IoT environment. The general scheme of the method is presented in Figure 3. At the first step, according to the performed by the user tasks, a mathematical model is constructed that relates these elements based on the contexts corresponding to these tasks. For the mathematical model it is proposed to use a weighted graph. Further, in the second step, the transformations of this model are performed, allowing to establish connections between each pair of tasks. And, finally, at the third step, a meaningful interpretation of the resulting transformation into the subject area is made, that is, groups of tasks are built. Based on the information about the groups of tasks the groups of users are calculated.

The weighted graph is calculated based on task context that is described by classes and attributes (see Figure 4). Therefore the weighted graph will be looks like as follows:

$$G_0 = \langle N, E \rangle = \langle (c, a, T), (ca, cc, cT, aT) \rangle,$$

where N is a set of graph vertexes and E – graph arcs. When the graph G_0 has three types of vertexes: c – classes, a – attributes, and T – tasks.

Arcs of the graph G_0 can be represented by the following matrix:

$$T[i,j] = \begin{cases} 0, \text{ if } i = j \\ c_{ij} \in \Re^+, \text{ if exists an arc fromi to } j \\ \infty, \text{ if an arc fromi to } j \text{ does not exist} \end{cases}$$

Figure 3. Ontology-based clusterization: Generic scheme

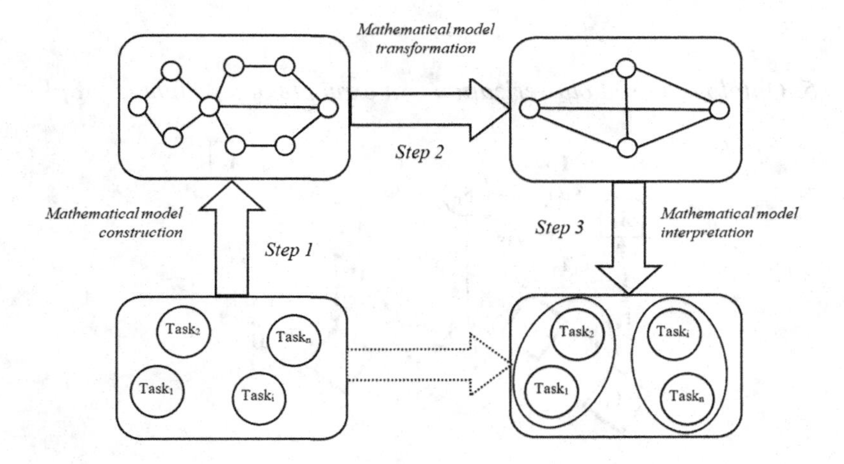

Figure 4. Ontology-based clusterization: Mathematical model construction

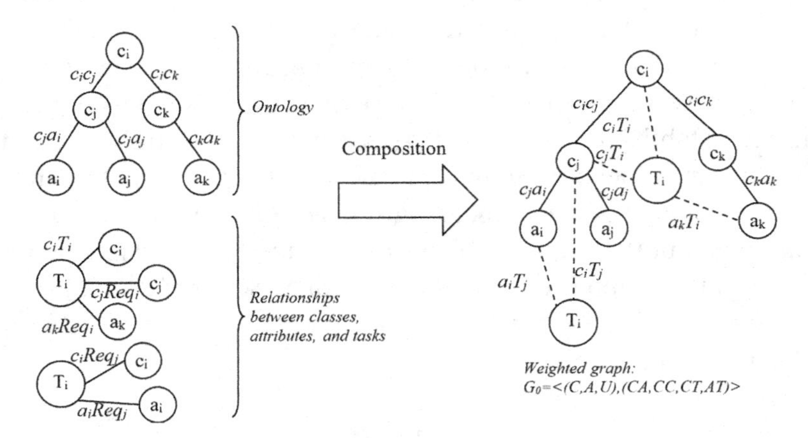

There are two types of arcs on the graph G_0. Type I (ca , cc) is determined by the taxonomy of classes and attributes of the ontological model. Type II (cT , aT) is defined by the relationship between the task and the class / attribute (see Figure 5). The weights of arcs between vertices representing classes and tasks (cT_{weight}) and attributes and queries (aT_{weight}) are determined by the similarity of task terms and class (attribute) terms:

$$cT_{weight} = 1 - cT_{sim} \quad aT_{weight} = 1 - aT_{sim} ,$$

where cT_{sim} is the similarity of task terms and class and aT_{sim} is the similarity of task terms and attribute. Arcs ca and cc that is linked classes and attributes

Figure 5. Ontology-based clusterization: An example of a weighted graph

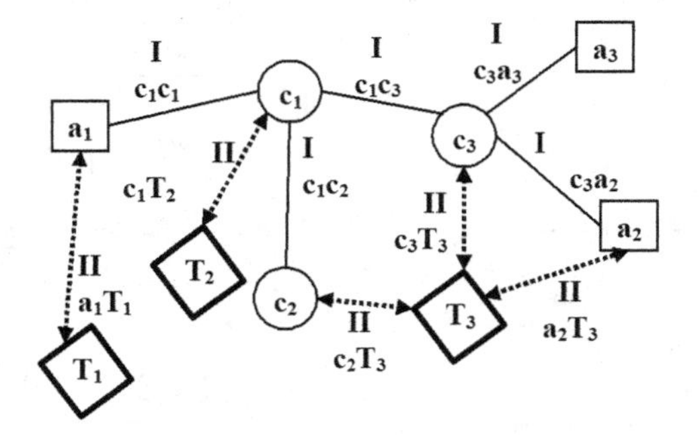

in the ontology has weights ca_{weight} and cc_{weight} that is determined by the ontology engineer.

At the second step the shortest paths calculation between every two tasks in graph G_0 is implemented (see Figure 6). For this purpose, the adapted Floyd algorithm is used for forming the graph G_1. In the considered case, it is needed to know only the weights of the shortest paths between each pair of tasks, for this reason the algorithm was simplified. The following parameters will be used for the proposed algorithm: matrix T that describes arcs of the graph G_0, p is the count of arcs on graph G_0.

```
for i from 1 to p do
 for j from 1 to p do
  for k from 1 to p do
   if i<>j and T[i,j]<> ∞ and i<>k and T[i,k]<> ∞ and
      (T[j,k]= ∞ or T[j,k]>T[j,i]+T[i,k]) then
        T[j,k] = T[j,i]+T[i,k]
   end if
  end for
 end for
end for
```

As a result, the matrix T contains the shortest paths between each pair of tasks. Based on this matrix the graph G_1 is built.

At the third step the interpretation of the results is implemented (see Figure 7). In order to cluster the tasks, it is needed to divide the graph G_1 into subgraphs G_{1i}, $i = 1,...,n$, where n is the number of clusters. The mass of the cluster $Dist\left[G_{1i}\right]$ is defined as the sum of the weights of all the arcs of

Figure 6. Ontology-based clusterization: mathematical model transformation

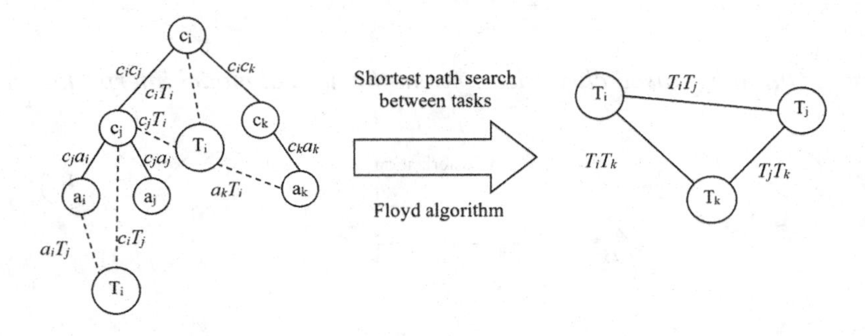

the subgraph G_{1i}. Feasible clustering can be achieved if the following conditions are met:

1. $n \rightarrow min$, i.e. it is necessary to minimize the number of clusters;
2. $W1i_{max}$, $i = 1,\ldots,n$, i.e. the maximum cluster mass for each subgraph is less than the constant W_{max}.

The algorithm is as follows:

1. $Dist\left[T_i\right] = 0$, $i = 1,\ldots,n$. At the initial stage of the algorithm, each vertex is considered a subgraph. The mass of each such subgraph $Dist\left[T_i\right] = Dist\left[G_{1i}\right]$ is zero.
2. The vector V is filled in such a way that: $V\left[z\right] = ARCwight\left[i, j\right] + Dist\left[G_{1i}\right] + Dist\left[G_{1j}\right]$; that is, each element $V\left[z\right]$ of vector V is equal to the sum of the following weights: the weight of the arc between T_i and T_j (ARCweight) and the masses of these subgraphs ($Dist\left[G_{1i}\right]$ and $Dist\left[G_{1j}\right]$).
3. Select the minimum element $V\left[z\right]$ from the vector V.
4. If $V\left[z\right] > W_{max}$, then the algorithm is completed, and the current clusterization satisfies the specified conditions. If $V\left[z\right] < W_{max}$, then the next step is performed.
5. The subgraphs G_{1i} and G_{1j}, corresponding to the element $V\left[z\right]$, are combined into G_{1i}, and the mass of the new subgraph $Dist\left[G_{1i}\right]$ will be equal to $V\left[z\right]$. The subgraph G_{1j} and the vector $V\left[z\right]$ are deleted.
6. The values of the vector V are updated for arcs adjacent to the subgraph G_{1i} (if the subgraph G_{1k} is adjacent to the subgraph G_{1i}, then the element

Figure 7. Ontology-based clusterization: mathematical model interpretation

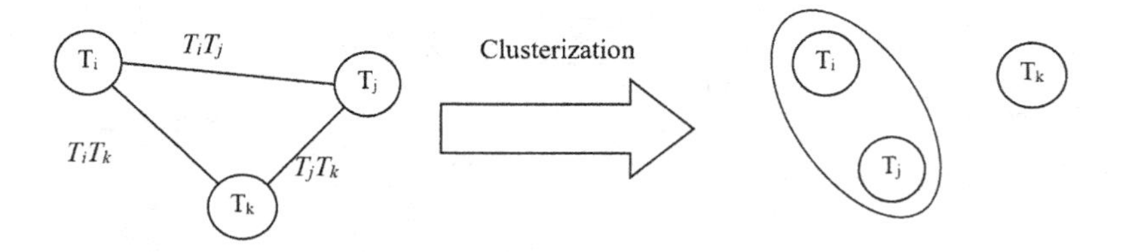

$V[z]$ corresponding to the arc between the subgraphs G_{1i} and G_{1k} will be: $V[z] = ARCwight[i,k] + Dist[G_{1i}] + Dist[G_{1k}]$.

7. Go to step 3.

SOLUTIONS AND RECOMMENDATIONS

There are five solutions have been identified for the proposed profiling and personalization technique: ontology utilization, context modelling, competence modelling, interaction history utilization, task clusterization (see Table 1). Proposed in the chapter profiling and personalization technique for the Internet of Things environments is based on these five solutions.

Table 1. Profiling and personalization solutions in respect to IoT and CPS

#	Solution	Comment
1	Ontology utilization	An ontology is a domain vocabulary completed with a set of precise definitions, or axioms, that constrain the meanings of the terms sufficiently to enable consistent interpretation of the data that use that vocabulary. Utilization of such vocabulary for description of the problem domain allows to formalize the processes in IoT environment.
2	Context modelling	The problem domain ontology allows to identify of the user and task contexts. Context is a description of a situation in which the resource is located and contains all the information that can be used to describe this situation. Task context is a slice of the problem domain ontology that is related to the task. The user context is a slice of problem domain ontology that is related to the user.
3	Competence modelling	The modelling of the competencies is implemented based on Knowledge, Skills, and Abilities model proposed by U.S. federal government. Modelling of the competencies is important to automate the interaction of the user with IoT environment. It is proposed to model the competence as a knowledge, skill, or ability with associated proficiency level in a certain context. The knowledge, skill, and ability is chosen by the user from problem domain ontology.
4	Interaction history utilization	Interaction history storing and its analysis in offline mode for user clustering provide possibilities of implicit preferences determination and utilization in further interaction of the user with IoT environment.
5	Task clusterization	Task clusterization solution has been proposed since every task is linked to the problem domain ontology. At the same time every task is linked to the user which implements it, so in this case task clusterization means the user clusterization.

FUTURE RESEARCH DIRECTIONS

Profiling and personalization are the emerging trends in modern life. Nowadays, modern information systems track user behavior and adapt their behavior based on this information. IoT environments also should understand the user needs and describe the resource competencies to automate the processes of resources search for task performing. The following open problems have been identified for profiling and personalization in IoT environments: problem domain ontology construction, cold start, and weighted ontology (see details in Table 2).

CONCLUSION

The chapter proposes profiling and personalization techniques in Internet of Things Environments. In scope of the chapter the user profile model has been presented that describes the user, his/her preferences, competencies, context, and stores the interaction history; resource profile model that describes the resource context and competencies and stores the interaction history; and the user clusterization method that is aimed at grouping users of the IoT environment into groups by preferences and update these preferences by analyzing the history of interaction the user with the Internet of Things environment. In contrast to the work (Amoretti, Belli, Zanichelli, 2017) user

Table 2. Open problems: profiling and personalization methods for IoT

#	Open Problem	Comment
1	Problem domain ontology construction	The successfulness of the problem domain construction is strictly depended on its complexity. Such IoT environment as smart car or smart home can be easily described by problem domain ontology but worldwide IoT is not possible to describe. Therefore, the presented profiling and personalization techniques are depended on the quality of the problem domain ontology.
2	Cold start	The cold start problem is the well-known problem for the recommendation systems. In the considered approach the same situation exists. The new user does not have any cluster groups and in this case he/she does not have an implicit preference.
3	Weighted ontology	In scope of the proposed clusterization algorithm the shortest path calculation step is proposed. For these purposes the weighted ontology is needed. Wight determination for the relations between ontology elements is a complicated task for the expert but can improve the quality of user clusterization. For the proposed algorithm the weights have been set as constants.

grouping is planned to be implemented using the ontology-based context-oriented clustering method. In contrast to the work (Du et al., 2016; Xiong et al., 2016) the user is described by a set of competencies, as well as explicit and implicit preferences. At these works the authors propose to describe the user by user preference vectors and calculate the similarity of user profiles using the k-nearest neighbors method.

ACKNOWLEDGMENT

The primary contributor to this chapter is Alexey Kashevnik from ITMO University, Russia. The research is funded by the Russian Science Foundation (project # 18-71-10065).

REFERENCES

Amoretti, M., Belli, L., & Zanichelli, F. (2017). UTravel: Smart Mobility with a Novel User Profiling and Recommendation Approach. *Pervasive and Mobile Computing*, *38*(2), 474–489. doi:10.1016/j.pmcj.2016.08.008

Delic, A. (2016). Picture-based Approach to Group Recommender Systems in the E-Tourism Domain. *2016 Conference on User Modeling Adaptation and Personalization*, 337–340. 10.1145/2930238.2930368

Dey, A. K., Salber, D., & Abowd, G. D. (2001). A Conceptual Framework and a Toolkit for Supporting the Rapid Prototyping of Context-Aware Applications. *Context-Aware Computing*, *16*. Retrieved from http://www.cc.gatech.edu/fce/ctk/pubs/HCIJ16.pdf

Du, Q., Xie, H., Cai, Y., Leungc, H., Lid, Q., Mina, H., & Wang, F. (2016). Folksonomy-based Personalized Profiles. *Neurocomputing*, *204*(5), 142–152. doi:10.1016/j.neucom.2015.10.135

Horgan, D. (2018). From here to 2025: Personalised medicine and healthcare for an immediate future. *Journal of Cancer Policy*, *16*, 6–21. doi:10.1016/j.jcpo.2017.12.008

Kaneko, K., Kishita, Y., & Umeda, Y. (2018). Toward Developing a Design Method of Personalization: Proposal of a Personalization Procedure. *Procedia CIRP*, *69*, 740–745. doi:10.1016/j.procir.2017.11.134

Korzun, D. G., Meigal, A. Y., Borodin, A. V., & Gerasimova-Meigal, L. I. (2017). On mobile personalized healthcare services for human involvement into prevention, therapy, mutual support, and social rehabilitation. Engineering, Computer and Information Sciences (SIBIRCON), 276–281.

Lepri, B., Staiano, J., Shmueli, E., Pianesi, F., & Pentland, A. (2016). The role of personality in shaping social networks and mediating behavioral change. *User Modeling and User-Adapted Interaction*, *26*(2), 143–175. doi:10.100711257-016-9173-y

Levashova, T., & Pashkin, M. (2017). Personalized Configuration of Immaterial Products. *Proceedings of the 20th Conference of Open Innovations Association FRUCT*, 228–235.

Lu, Y., Papagiannidis, S., & Alamanos, E. (2018). Internet of Things: A systematic review of the business literature from the user and organizational perspectives. *Technological Forecasting and Social Change*, *136*, 285–297. doi:10.1016/j.techfore.2018.01.022

Piccoli, G., Lui, T., & Grün, B. (2017). The impact of IT-enabled customer service systems on service personalization, customer service perceptions, and hotel performance. *Tourism Management*, *59*, 349–362. doi:10.1016/j.tourman.2016.08.015

Reh, J. (2018). *KSA: Using the Knowledge, Skills and Abilities Model*. Retrieved from https://www.thebalancecareers.com/understanding-knowledge-skills-and-abilities-ksa-2275329

Skillen, K., Chen, L., Nugent, C., Donnelly, M., Burns, W., & Solheim, I. (2014). Ontological user modelling and semantic rule-based reasoning for personalisation of Help-On-Demand services in pervasive environments. *Future Generation Computer Systems*, *34*, 97–109. doi:10.1016/j.future.2013.10.027

Smirnov, A., Kashevnik, A., & Ponomarev, A. (2017). *Context-based infomobility system for cultural heritage recommendation: Tourist Assistant—TAIS. In Personal and Ubiquitous Computing* (pp. 297–311). Heidelberg, Germany: Springer.

Smirnov, A., Kashevnik, A., Shilov, N., Oliver, I., Boldyrev, S., & Balandin, S. (2009). Profile-Based Context Aware Smart Spaces. *Proceedings of the XII International symposium on problems of redundancy in information and control systems*, 249 – 253.

Smirnov, A., Levashova, T., Kashevnik, A., & Shilov, N. (2009). Profile-based self-organization for PLM: approach and technological framework. *Proceedings of the 6th International Conference on Product Lifecycle Management (PLM 09).*

Smirnov, A., Levashova, T., Shilov, N., & Kashevnik, A. (2013). *Ubiquitous Computing in Emergencies: Profile-Based Situation Response Based on Self-Organizing Resource Network. In Prediction and Recognition of Privacy Efforts Using Collaborative Human-Centric Information Systems* (pp. 168–175). Amsterdam: IOS Press.

Smirnov, A., Shilov, N., Levashova, T., & Kashevnik, A. (2009). *GIS for profile-based context formation in situation management*. Information Fusion and Geographic Information Systems. doi:10.1007/978-3-642-00304-2_7

Tsai, C. (2016). A Fuzzy-Based Personalized Recommender System for Local Businesses, *Proceedings of the 27th ACM Conference on Hypertext and Social Media*, 297–302. 10.1145/2914586.2914641

Wei, J., Meng, F., & Arunkumar, N. (2018). A personalized authoritative user-based recommendation for social tagging. *Future Generation Computer Systems*, *86*, 355–361. doi:10.1016/j.future.2018.03.048

Wißotzki, M., Sandkuhl, K., Smirnov, A., Kashevnik, A., & Shilov, N. (2017). Digital Signage and Targeted Advertisement Based on Personal Preferences and Digital Business Models. *Proceedings of the 21st Conference of Open Innovations Association FRUCT*, 375–381. 10.23919/FRUCT.2017.8250206

Xiong, L., Lei, Y., Huang, W., Huang, X., & Zhong, M. (2016). An estimation model for social relationship strength based on users' profiles, co-occurrence and interaction activities. *Neurocomputing*, *214*, 927–934. doi:10.1016/j.neucom.2016.07.022

You, Q., Bhatia, S., & Luo, J. (2016). A picture tells a thousand words—About you! User interest profiling from user generated visual content. *Big Data Meets Multimedia Analytics*, *124*, 45–53.

Zhang, B., & Sundar, S. S. (2019). Proactive vs. reactive personalization: Can customization of privacy enhance user experience? *International Journal of Human-Computer Studies*, *128*, 86–99. doi:10.1016/j.ijhcs.2019.03.002

KEY TERMS AND DEFINITIONS

Competence: A set of knowledge, skill, and attitudes with the corresponding proficiency level that can be applied in a context.

Context: A description of a situation in which the resource is located and contains all the information that can be used to describe this situation.

Internet of Things (IoT): The internetworking of physical entities represented by devices that enable these entities to collect and exchange data for a achieving a common goal.

Ontology: A domain vocabulary complete with a set of precise definitions, or axioms, that constrain the meanings of the terms sufficiently to enable consistent interpretation of the data that use that vocabulary.

Personalization: An ability of a system to identify user needs and preferences and deliver to them the appropriate content, experience, or functionality.

Resource Profile: A set of characteristics that describes the resource in IoT environment including the user context, competencies, and interaction history.

User Profile: A set of characteristics that describes the user in IoT environment including the user context, competencies, preferences, and interaction history.

Chapter 5
Semantic Methods for Data Mining in Smart Spaces

ABSTRACT

This chapter shows the role of semantic methods in delivering AmI. The smart spaces paradigm applies ontological modeling for representing available IoT resources as shared information. This way, resources are virtualized by local information hubs, which are deployed on existing devices. The virtualization benefits from semantics since relations between resources are also represented, forming a semantic network. In turn, various ranking models can be implemented for information search and knowledge reasoning (e.g., based on such well-known algorithms as PageRank). The structural properties of the semantic network leads to advanced AmI support for constructing proactive services: discovery of certain structures (e.g., cycles) can be interpreted as formation of specific knowledge that initiates service construction and delivery.

INTRODUCTION

The Internet of Things (IoT) concept shows the role of distributed service construction based on the data produced from multiple heterogeneous sources by multiple dynamic participants (Sethi & Sarangi, 2017). The smart spaces suit of technologies is used for creating a certain class of intelligent service-oriented environments (Augusto, Callaghan, Cook, Kameas, & Satoh, 2013).

DOI: 10.4018/978-1-5225-8973-0.ch005

A shared view on information is provided to all participants via a semantic information broker (SIB), which supports the information-driven interaction by producing, processing, and consuming this shared information with focus on its semantics (Korzun, Balandin, Kashevnik, Smirnov, & Gurtov, 2017).

In IoT environments, a service-oriented application can be created as a smart space. The latter forms a sparse-connected multi-agent system deployed on various digital devices, including mobile and embedded IoT-enabled equipment (Augusto, Callaghan, Cook, Kameas, & Satoh, 2013; Korzun, Balandin, Kashevnik, Smirnov, & Gurtov, 2017). Software agents run on the devices and interact over the shared information content to create services together.

This type of interaction involves—in parallel and asynchronously—many informational sources and destinations. Information sharing makes the interaction indirect, based on a semantic information broker (SIB) that supports publish/subscribe (pub/sub) model (Eugster, Felber, Guerraoui, & Kermarrec, 2003). The pub/sub model is widely accepted for organizing multi-part interactions in distributed systems and now become applied in development of smart spaces in IoT environments (Pellegrino, Huet, Baude, & Alshabani, 2013; Esposito, Platania, & Beraldi, 2014; Roffia et al., 2016).

Smart services can be developed based on a semantic network interlinking the set of available resources in IoT environment. The semantic network enhances the shared vision on information. The network is subject to data mining needed for selection of appropriate information as a result provided by services constructed by agents in a smart space.

A service can be considered as providing a search extend of the shared information collected in the smart space. Several most appropriate information facts are found for a given problem. It is close to the *k*-optimization approach (several top solutions are used).

BACKGROUND

Service construction in a smart space can be formulated in terms of flows of information changes (Korzun, 2014). It follows the vision of event-driven and information-driven programming. The events to react are ontologically represented in the smart space. This event-based interaction can be enhanced to information-driven interaction. The reaction is not on a simple event (some values are updated) but on forming a certain informational or knowledge fact, e.g., interaction models of emergent semantics (Aiello et al., 2008) and semantic connections (Vlist, Niezen, Rapp, Hu, Feijs, 2013).

Semantic integration of available resources is needed for creating smart services in smart space (Ovaska, Cinotti, & Toninelli, 2012). It supports creating new knowledge, working with users on a personal or mini-group level, contributing to the realization of their expectations.

A mediation layer is introduced for semantic integration where knowledge is derived based on a distributed set of multiple data sources, e.g., including such services as DBpedia (Bizer et al., 2009) and other services for semantic information publishing, enrichment, search, and visualization. We apply the semantic network model for resource integration. The smart space needs the following components.

1. Ontological model for structural representation of available resources (i.e., information or knowledge about such resources) as well as their various descriptions and relations with other objects (Palviainen & Katasonov, 2011).
2. The system to transform the semantics from the descriptions to the semantic network using the ontological model (Augusto, Callaghan, Cook, Kameas, & Satoh, 2013). Human experts can be introduced into this transformation (e.g., based on a wiki system).
3. Cooperative constructing and maintaining the semantic network by many dynamic participants (Korzun, 2014).
4. Semantic data mining in the constructed semantic network to take into account existing relations between collected descriptions (Korzun, 2016).
    1. The ontological model for the semantic network is defined by ontology O. First, O describes a system of concepts C_i (ontology classes) for $i=1, ..., n$. Any particular node v in V (ontology class object, instance or individual) belongs to one or more concepts. Second, O describes the interlinking structure for L, i.e., between which concepts a relation can be and possible types of such relations. The links represent the primary semantics. Third, O describes attributes that v in V and l in L may have to reflect additional semantics (e.g., keywords).

Semantic network construction can be implemented as a collective process (Korzun, Varfolomeyev, Yalovitsyna, & Volokhova, 2017). On the one hand, many nodes v are straightforwardly derived from existing descriptions (e.g., collected in the smart space or in local information systems virtualized in the smart space). Also, nodes correspond to descriptions available in various remote sources (e.g., web pages or photos in the Internet). On the other hand, for nodes v in V the expert defines semantic relations (i.e., links l in L) and their attributes.

An information service needs to find $k > 0$ the most appropriate information facts. A fact can be a node v in V, a link l in L, or a connected graph structure s in G (e.g., a path from u to v can have valued interpretation for some u and v in V). This data mining can be reduced to the ranking problem when rank values $r_v > 0$ or $r_l > 0$ are associated with nodes or links. The higher rank the better is appropriateness of the information. The rank of a connected graph structure is calculated based on ranks of the composed nodes and links.

From the scenario-driven point of view, we can consider a service as knowledge reasoning over the content I and delivering the result to the users (Korzun, 2014). Conceptual steps of the service construction are formalized in the algorithm presented in Figure 1.

SMART SPACE BASED PRINCIPLES OF SERVICE CONSTRUCTION IN IOT ENVIRONMENTS

Principle 1 (Information Hub)

For a given IoT environment a knowledge base is created in the smart space with ontological representation of involved participants, ongoing process, and available resources.

The principle leads to the following options for designing a smart space based service-oriented information system (see Figure 2).

Figure 1. Information service

Algorithm 1 Information delivery actions of service

Require: Ontology o to access information content I of the smart space. The set U of available UI devices.

1: Await $[q_{\text{act}}(o) \to I] = \text{true}$ {event-based activation}
2: Query $x := [q_{\text{info}}(o) \to I]$ {information selection}
3: Select $d \in U$ {target UI devices}
4: Visualization $v_d := v_d + x$ {service delivery}

Figure 2. Information hub

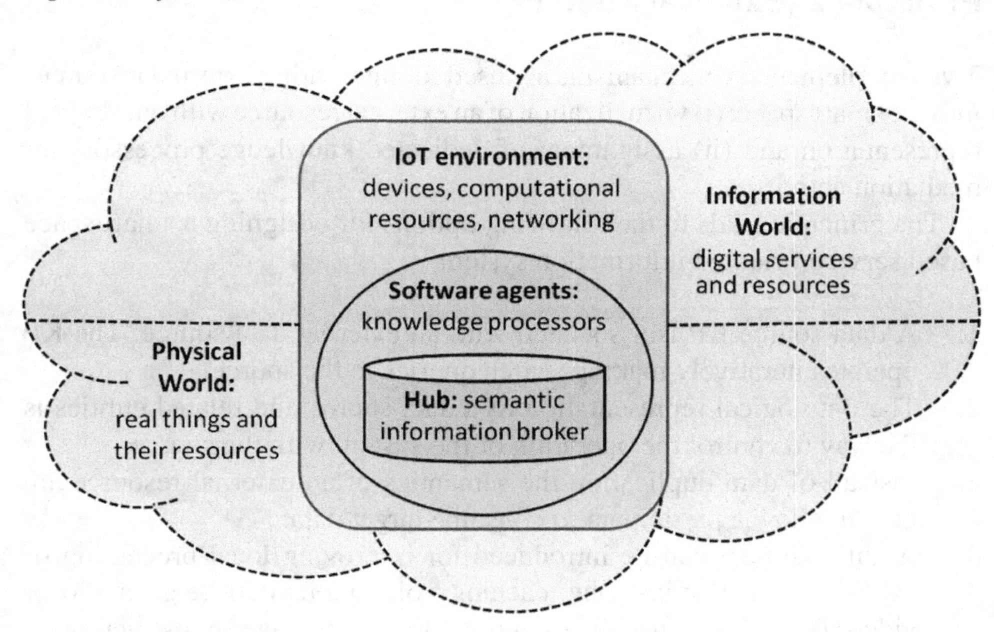

1. Many surrounding devices of the IoT environment as well as personal mobile devices of the users are involved to participate.
2. Semantic interoperability is achieved due to the ontological representation understandable by the participants.
3. The knowledge base is created as ad-hoc and then maintained cooperatively by the participants themselves.
4. The created knowledge base is localized and customized for a given IoT environment and application needs.

The principle of information hub supports virtualization of all related processes and resources in the smart space. In addition to the straightforward virtualization, the semantics are also shared to describe relations observed by involved participants in ongoing processes and available resources. The shared content forms a semantic network of represented objects and their relations. The content becomes a dynamic evolving system with properties similar to peer-to-peer systems. In particular, a service construction process is reflected in the smart space (and can observed by interested participants) as some routes in the semantic network.

Principle 2 (External Resources)

Two complementary mechanisms are used for integrating external resources into the smart space: (i) virtualization of an external resource with ontological representation and (ii) assignment of dedicated knowledge processors for mediation activity.

The principle leads to the following options for designing a smart space based service-oriented information system.

1. A data source KP is associated with an external data source. The KP operates iteratively making search queries to the source.
2. The ontological representation of a data source and related entities is the way to control the operation of the system with the source.
3. Instead of data duplication the semantics of an external resource are kept to allow a participant to consume target data.
4. Additional KPs can be introduced for improving local processing of external data. For instance, caching voluminous data (e.g., audio or video) or dynamic visualization (e.g., local web pages construction).

The principle of external resources opens a smart space for constructing enhanced services. The today's Internet has enough services to solve many everyday problems. However, the puzzle of their combination when solving a given problem is still performed by the users manually because of the high fragmentation of exiting Internet services. Based on the discussed principle, a service-oriented information system provides means for solving such puzzles within the smart space in an automated manner.

Principle 3 (Information-Driven Programming)

In the service construction, a participating KP implements two basic steps: (i) detection of the specified knowledge formation in the smart space and (ii) reaction for producing new knowledge to share in the smart space.

The principle leads to the following options for designing a smart space based service-oriented information system.

1. Search query is the basic mechanism for specifying the knowledge and detecting its formation in the smart space.

2. Some variants of detecting the specified knowledge formation can be implemented by subscription operation, including SPARQL-based subscription.
3. One or more reasoning KP can be associated for detecting the specified knowledge formation and reflecting the informational fact in the smart space.

The principle of information-driven programming provides a way to make semantic-driven design of needed interactions to cooperatively construct a service in the smart space. From programming point of view, for each participating KP its input and output interfaces with the smart space should be defined: the output interface design describes the events that the KP initiates, the input interface design describes the reaction that the KP is responsible. The principle supports moving the system design beyond the traditional case when one programmable component (a KP in our smart space terminology) is assigned for constructing one predefined service.

INDIVIDUAL STRATEGIES IN SERVICE CONSTRUCTION

When a service is constructed by multiple participants in the smart space the service (the information it provides for consumption) needs delivering to appropriate clients, which is typically implemented using the subscription operation (Eugster, Felber, Guerraoui, & Kermarrec, 2003). The basic mechanism for notifying the clients on information updates is "passive" subscription. The smart space SIB (as "a centralized element") controls all ongoing service construction updates and notifies all interested clients, i.e., the clients passively consume information. This centralized solution easily suffers from notification losses due to the IoT settings (Esposito, Platania, & Beraldi, 2014). Additional mechanisms are needed to better control of such information-driven service construction in IoT-enabled smart spaces.

The following model formalizes the key properties of the subscription notification loss problem (Korzun, Pagano, & Vdovenko, 2016). Let i=1,2,... be the event-based time evolution on the client side, where i denotes the index (i.e., sequence numbering) of notification events. In the basic subscription, an event i corresponds to a passive notification (i.e., received from SIB). As we shall see in the next section, i can correspond to an explicit check of the notification delivery (made by the client within its active control). Denote by t_i and k_i the time elapsed and the number of losses occurred between i and $i+1$, respectively. Assume that some initial value t_0 is always defined. The values for k are non-negative integers.

The basic scheme of introducing the active control into the smart space subscription operation is illustrated in Figure 3 (Vdovenko, Bogoiavlenskaia, & Korzun, 2017).

Constant Strategy

The simplest option of active control for a client to check for the information updates regularly after a constant time interval t_C. After each notification event i the client starts the timer, and either $t_{i+1}=t_C$ (if the timer has expired) or $t_{i+1}<t_C$ (if the passive notification has arrived from SIB). The strategy does not take into account the history of losses and the system state, i.e., no adaptability is provided. Notification loses $k_i \geq 1$ can occur between i and $i+1$, more likely for larger t_C.

Random Strategy

In contrast to the deterministic strategy, the client applies the randomization approach when selecting the time t_{i+1} to wait after the notification event i. The efficiency of such randomization has been demonstrated for other scheduling problem in networking (Korzun, Kuptsov, & Gurtov, 2016). For simplicity we assume the random strategy applies the uniform distribution when t_{i+1} is selected uniformly from interval (a,b) for the fixed strategy parameters $0 \leq a < b < \infty$.

Figure 3. Subscription notification loss in a smart space with many mobile clients

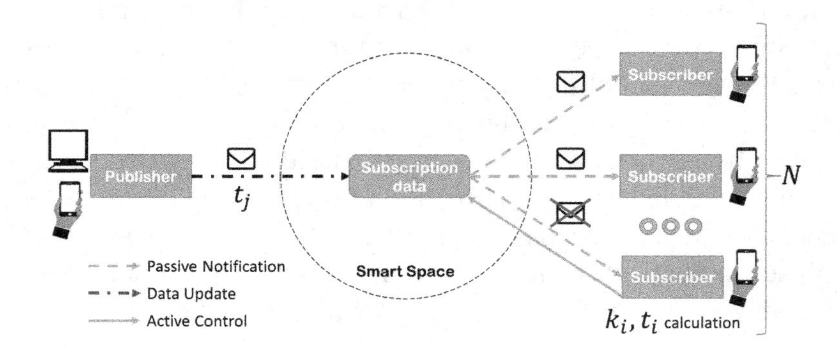

Adaptive Strategy

The adaptation uses the observed value of losses k_1. When no losses occur (i.e., k_i=0) then, aiming at saving its resources, the client increases additively the check interval $t_{i+1}=t_i+\delta$ for the fixed strategy parameter $\delta>0$. The additive increment is conservative, since further growth in t_{i+1} can lead to suffering a burst of losses.

If the client has observed losses (i.e., $k_i>0$), then, trying to decrease the number of further losses, the client decreases essentially the check interval

$$t_{i+1} = \pm\, t_i + \left(1-\alpha\right)\frac{t_i}{k_i+1} \quad (1)$$

First, the decrease in (1) is multiplicative (and depending on the particular value of losses) since the client is interested in quickly achieving the "no-loss" state. Second, the exponential moving average is applied in (1) to take the previous process states into account for the fixed strategy parameter $0\leq\alpha<1$. The case $\alpha=0$ is pure multiplicative decrease.

Therefore, the adaptive strategy follows the recurrent system when the check interval t_{i+1} is reduced (multiplicative decrease) in case when losses are observed and incremented (additive increase) otherwise.

$$t_{i+1} = \begin{cases} t_i+\delta & \text{if } k_i=0 \\ \dfrac{1+\alpha k_i}{k_i+1}t_i & \text{if } k_i>0 \end{cases} \quad (2)$$

The adaptive strategy is based on the Additive–Increase/Multiplicative–Decrease (AIMD) method, which is used for congestion control in Internet, e.g., see (Callegari, Giordano, Pagano, & Pepe, 2014). The strategy can be reduced to the following two important variants: AIMD-like strategy and semi-adaptive strategy.

AIMD-Like Strategy

Let us interpret t_{i+1} in (2) as congestion window size (for data sent through the network), as accepted in TCP. First, TCP congestion avoidance uses $\delta=1$, i.e., the additive increment is done by one full-sized segment. Second, $\alpha=0$, i.e., TCP does not use the exponential moving average. Third, $k_i \in \{0,1\}$, i.e., a packet can be either lost or not. Consequently, when a lost packet is observed the congestion window size is halved. Based on these three points we consider the following reduction of (2) to define the AIMD-like strategy.

$$t_{i+1} = \begin{cases} t_i + \delta & \text{if } k_i = 0 \\ t_i / \kappa & \text{if } k_i > 0 \end{cases} \tag{3}$$

The strategy parameters define the additive increase with fixed $\delta>0$ and the multiplicative decrease with fixed $\kappa>1$.

$$\begin{cases} t_i + \delta & \text{if } k_i = 0 \\ t_i / \kappa & \text{if } k_i > 0 \end{cases} \tag{4}$$

The strategy parameters define the additive increase with fixed $\delta>0$ and the multiplicative decrease with fixed $\kappa>1$.

Semi-Adaptive Strategy

Another simplification is always halving the check interval in case of losses, i.e., set $\kappa=2$ in (3). When no loss is observed then return the initial (reference) value t_0.

$$t_{i+1} = \begin{cases} t_0 & \text{if } k_i = 0 \\ t_i / 2 & \text{if } k_i > 0 \end{cases} \tag{5}$$

Note that this semi-adaptive strategy allows advancing. In particular, as in (3) any fixed $\kappa>1$ can be used for the multiplicative decrease. Also, similarly to the random strategy, some randomized value (e.g., close to t_0) can be used if $k_i=0$.

RANK BASED SERVICE CONSTRUCTION

An information service provides a search extend of the collected shared information in the smart space. The service aims at finding several the most appropriate information facts for a given problem. This property is close to the k-optimization approach (when several top solutions are used). To mention as examples, some particular semantic properties of such services are as follows.

- **Semantic Clustering:** A set of thematically related objects.
- **Semantic Filtering:** Most appropriate descriptions for a given object.
- **Semantic Neighborhood:** Closely related objects for a given object.

The properties can be achieved based on certain information arrangements, when the order describes the relevance of information fragment. Mathematically, this way of data mining can be implemented using ranking models. Arranged information is provided with numerical rank values. Objects with similar ranks can be considered as forming a cluster. Highest-rank objects are selected in filtering. For a given objects, its rank-based neighborhood includes the objects having similar rank value.

The following three classes of ranking methods (Petrina et al., 2017): 1) local ranking, 2) collaborative filtering, 3) structural ranking. The role of these methods for creating smart services for smart museum domain is discussed in (Petrina et al., 2017). A ranking algorithm runs within a search request when semantic network $G=(V,L)$ is traversed. The corresponding nodes $v \in V$ and links $l \in L$ are assigned with rank values $r_v \geq 0$ and $r_l \geq 0$. Then k highest-rank facts are extracted to be used in service construction as the most relevant to the current need of the user.

Local Ranking

Two or more objects are analyzed for similarity based on their content and overlapping of this content. In this case, the rank is computed in respect to some fixed node u in V and reflects distance of other nodes from u.

$$r_v(u) = \frac{1}{\rho(u,v)}, \tag{6}$$

where u and v are nodes, links, or even some connected substructures in G.

For instance, if u and v have sets K_u and K_v of annotating keywords (or tags, or other discrete semantic attributes associated with the stored content) then the rank reflects the size of content overlapping for u and v:

$$\acute{A}(\boldsymbol{u},\boldsymbol{v}) = \left|K_u \cap K_v\right|,$$

i.e., the larger the number of shared keywords the higher is the similarity.

In particular, from the service construction point of view, if u is the recent object that the user studies then the information service can provide the highest rank nodes $v_1, v_2, ..., v_k$ as a multi-option recommendation for the further study. In addition to the mathematical rank-based evaluation of the information relevance, the role of delivery of the information (service) to the user is essential. The latter problem needs problem-oriented visual models. In particular, a star graph model can be used with u in the central node and $v_1, v_2, ..., v_k$ are rays of length $r_{v1}, r_{v2}, ..., r_{vk}$. The angle position of rays can be used for reflecting geo-location information about objects $v_1, v_2, ..., v_k$.

Collaborative Filtering

This ranking model assumes that many users generate opinions about each object. The opinions are transformed to some community based scores (normalized $0 \le r_v^* \le 1$). Then the scores can be combined with other ranking requirements. For instance,

$$r_v = \alpha r_v^* + (1-\alpha)\left(1 - \frac{d_v}{\max_{w \in W} d_w}\right), \tag{7}$$

where W is a set of objects of potential interest for the user, $\boldsymbol{d}_w > 0$ is an individual (personalized) user's interest for object w, $0 \le \alpha \le 1$ is a tradeoff parameter between community scores and individual interest.

In particular, if W is a set of points of interest for the tourist and $\boldsymbol{d}_w$ is the time to reach w from the current location then the information service can provide the highest rank nodes $v_1, v_2, ..., v_k$ as recommendation for the next object to study.

Structural Ranking

This ranking model utilizes the connectivity properties of the semantic network $G=(V,L)$, similarly as it happens in the well-known PageRank algorithm (for web networks analysis). For instance, node ranks r_v for all $v \in V$ are computed iteratively starting from some initial values $r_u^{(0)}$:

$$r_v^{(i+1)} = \alpha \sum_{\forall v \to w} p_{wv} r_w^{(i)} + (1-\alpha)\pi_v, \tag{8}$$

where p_{wv} is weight of the link $l(v \to w)$, $0 \leq \alpha \leq 1$ is the damping factor denoting the probability of following the connectivity structure of G, and π is a jump probability vector for all $v \in V$.

In particular, if p_{vu} is relative weight of v's role to u then the information service can provide the highest rank objects $v_1, v_2, \ldots, v_k$ as recommendation for the most appropriate information facts to study.

SOLUTIONS AND RECOMMENDATIONS

Consider several important classes of information services for the domain of smart museum. Such services provide information assistance needed for cultural heritage preservation, transmission, and research (Korzun, Yalovitsyna, & Volokhova, 2018).

Visit Service

The service constructs a personalized exposition of recommended exhibits for a visitor to study. Such a recommendation is a small set of selected objects from the presented ones in the museum exhibition room. This set V_U is constructed from the available knowledge such that the set represents the most interesting facts for the particular visitor u or their group U. This way, a visit program is constructed for a museum visitor before the visit. The service is also responsible for program adaptation during the visit depending on the preferences of the visitor and on the dynamically changing situation.

Exhibition Service

The service shows selected descriptions and visual information about the studied exhibits on exhibition touch screens or on personal mobile devices of the visitors. In fact, the service creates a kind of virtualization when a physical exhibition is augmented with digital representation (i.e., implementing multimodal interface). As in Visit service, Exhibition service acts as a recommender since the screens show the recommended (most interesting) facts derived from the available museum collection knowledge for the current context and situation.

Enrichment Service

The service supports modification (evolution) of the semantic network by museum personnel and visitors (i.e., implementing collective intelligence). A museum visitor can enrich descriptions of studied exhibits (e.g., adding annotations). A personal mobile device (e.g., smartphone) becomes a primary access tool for this service. First, annotation is useful when the visitor adds descriptions about an object (e.g., facts from an eyewitness of the event), which is particularly important in everyday life history. Second, visitors can make the routine work on establishing known history-valued relations between objects. The visitor adds some relation (together with its description), and museum personnel moderate the correctness and value.

FUTURE RESEARCH DIRECTIONS

Base on the rank models the following semantic properties can be analyzed using mathematical technique (semantic methods of data mining).

- Semantic clustering: a set of thematically related objects.
- Semantic filtering: most appropriate descriptions for a given object.
- Semantic neighborhood: closely related objects for a given object.

The key open problem is development of particular methods to apply the properties when developing smart space solutions to applications. The development needs solving a generic selection problem in the settings of IoT environments. Then a kind of decision-making procedure is performed (based on the selected information).

CONCLUSION

This chapter introduced the role of semantic methods in delivering AmI. The smart spaces paradigm applies ontological modeling for representing available IoT resources as shared information. This way, resources are virtualized by local information hubs, which are deployed on existing devices.

The virtualization benefits from semantics since relations between resources are also represented, forming a semantic network. We study an individual strategy of active control for information updates. The strategy is applicable when the selection decision depends on latest information from others. We present ranking methods for semantic data mining. Up-to-date information is evaluated to select the most relevant facts to the participant. In turn, various ranking models can be implemented for information search and knowledge reasoning, e.g., based on such well-known algorithms as PageRank. The structural properties of the semantic network leads to advanced AmI support for constructing smart services.

ACKNOWLEDGMENT

The primary contributor to this chapter is Dmitry Korzun from Petrozavodsk State University (PetrSU), Russia. We also used materials kindly provided by Alexey Varfolomeyev (Independent researcher, Ukraine).

REFERENCES

Aiello, C., Catarci, T., Ceravolo, P., Damiani, E., Scannapieco, M., & Viviani, M. (2008). Emergent semantics in distributed knowledge management. In Evolution of the Web in Artificial Intelligence Environments (pp. 201-220). Springer-Verlag. doi:10.1007/978-3-540-79140-9_9

Augusto, J. C., Callaghan, V., Cook, D., Kameas, A., & Satoh, I. (2013). Intelligent Environments: A Manifesto. *Human-centric Computing and Information Sciences*, *3*(1), 1–18. doi:10.1186/2192-1962-3-12

Bizer, C., Lehmann, J., Kobilarov, G., Auer, S., Becker, C., Cyganiak, R., & Hellmann, S. (2009). DBpedia - a crystallization point for the Web of Data. *Journal of Web Semantics*, *7*(3), 154–165. doi:10.1016/j.websem.2009.07.002

Esposito, C., Platania, M., & Beraldi, R. (2014). Reliable and timely event notification for publish/subscribe services over the internet. *IEEE/ACM Transactions on Networking*, *22*(1), 230–243. doi:10.1109/TNET.2013.2245144

Eugster, P. T., Felber, P. A., Guerraoui, R., & Kermarrec, A.-M. (2003). The many faces of publish-subscribe. *ACM Computing Surveys*, *35*(2), 114–131. doi:10.1145/857076.857078

Kiljander, J., Ylisaukko-oja, A., Takalo-Mattila, J., Etelapera, M., & Soininen, J.-P. (2012). Enabling semantic technology empowered smart spaces. *Journal of Computer Networks and Communications*, *2012*, 1–14. doi:10.1155/2012/845762

Korzun, D. (2014). Service formalism and architectural abstractions for smart space applications. In *Proceeding of 10th Central & Eastern European Software Engineering Conference in Russia* (pp. 19:1–19:7). ACM. 10.1145/2687233.2687253

Korzun, D. (2016). On the smart spaces approach to semantic-driven design of service-oriented information systems. In *Proceedings of 12th International Baltic Conference on Databases and Information Systems (DB&IS)* (pp. 181-195). Academic Press. 10.1007/978-3-319-40180-5_13

Korzun, D., Balandin, S., Kashevnik, A., Smirnov, A., & Gurtov, A. (2017). Smart spaces-based application development: M3 architecture, design principles, use cases, and evaluation. *International Journal of Embedded and Real-Time Communication Systems*, *8*(2), 66–100. doi:10.4018/IJERTCS.2017070104

Korzun, D., Pagano, M., & Vdovenko, A. (2016). Control Strategies of Subscription Notification Delivery in Smart Spaces. *Communications in Computer and Information Science*, *601*, 40–51. doi:10.1007/978-3-319-30843-2_5

Korzun, D., Varfolomeyev, A., Yalovitsyna, S., & Volokhova, V. (2017). Semantic infrastructure of a smart museum. *Personal and Ubiquitous Computing*, *21*(2), 345–354. doi:10.100700779-016-0996-7

Korzun, D., Yalovitsyna, S., & Volokhova, V. (2018). Smart Services as Cultural and Historical Heritage Information Assistance for Museum Visitors and Personnel. Baltic J. *Modern Computing*, *6*(4), 418–433.

Ovaska, E., Cinotti, T.S., & Toninelli, A. (2012). The design principles and practices of interoperable smart spaces. *Advanced Design Approaches to Emerging Software Systems: Principles, Methodology and Tools*, 18–47.

Palviainen, M., & Katasonov, A. (2011). Model and ontology-based development of smart space applications. In *Pervasive Computing and Communications Design and Deployment* (pp. 126–148). Technologies, Trends, and Applications. doi:10.4018/978-1-60960-611-4.ch006

Pellegrino, L., Huet, F., Baude, F., & Alshabani, A. (2013). A Distributed Publish/Subscribe System for RDF Data. Lecture Notes in Computer Science, 8059, 39-50.

Petrina, O. B., Korzun, D. G., Volokhova, V. V., Yalovitsyna, S. E., & Varfolomeyev, A. G. (2017). Semantic approach to opening museum collections of everyday life history for services in Internet of Things environments. *International Journal of Embedded and Real-Time Communication Systems*, *8*(1), 31–44.

Roffia, L., Morandi, F., Kiljander, J., D'Elia, A., Vergari, F., Viola, F., ... Cinotti, T. S. (2016). A Semantic Publish-Subscribe Architecture for the Internet of Things. *IEEE Internet of Things Journal*, *3*(6), 1274–1296. doi:10.1109/JIOT.2016.2587380

Sethi, P., & Sarangi, S. R. (2017). Internet of Things: Architectures, Protocols, and Applications. *Journal of Electrical and Computer Engineering*, *2017*, 9324035. doi:10.1155/2017/9324035

Vlist, B., Niezen, G., Rapp, S., Hu, J., & Feijs, L. (2013). Configuring and controlling ubiquitous computing infrastructure with semantic connections: A tangible and an AR approach. *Personal and Ubiquitous Computing*, *17*(4), 783–799. doi:10.100700779-012-0627-x

KEY TERMS AND DEFINITIONS

Data Mining: The process of discovering patterns in large data sets involving methods at the intersection of machine learning, statistics, and database systems.

Information Service: A search extend of the shared information collected in the smart space.

Internet of Things (IoT): The internetworking of physical entities represented by devices that enable these entities to collect and exchange data for a achieving a common goal.

Recommender System (or Recommendation System): An information filtering system that seeks to predict the "rating" (or "preference", "score", "rank") a user would give to an item (e.g., to an information fact).

Semantic Network: A knowledge base that represents semantic relations between concepts. Formally, the underlying representation model is a directed graph consisting of nodes, which represent concepts, and links, which represent semantic relations between concepts, mapping or connecting semantic fields.

Smart Space: A set of communicating nodes and information storages, which has embedded logic to acquire and apply knowledge about its environment and adapt to its inhabitants in order to improve their experience in the environment.

Chapter 6
Internet of Things Resources Interaction for Service Construction and Delivery

ABSTRACT

Semantic interaction support for internet of things (IoT) resources is a key point of the service construction and delivery for the users. Semantic interoperability between interacted resources provides possibilities for them to understand each other. One of the possible approaches to enrich the semantic interoperability is the ontology modeling. Every resource is described by an ontology. The ontology formally represents knowledge as a set of concepts within a domain, using a shared vocabulary to denote the types, properties, and interrelationships of those concepts. Based on the ontology matching techniques, resource ontologies are matched, and resources operate in accordance with this matching. Context is any information that can be used to characterize the situation of an entity. An entity in the considered case is the resource of IoT environment. It is proposed to use the ontologies to describe the context of resource and take this information for task performing. For the service construction, the coalitions of IoT resources that can jointly provide the needed service for a task performing need to be created.

DOI: 10.4018/978-1-5225-8973-0.ch006

INTRODUCTION

Interaction of IoT resources is the important task for the joint service construction and delivery. Different resources should "understand" each other to perform task together that requires the interoperability support between them. The chapter considers different levels of interoperability, discuss the context model creation for the resource, and presents an approach to coalition creation of IoT resources for joint service construction.

There are following levels of interoperability between software resources are distinguished (see Kubicek, Cimander, & Scholl, 2011; Kubicek & Cimander, 2009): technical level, syntactic level, level of semantic interoperability, and level of organizational interoperability (or interoperability of business processes). The technical layer provides connection information transfer between software components (interfaces, communication protocols and the infrastructure necessary for the operation of these protocols). The syntactic layer includes data transfer formats from one program component to another. The semantic level provides an understanding of the meaning of the information exchanged between software components. The organizational level provides an understanding of the business processes arising from the interaction of software components. The first two levels are related to the technical equipment and the basic software of the interacting components, while the third level is the basic one when they interact to harmonize the behavior of the components. The fourth level allows the software components to reconcile business processes between them when performing joint tasks. The third level is the base for support "understanding" of each other by IoT resources. In this regard, this chapter focuses on ensuring the semantic interoperability of IoT resources, which will allow the formation of coalitions for the joint task performing by different IoT resources. The second aspect for coalition creation is the context modelling. The task that should be performed has to be modelled as soon as current situation that is related to this task. Therefore, authors propose to use the context management technology for the context modelling and utilization. In scope of the chapter it is proposed to use ontologies to ensure the semantic interoperability between Internet of Things resources. The ontology formally represents knowledge as a set of concepts within a domain, using a shared vocabulary to denote the types, properties, and interrelationships of those concepts. Ontology management techniques cover processes of acquisition, storage, updating, and utilization of ontologies.

Special issue ''Intelligent Algorithms and Standards for Interoperability in Internet of Things" of the Future Generation Computer Systems journal (Ahmad, Cuomo, Wu, & Jeon, 2019) consider the intelligent algorithms and standards development for interoperability in Internet of Things. The issue highlights the popularity of the topic and a lot of research done in this area.

The chapter is structured as follows. Background section presents broad definitions and discussions of the semantic interoperability for IoT resources topic. The section semantic interoperability support between interacting resources discusses the proposed the ontology matching method that aimed at "understanding" support between two resources described by ontologies in a shared space. The section context model and coalition creation of internet of things resources proposes the model that is aimed to take into account current situation and utilize it during the interaction process for coalition creation aimed at service construction for task performing in IoT environment. The section multi-level self-organization technique of resources in IoT environment presents a technique for multi-level self-organization support in IoT environment. Solutions and recommendations section discuss questions in dealing with the issues, controversies, or problems presented in the preceding section. The section future research directions discuss the future work in the area of personalization. Conclusion summarize the chapter.

BACKGROUND

Modern research works in the area of intelligent agent interaction have been presented. Interoperability still remains one of the main challenges towards realizing the grand vision of IoT (Negash, Westerlund, & Tenhunen, 2019). The paper presents an approach that considers various types of IoT application domains, architecture of the IoT, and the works of standards organizations to give a holistic abstract model of IoT. Authors propose three computing layers: technical, syntactic, and semantic in contrast to (Kubicek, Cimander, & Scholl, 2011; Kubicek & Cimander, 2009) considered in this chapter. Authors present a Web of Virtual Things (WoVT) server that can be deployed at the middle layer of IoT (Fog layer) and Cloud to address the problem of interoperability.

In the paper (Iqbal et al., 2018) authors propose an interoperable IoT platform for a smart home system using a web-of-objects and cloud architecture. Authors propose to control the home appliances from anywhere using the platform.

To implement this functionality they developed a platform to integrate the information from smart home sensors to the cloud. Authors proposed a Raspberry PI based gateway for interoperability among various legacy home appliances, different communication technologies, and protocols and bring the smart home appliances to the web and make it accessible through the representational state transfer framework. Then the cloud server to store the information has been provided.

In the paper (Baca et al., 2015) authors discuss the coordination mechanisms of a group of modular robots for joint task performing. The presented by authors system architecture is divided into modules and modular robots. Modules are basic system components that are classified into three types: power / control, joint, and specialized. A modular robot is an autonomous object composed of at least one power / control module, one or more connecting modules, and / or special modules. The approach is based on two types of interaction between software components: inter robot (between different configurations of the modular robot and the control station) and intra robot (inside the configuration of the modular robot). Through this communication architecture, synchronization of modules in the modular robot configuration and coordination of the modular robot group is implemented. Under the group in this case refers to a set of modular robots, collaborating to perform the task. Coordination mechanisms and cooperation strategies are implemented in the developed modular system that is a reconfigurable inhomogeneous modular robot system consisting of a series of interchangeable modules that form different robots.

The paper (Ono & Ogawa, 2014) describes the interaction of the smartphone with mobile robot developed based on the LEGO Mindstorms robotic kit. Authors propose to connect the smartphone to the NXT controller via the Bluetooth protocol. Smartphone interacts with the robot and determined necessary actions based on information from the controller. The developed robot consists of two motors, rotating wheels to control the speed and direction, one motor to change the angle of the smartphone and two sensors (one ultrasonic and one touch sensor). A smartphone based on the Android operating system sets the behavior of the robot and sends data to the NXT controller, which controls the motors and reads the readings from the sensors.

A multi-level hybrid navigation strategy for set of robots is proposed by authors of the paper (Zhu et al., 2013). The authors consider the situation when there are several robots and static obstacles in two-dimensional space. Each robot starts from the starting position and has its own task. All robots are equipped with distance sensors, and can communicate with other robots to exchange information about their location, direction of motion, speed, obstacles, and behavior coordination. The hybrid navigation system consists of three levels: the level of action, the level of low-level communications and the level of high-level communications. The level of action directly controls the movement of the robot. The level of low-level communications initially performs route planning based on prior knowledge. At this level, typical conflict situations are also resolved. If the situation at this level cannot be resolved, then it is transferred to the level of high-level communications. A key feature of the system is a bottom-up management architecture, where a high-level layer is activated only when necessary. In this architecture, the level of action is the most loaded level that works at each stage of management.

The authors of the paper (López et al., 2013) describe a building maintenance and monitoring system using mobile robots abd control them through the Internet. Authors propose the centralized architecture: the robots and the building maintenance system is connected to a central server. Navigation modules have been developed based on CARMEN system (see Fernández et al., 2004). In contrast to CARMEN in the proposed system the motion control of robots is divided into high-level (strategic) and low-level (tactical) planning.

The paper (Rodić et al., 2015) discusses the control architecture for hierarchical distributed structure of the robot controllers. In such architecture the controller at the highest level coordinates all robot functions, data collection, and data exchange traffic. Other controllers of lower levels are subordinated to this controller.

The paper (Chand & Carnegie, 2013) focused on local area map creation by the set of robots and it investigation. The approach presented in the paper allows robots with limited information processing and / or object recognition capabilities to scan large spaces. The approach includes computing robots at the top level and robots with limited computing capabilities (workers) at the bottom level. The terrain contains obstacles that is divided by computing robots into local areas. Obstacles are investigated by workers. Workers perform two types of tasks: moving between local areas and movement within the local area and his research. Robots can perform both tasks, but because of the limited computational capabilities they can usually perform only one. In this case, the robot can dynamically change its role during the study to improve the efficiency of the system.

Authors of the paper (Zhang & Ueno, 2007) presents a model of a system of inhomogeneous robots using a frame representation of knowledge to describe the functions and behavior of such a robot. The knowledge required to build a robot system is integrated into a single model for sharing between robots and users. The proposed system allows to integrate heterogeneous robots and various methods as soon as automatically perform human-robot interaction and plan the behavior of the robot. The paper presents a system of heterogeneous robots, consisting of a humanoid robot, a mobile robot, and a dog robot. The interaction of robots is based on the SPAK platform, which provides (a) a central module that acts as a blackboard, (b) a knowledge module and (c) a task scheduler. The platform provides the software tools needed to integrate various existing modules over a wireless network. According to user requests, the behavior of the robot can be automatically generated as a behavioral frame in SPAK. Commands defined in such frames are sent to robots. In addition, all robots have their own local control programs that control their behavior. During the execution of tasks by robots, instructions from SPAK are converted into a command for the robot so that the robot can execute it. In order to improve performance and ensure the reliability of joint operation of heterogeneous robots, feedback from robots is necessary to evaluate their actions. Feedback signals about the actions of robots can be obtained in two ways. In the first case, in an environment where the user and robots are located, sensors are installed to monitor the actions of the robots. In the second case, feedback is received from the robots themselves, when they finish their actions and is transmitted back to SPAK.

SEMANTIC INTEROPERABILITY SUPPORT BETWEEN INTERACTING RESOURCES

In the concept of Semantic Web ontology language (OWL) has been introduced as a knowledge representation language to encode ontologies. It is based on description logic, enabling structural knowledge representation and reasoning (Horrocks, 2008; Baader, Calvanese, McGuinness, Nardi, & Patel-Schneider, 2003). The formalism follows an object-oriented model: knowledge is described in terms of individuals (instances), classes (concepts), and properties (roles and attributes).

Although ontologies and OWL in particular provide a powerful tool for developers, the OWL syntax is too complicated for machine-based processing. The Semantic Web introduced RDF, a foundation for machine-aware representation and processing of semantic data. On the one hand, RDF provides interoperability between applications, making data interchange machine understandable. On the other hand, RDF supports ontologies and allows extensions with OWL constructions.

To achieve the semantic interoperability between different heterogeneous resources built on top of different ontologies the ontology matching method has been proposed (Figure 2). Based on the presented ontology matching model authors have the USA patent (S. Balandin et al., 2012; Smirnov et al., 2010).

The proposed approach allows to match two ontologies for the interoperability support of resources in IoT environment. The approach takes into account that the matching procedure has to be done in three steps. It is considered, that when a resource joins an IoT environment, it performs a matching of its own ontology with the IoT knowledge base. If all ontology classes that characterize resource capabilities and requirements are matched with knowledge base then it is conducted that resource ontology has been successfully matched with the IoT environment (ontologies of other resources).

The approach consists of the following steps:

1. Compare all elements between two ontologies and fill the matrix ***M*** using information about the same words and synonims.
2. Compare all elements between two ontologies and fill the matrix ***M*** using similarity-based model. The matrix ***M*** shows the degree of similarity of elements of the first ontology to the second. It has size ***m*** to ***n***. where ***m*** is the number of elements in the first ontology and ***n*** is the number of elements in the second one. Each element of this matrix contains the degree of similarity between the string terms of two ontology elements using the fuzzy string comparison method.
3. Calculate semantic distances, using the background knowledge, e.g., WordNet or Wiktionary and fill the matrix M'. The matrix M' is of size of ***m*** to ***n*** too as the matrix ***M***.
4. Update values in matrix ***M*** where each new value of elements of ***M*** is the maximum value of $(M\ M')$.
5. Improve distance values in the matrix ***M*** using the graph-based distance improvement model.

As a result, the matrix ***M*** contains the degrees of similarity between every two elements in matched ontologies. Based on information from matrix ***M*** it is possible to determine correspondences between elements by selecting higher than a threshold value degrees of similarities. The threshold value has to be set by the responsible person based on the problem domain area where the resources are operated.

Figure 1. Ontology matching method general scheme

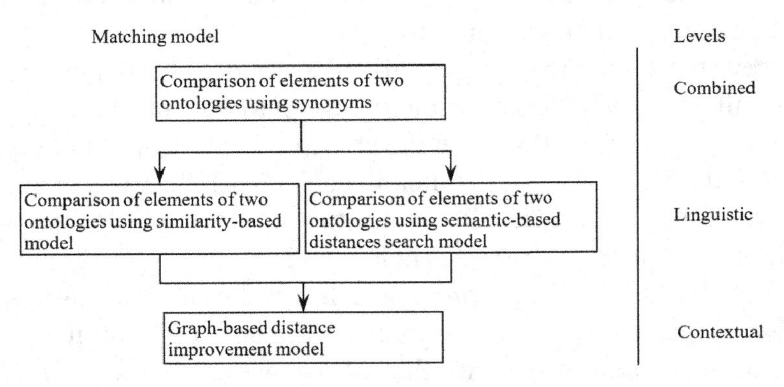

The similarity-based model for the ontology matching is presented in Figure 2. It contains a stemming procedure to normalize words, improved fuzzy string comparison procedure, and normalization procedure. To improve the matching quality, the application of the stemming procedure is proposed. This operation makes it possible to identify ontology elements even if they are written in different forms. The following conversions can be done: “looking” → “look”, “device” → “devic”, “vertical” → “vertic”, and “horizontal” → “horizont”. The basis of the string comparison algorithm is the well-known conventional algorithm that calculates occurrence of substrings from one string in the other string. However, this algorithm does not take into account the length of the second string. As a result, it was decided to introduce the comparison based on the above algorithm twice:

$$\boldsymbol{FC_1 = FuzzyCompare\left(Element_1, Element_2\right)}$$

and

$$\boldsymbol{FC_2 = FuzzyCompare\left(Element_2, Element_1\right)}$$

After that we calculate the result as an aggregation of the above results in accordance with the following formula:

$$\boldsymbol{Re' = n \times FC_1 + \left(1 - n\right) * FC_2}.$$

Figure 2. Similarity-based model

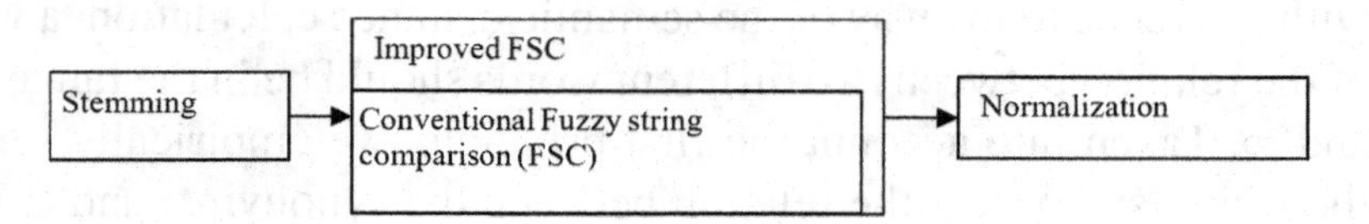

where n is a weight, n∈[0;1] determined by the responsible person based on problem domain area takig into account the following rules: $n = 0.5$ .means the same weight to the both strings, $n = 0$ .searches only terms of first ontology elements inside the terms of the second ontology, and $n = 1$ .vise versa. It is proposed by default to set $n = 0.5$.

To measure semantic distances between ontology elements the machine-readable dictionary is used (Wiktionary or WordNet).

These dictionaries include: a set of words defined in dictionary along with, definitions given for each word, a set of synonyms for each word, and a set of associated words for each word. Words associated with a word are considered as hyperlinked words occurring in the dictionary definition given for this word. The nodes of ontology are linked to nodes representing their synonyms and associated words as this is given in the machine-readable dictionary. The links between the nodes are labeled by the distance of relations specified between the concepts represented by these nodes in the machine-readable dictionary. Weight w .of a relation specified between two ontology elements t_i .and t_j .is assigned as:

$$w = \begin{cases} 0.5, if\ t_i\ and\ t_j\ are\ synonms \\ 0.3, if\ t_i\ and\ t_j\ are\ associative\ words \\ \infty, if\ t_i\ and\ t_j\ are\ the\ same\ words \end{cases}$$

The values for the weights were evaluated based on the following principles:

1. Semantic distances between synonyms are assumed to be smaller than semantic distances between associated words;
2. Semantic distance is proposed to be calculated as inversely proportional to weights raised to a power. The power is proportional to the path between the compared words. The longer the path, the greater the semantic distance

for the two different words is expected to be. To meet this expectation with reference to the way of the semantic distance calculation, a weight of the relation between two different words should be in the range *(0, 1)* and ∞. Taken into account the first principle, we empirically selected the weights: 0,5 - for the relation between the synonyms; and *0,3* - for the relation between the associated words;

3. The semantic distance between the same words is equal to *0*.

To search the semantic distance between the elements of two ontologies, the nodes of the first ontology are checked for their similarity to nodes of the second ontology. As a measure of similarity, the semantic distance (Dist) is used.

$$\boldsymbol{Dist}\left(\boldsymbol{t}_i,\boldsymbol{t}_j\right)=\frac{1}{\sum_S \prod_{k=s_i}^{s_j} \boldsymbol{w}_k}$$

Where $\boldsymbol{t}_i$, $\boldsymbol{t}_j$ – ontology elements; $\mathbf{w}$ – weight of lexical relation existing between $\boldsymbol{t}_i$ and $\boldsymbol{t}_j$; $\mathbf{S}$ – a set of paths from $\boldsymbol{t}_i$ to $\boldsymbol{t}_j$, where a path $\mathbf{S}$ is formed by any number of links that connect $\boldsymbol{t}_i$ and $\boldsymbol{t}_j$ passing through any number of nodes. The degree of similarity depends inversely on distance.

The graph-based improvement model for propagation similarities from one ontology element to another is presented in Figure 3. The main goal of this model is to propagate the degree of similarity between closely matching ontology elements to ontology elements related to them through RDF triples.

Let $\mathbf{X}=\left(\mathbf{x}_1,\mathbf{x}_{21},\ldots,\mathbf{x}_n\right)$ is the set of subjects and objects in the ontology of two knowledge processors. Let $\mathbf{D}_x=\left(\mathbf{d}\left(\mathbf{x}_i,\mathbf{x}_j\right),\ldots\right)$ is a degree of similarity between $\mathbf{x}_i$ and $\mathbf{x}_j$. Let $\mathbf{R}=\left(\mathbf{r}_1,\mathbf{r}_2,\ldots,\mathbf{r}_n\right)$ is a set of predicates in the ontology of two knowledge processors. Let $\mathbf{D}_r=\left(\mathbf{d}\left(\mathbf{r}_i,\mathbf{r}_j\right),\ldots\right)$ is a set of degrees of similarity between $\boldsymbol{r}_i$ and $\boldsymbol{r}_j$. Constant $\mathbf{Tr}$ is a threshold value that determines whether two ontology elements mapped to each other or not.

The following algorithm propagates similarity distance to RDF subjects and objects.

```
d(xi, xj) = maximum(Dx)
while (d(xi, xj) > Tr) do
```

Figure 3. Matching of two ontologies

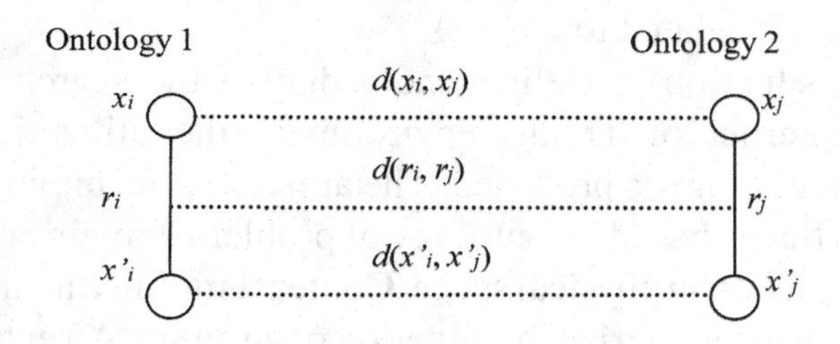


```
        for each d(x'_i, x'_j) as x_i r_m x'_i and x_j r_l x'_j do
                if d(r_m, r_l) > Tr then
                        d(x'_i, x'_j) = sqrt[2](d(x_i,x_j) * d(x'_i,x'_j))
                endif
        endfor
        Exclude d(x_i, x_j) from D_x
        d(x_i, x_j) = maximum(D_x)
endwhile
```

$$d(x'_i, x'_j) = \sqrt[2]{d\left(x_i, x_j\right) * d\left(x'_i, x'_j\right)}$$

The following algorithm allows propagating similarity distance to RDF predicates.

```
for each d(x_i, x_j) > Tr do
        for each d(x'_i, x'_j) > Tr as x_i r_m x'_i and x_j r_l x'_j do
                d(r_m, r_l) = sqrt[3](d(x_i,x_j) * d(x'_i,x'_j) * d(r_m,r_l))
        endfor
endfor
```

$$d(r_m, r_l) = \sqrt[3]{d\left(x_i, x_j\right) * d\left(x'_i, x'_j\right) * d\left(r_m, r_l\right)}$$

CONTEXT MODEL AND COALITION CREATION OF INTERNET OF THINGS RESOURCES

Coalition creation is important task for IoT environment. Since the centralized architecture usually is not applicable for the resource interaction, the resources have to find possibilities to interact with each other for joint task performing. Lets consider the example the a task appears in IoT environment and it has to be implemented by set of resources. Using the ontology matching approach and context model described in previous sections the resources can interact each other, enrich the semantic interoperability, and identify the context model that describes the task formally as soon as current situation in IoT environment that is related to the task.

For current situation modeling and reducing the search space for the resources in Internet of Things environment the utilization of context management technology is proposed. The aim of this technology is a context model creation that is based on ontology of problem domain and information about current situation in physical space. Context is defined as any information that can be used to characterize the situation of an entity. An entity is a person, place or object that is considered relevant to the interaction between a user and an application, including the user and application themselves (Dey et al., 2001). Context is suggested being modeled at two levels: abstract and operational. These levels are represented by abstract and operational contexts, respectively.

Abstract context is an ontology-based model integrating information and knowledge relevant to the current problem situation. Such knowledge is extracted from the application ontology it specifies domain knowledge describing the situation and problems to be solved in this situation. The abstract context reduces the amount of knowledge represented in the ontology to the knowledge relevant to the current problem situation. In the ontology this knowledge is related to the resources via the matching of their descriptions and ontology elements, therefore the abstract context allows the set of resources to be reduced to the resources needed to instantiate knowledge specified in the abstract context. The reduced set of resources is referred to as contextual resources.

Operational context is an instantiation of the domain constituent of the abstract context with data provided by the contextual resources. This context reflects any changes in environmental information, so it is a near real-time picture of the current situation. The context embeds the specifications of the problems to be solved. The input parameters of these problems, which correspond to properties of the classes of the domain constituent, are instantiated.

Constraint satisfaction techniques can be used to take into account dynamic environmental conditions and other possible constraints that have an impact on the problem. These techniques are naturally combined with ontology-based problem definition, and allow setting context parameters so that they would be taken it into account when the current situation constraints are applied. Thus, the problems embedded in the operational context are processed as constraint satisfaction problems in its enumeration form (the result is a behavior model of the IoT resource).

The proposed approach to context modelling consists of two steps (see Figure 4). At the first phase the resources are described by ontologies.

At the second step the context model is built for every resource of IoT environment based on ontology models of resources, task that appears in IoT environment, and current situation in the environment. The aim of abstract context creation is to identify the elements of ontology that is relevant at the moment for the task. Abstract context describes only the functions of a resource that are needed for the current task. For example, imagine that the resource is implemented by a robot. The robot can implement motion (3 axis), gripping, and measurement that is described by its ontology. For abstract context, only motion (2 axis) and gripping can be relevant since other capabilities does not relevant to the current situation.

At the third step the matching of the context models is implemented and based on this matching the resources can "understand" each other for

Figure 4. A proposed context creation model

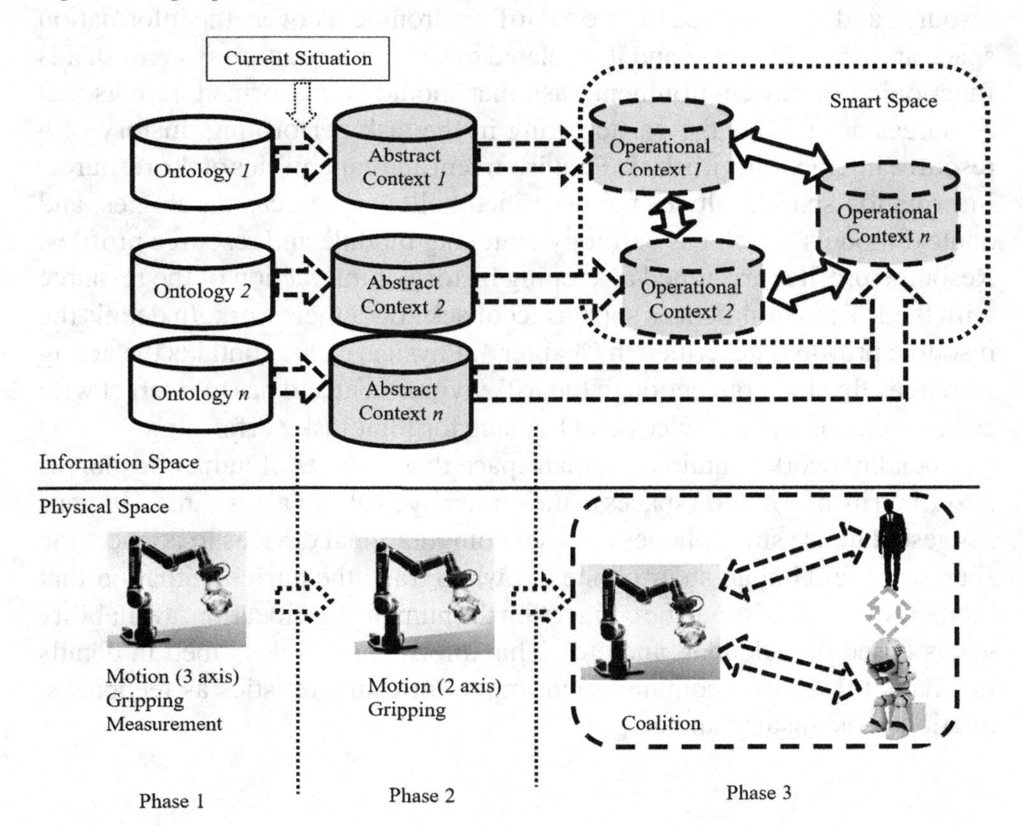

joint task performing. The matching method is described in details in the previous section. For the robot example imagine that robot should pick the object and transfer it in two axis and place. In such example robot should know when the object appears in the position and which coordinates is the destination point. IoT environment can have two resources for this purposes. One resource is a sensor that determines that object appears in the position point. Another one is the user interface or calculation resource that should determine the destination point. To support the understanding of the robot with the resources the ontology matching is implemented. Robot requires information about the presence of object. This information is described in the requirement part of ontology by a class and attributes. The resource has also has the class and attributes that describes presence of the object. In this simple example these classes should be matched and in case of successful matching the robot understands the resource and know when the object appears in the position point.

The presented approach provides possibilities to support semantic interoperability between physical devices (robots, sensors, and etc.), software resource and humans (see Figure 5). IoT environment covers the information space and physical space and it is related to some information systems that is functioning in this environment, task that should be performed, ratings that resources are got for the participating in the task performing, history of a resource interaction with the IoT environment and capabilities of the resource. Information space includes the described bellow resources ontologies, and context models as soon as ontology matching module and resource profiles. Resource profiles are aimed at keeping history of interaction of the resource with the IoT environment as soon as feedback about their work. In details the resource profile is described in Chapter 4. Physical space contains the acting resources that has connection to the IoT environment and has to interact with each other, software services and humans for joint task performing.

Social network contains a human space that consists of human resources described in information spaces in the same way as physical resource. Humans suggested to use smartphones or other computational devices to connect the shared space. Human smartphone allows to track the current situation that human is located without the connection the human (e.g., location, availability status based on calendar, and etc), This information is described in details in Chapter 4. Profile contains such important characteristics as feedbacks, relationships, history and etc.

Figure 5. Operational context creation in IoT environment

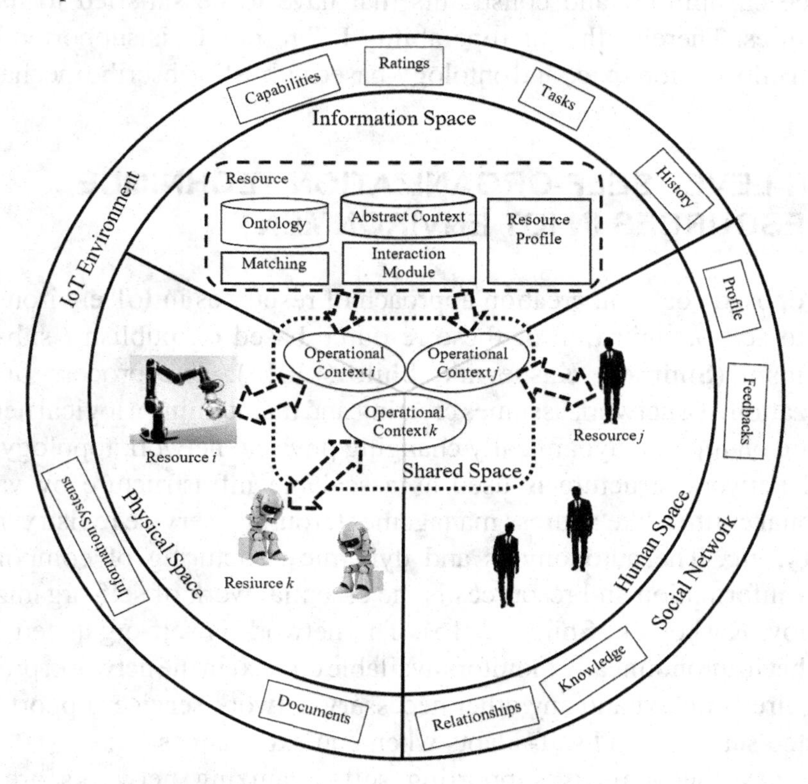

For the task performing firstly in information space resources are creating the virtual coalition by implement the ontology matching of their operational context. After that the physical coalition is organized and resources construct a service that performs the task. The operational context is published in information space and becomes accessible for other potential coalition participants. Information space is organized based on black board architecture that provides possibilities for potential coalition participants implement indirect interaction. Thereby, virtual coalition is created in information space and then physical coalition appears in physical space. Interaction of potential coalition participants in information space is implemented based on ontology based publish/subscribe mechanism that provides possibilities for mobile robots and humans publishing their information and knowledge and subscribing on interesting information using ontologies. When an IoT resource registers to be a potential coalition participant it uploads the own ontology to the information space. This ontology formalizes the main IoT resource capabilities and constraints that have to be satisfied to use the capabilities. Thereby, the interoperability IoT resources is supported based on open information space and ontology-based publish/subscribe mechanism.

MULTI-LEVEL SELF-ORGANIZATION TECHNIQUE OF RESOURCES IN IOT ENVIRONMENT

The proposed coalition creation approach of resources in IoT environments refers to self-organization of these resource based on publish / subscribe mechanism (Smirnov, Kashevnik, Shilov, 2015). The process of self-organization of a network assumes creating and maintaining a logical network structure on top of a dynamically changing physical network topology. This logical network structure is used as a scalable infrastructure by various functional entities like address management, routing, service registry, media delivery, etc. The autonomous and dynamic structuring of components, context information and resources is the essential work of self-organization (Smirnov, Kashevnik, Shilov, 2015). The network is self-organized in the sense that it autonomically monitors available context in the network, provides the required context and any other necessary network service support to the requested services, and self-adapts when context changes.

The key mechanisms supporting self-organizing networks are self-organization mechanisms and negotiation models. The following self-organization mechanisms are selected (De Mola, Quitadamo, 2006): intelligent relaying, adaptive cell sizes, situational awareness, dynamic pricing, and intelligent handover.

The presented multidisciplinary research aiming at multilevel self-organization is based on the idea from the new multidisciplinary of 21st Century science. The idea is designing sociologically-inspired computing systems since social systems perform well by continuous organized adaptation. The research assumes investigation of how solutions to structurally similar problems of organized adaptation found in social systems can be applied to cyber-physical-social systems. Thus, combining information and communication technologies with the theory of social systems and knowledge of multiple disciplines would enable new methods and mechanisms for efficient self-organization of resources.

To guide such self-organizing groups / systems a certain guiding control is needed (e.g. via policy transfer) from an upper level to lower. The multilevel self-organization has not been addressed yet in research. This approach would enable a more efficient self-organization based on the "top-to-bottom" configuration principle, which assumes conceptual configuration followed by parametric configuration. In this regard, each level can be considered as a scenario-based decision arena following certain complex knowledge patterns related to adaptable business models.

The approach is based on the following principles: self-management and responsibility, decentralization, as well as integration of chain policy transfer (a formal chain of policies running from top to bottom) with network organization (without any social hierarchy of command and control within a level), initiative from an upper level and co-operation within one level. The idea can be interpreted as producing "guided order from noise". In accordance with (Jantsch, 1975) such system falls into the class of purposeful systems.

Intra-level self-organization is considered as a threefold process of (i) cognition (where subjective context-dependent knowledge is produced), (ii) communication (where system-specific objectification or subjectification of knowledge takes place), and (iii) synergistical co-operation (where objectified, emergent knowledge is produced). The Individually acquired context-dependent (subjective) knowledge is put to use efficiently by entering a social co-ordination and co-operation process. The objective knowledge is stored in structures and enables time-space distinction of social relationships.

In order to achieve the dynamics and self-organization of the IoT resource they have to be creative, knowledgeable, active, and social. The resources that are parts of a system permanently change their joint environment what results in a synergetic collaboration and leads to achieving a certain level of collective intelligence. This is also supported by the fact that individual resource behavior is partially determined by the social environment the resources are contributing to (called "norms"). For this purpose a protocol has been developed based on the BarterCast approach (see Meulpolder et al., 2009) that originates from the following ideas: (i) each resource builds a network representing all interactions it knows about; (ii) the reputation of a resource depends on the reputation of other resource in the path between this resource and the resource connecting to it. The overall scheme of the approach is shown in Figure 6. In according to the approach it is proposed to implement self-organization in three levels: physical level, planning level, and strategic level. Based on the self-organization in higher level the policies are identified and distributed to the lower level.

SOLUTIONS AND RECOMMENDATIONS

There are six solutions have been identified for the proposed IoT resources interaction for service construction and delivery: semantic interoperability support, ontology utilization, context modelling, coalition creation, multi-level self-organization, ontology matching (see Table 1). Proposed in the chapter models and methods are based on these solutions.

Table 1. AmI solutions spectrum for IoT resources interaction

#	Solution	Comment
1	Semantic interoperability support	Semantic interoperability support for IoT resources is a key point of the service construction and delivery for the users since IoT network is a union of resources connected to the internet and there are know standard protocols and standards that can be used for resource interaction.
2	Ontology utilization	An ontology, is a domain vocabulary completed with a set of precise definitions, or axioms, that constrain the meanings of the terms sufficiently to enable consistent interpretation of the data that use that vocabulary. Utilization of such vocabulary for description of the problem domain allows to formalize the processes in IoT environment.
3	Context modelling	The problem domain ontology allows to identify of the user and task contexts. Context is a description of a situation in which the resource is located and contains all the information that can be used to describe this situation. Task context is a slice of the problem domain ontology that is related to the task. The user context is a slice of problem domain ontology that is related to the user.
4	Coalition creation	Coalition creation is the required task for IoT resource service construction and delivery. Finding the feasible set of resource to construct the service needed for the task performing is the complicated and not trivial task. It is proposed in the chapter to use such technologies as ontology management, context modelling, self-organization, and ontology matching to support this task.
5	Multi-level self-organization	Self-organization solution assumes of creating and maintaining a logical network structure on top of a dynamically changing physical network topology. Proposed multi-level self-organization solution allows to support the self-organization of the IoT resources in different levels and provides policies from the upper level to the lower.
6	Ontology matching	Ontology matching solution is aimed to match two ontologies that formally describer the two IoT resources tow support the semantic interoperability between these resources. Such matching provides possibilities for IoT resources to “understand” each other and interact for coalition creation and task performing.

FUTURE RESEARCH DIRECTIONS

Interaction and interoperability support of IoT resources for service construction and delivery are the important tasks and emerging trends last years. Nowadays, such IoT concepts as smart homes, smart cars, smart offices, and other appearing in the human daily life. However, the accessible in market systems has a limited functional as the devices of different producers cannot be connected to each other since the do not support the semantic interoperability between them. The following open problems have been identified (see details in Table 2).

CONCLUSION

This chapter introduced IoT resources interaction approach for service construction and delivery. The approach is based on semantic interoperability support based on proposed ontology matching method, developed context model, reference model for coalition creation of IoT resources, and multi-level

Table 2. Open problems: AmI methods for IoT resources interaction

#	Open Problem	Comment
1	Ontology and ontology matching	Ontology management is a powerful approach that allows to formally describe interacting resources in machine readable form with purposes of semantic interoperability between them. If the resources have been created on top of common ontology the matching between them is a simple task. If the ontologies have been created by different experts the ontology matching becomes a complicated task. The successfulness of the matching depends on the several factors including the qualification of the ontology engineers. But it is possible to imagine the cases where the ontologies will not be matched and the service will not be constructed. In this case the experts should be attracted to implement this process manually.
2	Computation complexity	Knowledge-based interaction of the services requires a higher computation complexity in contrast to the usual one based on exchange the predefined structures of data. Knowledge based computation requires additional tasks such as ontology matching and requires to exchange more information. In this case the applicability of such approach strongly depends on the scenario. The developed should thing and choose between speed and universalism.
3	Task definition	Task definition in a formal form requires additional background from the person who specifies it. In this case the applicability of the presented also requires of a human who specifies the task and how qualitatively he/she specifies the task.

self-organization technique. The approach is based on ontology management technique and resource interaction support based on shared space. Ontology matching method is based on syntactical and semantical matching as soon as graph based distance improvement model that takes into account context in the ontologies. Context is suggested being modeled at two levels: abstract and operational. Abstract context is the ontology based description of the task appearing in the IoT environment taking in the account the current situation. The operational context is the instantiation of the domain constituent of the abstract context with data provided by the contextual resources. It is proposed for the resources to share the operational context in the shared space. The proposed multi-level self-organization technique is aimed at three level of resource identification: physical, planning, and strategic. Self-organization of the resources is implemented in every level and policies are proposed from the higher level to the lower one based on this self-organization.

ACKNOWLEDGMENT

The primary contributors to this chapter are Alexey Kashevnik from SPIIRAS, Russia as well as Dmitry Korzun and Anton Shabaev from Petrozavodsk State University (PetrSU), Russia. Authors thank to Alexander Smirnov, Nikolay Shilov, and Tatiana Levashova for their help during the preparation of this chapter. The presented results are part of the research carried out within the project funded by grants N° 16-29-04349, N° 16-29-12866, and N° 19-07-00670 of the Russian Foundation for Basic Research.

REFERENCES

Ahmad, A., Cuomo, S., Wu, W., & Jeon, G. (2019). Intelligent algorithms and standards for interoperability in Internet of Things. *Future Generation Computer Systems*, *92*, 1187–1191. doi:10.1016/j.future.2018.11.015

Baader, F., Calvanese, D., McGuinness, D., Nardi, D., & Patel-Schneider, P. (2003). *The description logic handbook: theory, implementation, and applications*. New York, NY: Cambridge University Press.

Baca, J., Pagala, P., Rossi, C., & Ferre, M. (2015). Modular robot systems towards the execution of cooperative tasks in large facilities. *Robotics and Autonomous Systems*, *66*, 159–174. doi:10.1016/j.robot.2014.10.008

Balandin, S., Boldyrev, S., Oliver, I., Turenko, T., Smirnov, A., Shilov, N., & Kashevnik, A. (2012). *Method and apparatus for ontology matching*. US Patent 2012/0078595 A1.

Chand, P., & Carnegie, D. A. (2013). Mapping and exploration in a hierarchical heterogeneous multi-robot system using limited capability robots. *Robotics and Autonomous Systems*, *61*(6), 565–579. doi:10.1016/j.robot.2013.02.009

De Mola, F., & Quitadamo, R. (2006). Towards an Agent Model for Future Autonomic Communications. *Proceedings of the 7th WOA 2006 Workshop From Objects to Agents*.

Dey, A., Salber, D., & Abowd, G. (2001). A Conceptual Framework and a Toolkit for Supporting the Rapid Prototyping of Context-Aware Applications. *Human-Computer Interaction, 16*(2), 97–199. doi:10.1207/S15327051HCI16234_02

Fernández, J. L., Sanz, R., Benayas, J. A., & Diéguez, A. R. (2004). Improving collision avoidance for mobile robots in partially known environments: The beam curvature method. *Robotics and Autonomous Systems*, *46*(4), 205–219. doi:10.1016/j.robot.2004.02.004

Horrocks, I. (2008). Ontologies and the semantic web. *Communications of the ACM*, *51*(12), 58–67. doi:10.1145/1409360.1409377

Iqbal, A., Ullah, F., Anwar, H., Kwak, K. S., Imran, M., Jamal, W., & Rahman, A. (2018). Interoperable Internet-of-Things platform for smart home system using Web-of-Objects and cloud. *Sustainable Cities and Society*, *38*, 636–646. doi:10.1016/j.scs.2018.01.044

Jantsch, E. (1975). *Design for Evolution*. New York: George Braziller.

Kubicek, H., & Cimander, R. (2009). Three dimensions of organizational interoperability: Insights from recent studies for improving interoperability frame-works. *European Journal of ePractice, 6*.

Kubicek, H., Cimander, R., & Scholl, H. (2011). Organizational Interoperability in E-Government: Lessons from 77 European Good-Practice Cases. Academic Press.

López, J., Pérez, D., Paz, E., & Santana, A. (2013). WatchBot: A building maintenance and surveillance system based on autonomous robots. *Robotics and Autonomous Systems*, *61*(12), 1559–1571. doi:10.1016/j.robot.2013.06.012

Meulpolder, M., Pouwelse, J., Epema, D., & Sips, H. (2009). BarterCast: A practical approach to prevent lazy freeriding in P2P networks. *IEEE International Symposium on Parallel & Distributed Processing*.

Negash, B., Westerlund, T., & Tenhunen, H. (2019). Towards an interoperable Internet of Things through a web of virtual things at the Fog layer. *Future Generation Computer Systems*, *91*, 96–107. doi:10.1016/j.future.2018.07.053

Ono, K., & Ogawa, H. (2014). Personal Robot Using Android Smartphone. *Procedia Technology*, *18*, 37–41. doi:10.1016/j.protcy.2014.11.009

Rodić, A., Jovanović, M., Stevanović, I., Karan, B., & Potkonjak, V. (2015). *Building Technology Platform Aimed to Develop Service Robot with Embedded Personality and Enhanced Communication with Social Environment*. Digital Communications and Networks.

Smirnov, A., Kashevnik, A., & Shilov, N. (2015). *Cyber-Physical-Social System Self-Organization: Ontology-Based Multi-level Approach and Case Study*. 2015 IEEE 9th International Conference on Self-Adaptive and Self-Organizing Systems, Cambridge, MA.

Smirnov, A., Kashevnik, A., Shilov, N., Balandin, S., Oliver, I., & Boldyrev, S. (2010). On-the-Fly Ontology Matching in Smart Spaces: A Multi-Model Approach. *Proceedings of the Third Conference on Smart Spaces*, 72-83. 10.1007/978-3-642-14891-0_7

Zhang, T., & Ueno, H. (2007). Knowledge model-based heterogeneous multi-robot system implemented by a software platform. *Knowledge-Based Systems*, *20*(3), 310–319. doi:10.1016/j.knosys.2006.04.019

Zhu, Y., Zhang, T., Song, J., & Li, X. (2013). A hybrid navigation strategy for multiple mobile robots. *Robotics and Computer-integrated Manufacturing*, *29*(4), 129–141. doi:10.1016/j.rcim.2012.11.007

KEY TERMS AND DEFINITIONS

Abstract Context: The ontology-based description of the task appearing in the IoT environment taking in the account the current situation.

Context: Any information that can be used to characterize the situation of a resource of IoT environment.

Internet of Things (IoT): The internetworking of physical entities represented by devices that enable these entities to collect and exchange data for a achieving a common goal.

Ontology: Formally represents knowledge as a set of concepts within a domain, using a shared vocabulary to denote the types, properties, and interrelationships of those concepts.

Ontology Matching: Set of techniques combined together for identified the similar elements in two ontologies.

Operational Context: The instantiation of the domain constituent of the abstract context with data provided by the contextual resources.

Semantic Interoperability: An understanding of the meaning of the information exchanged between software components.

Chapter 7
Evolution of the Smart Spaces Paradigm Toward the Semantic Web of Things

ABSTRACT

This chapter describes how the Smart-M3 platform evolved in the direction of supporting web standards (e.g., HTTP and Websockets) to be ready for the (Semantic) Web of Things. The latest step in the Smart-M3 progress is named SEPA (SPARQL Event Processing Architecture). Employing SEPA as a mean for semantic interoperability in the Web of Things means allowing heterogeneous devices to be discovered, accessed, and controlled through a set of SPARQL queries, subscriptions, and updates according to a given ontology. In this chapter, an ontology for the (Semantic) Web of Things is presented. Using web standards solves the issues of interoperability but poses new challenges with respect to the typical constraints of IoT applications.

INTRODUCTION

The Web of Things (WoT) is a very recent research area that tries to face the challenges to interoperability posed by the Internet of Things (IoT) through the use of Web Standards (Guinard and Trifa, 2016). Semantic Web of Things (SWoT), is instead the name of the research area investigating the use of Semantic Web technologies in the IoT to face this challenge (Jara et al., 2014). In this Chapter we discuss about the evolution of the Smart-M3

DOI: 10.4018/978-1-5225-8973-0.ch007

platform (Viola et al., 2016) towards the new scenarios of the WoT and SWoT. The main pillar guiding our research is the ability to seamlessly discover and interact with (physical or virtual) devices, from now on *Web Things*, despite their heterogeneity. According to (Charpenay, Käbisch, and Kosch, 2016), we will then rely on a *Thing Description* to state the properties, actions and events exposed by a Web Thing and to solve the problem of discoverability (Guinard and Trifa, 2016) (i.e., discovering new devices in a network).

The Semantic Web of Things, as well as the Internet of Things, should support many different application domains, with very different characteristics. Among these requirements, it is worth mentioning the scaleability, the interoperability and the timeliness of messages. Scalability is essential to permit the seamless growth of an application in terms of devices taking part in a Smart Space as well as in terms of data exchanged by the involved entities without a noticeable degradation of performance. Interoperability at information level is an essential requirement in scenarios that are intrinsically heterogeneous being them developed by different vendors and supporting different protocols. Lastly, SWoT/IoT applications usually require that new data is notified as soon as possible to the interested entities (e.g., let's consider for example Vehicular Ad-hoc NETworks, also known as VANETs). The Smart-M3 platform (Viola et al., 2016) provides an environment for the development of reactive interoperable applications. Started in 2006 from NOKIA, the development of the Smart-M3 project is now carried on by several Universities in Europe (mainly in Italy, Russia and Finland). Smart-M3 has been successfully employed in vast European Projects like Internet of Energy (Bedogni et al., 2013), Chiron (Vergari et al., 2011), Recocape (Hamza et al., 2014), Arrowhead (D'Elia et al., 2015), and demonstrated its validity and maturity over a wide spread of application domains. Smart-M3 could then represent an ideal building block for the Semantic Web of Things. Nevertheless, a set of requirements should be met. This is the purpose of the latest evolution of the Smart-M3 platform, named SPARQL Event Processing Architecture (SEPA) (Roffia et al., 2018).

The development of the SEPA platform has started in 2016 with the aim of producing a reactive and reliable infrastructure for big data environments, like the Semantic Web of Things. SEPA supports W3C standards for the communication with a SPARQL Endpoint and provides, as also Smart-M3 does, a publish-subscribe interface that is now based on another standard protocol, Websockets (standardized by IETF as RFC 6455). Moreover, SEPA is now able to attach to whatever SPARQL Endpoint, thus allowing for the provision of a subscription mechanism on top of existing endpoints. The first prototype of the SEPA platform was presented at the W3C Web of Things Working and Interest Group meeting (Dusseldorf, July 2017) and later on at the 21st FRUCT Conference (Helsinki, November 2017). The broker of the SEPA platform has been equipped with an ontology to represent and control devices in the Semantic Web of Things, a framework for the automated deployment of Web Things. This Chapter then, describes the core of SEPA and the tools that permit its adoption for the creation of Semantic Web of Things applications.

The rest of the Chapter is organized as follows: in the next Section, the motivation behind an evolution of the Smart-M3 platform is proposed. Then, the next Section, proposes the solutions adopted to face the challenges of the new scenarios. The fourth future research direction are hypothesized, while in the fifth Section conclusions are drawn.

BACKGROUND

Originated by a visionary sentence of Xerox' pioneering researcher Mark Weiser (Weiser, 1991), the Internet of Things (Ashton, 2009) can be considered as a large scale evolution of the former pervasive/ubiquitous computing and context-aware computing. Up to now the importance of the context is unchanged, being the context any information characterizing the situation of an entity, being it a person, place or object that is relevant to the interaction between a user and an application and including the user and the application (Abowd et al., 1999). Even if the context is still playing a central role in the development of IoT applications, the surrounding technologies are profoundly changing. The IoT is indeed the result of twenty years of worldwide research carried on from universities and enterprises. As a result, technologies and protocols proliferated making interoperability a great challenge. Furthermore IoT is now a pervasive research area involving more than 50 application domains (Asin and Gascon, 2012). In fact, one of the causes of the success of the IoT paradigm is its ability to fit the need of very different domains. Evidences come from the growing number of smart cities where the IoT is used (among others) to support electric mobility (D'Elia et al., 2015), avoid traffic congestion (Talari et al., 2017), monitor parking availability (Rao, 2017), deal with waste collection (Medvedev et al., 2015). But IoT has also a strong connection to eHealth (Sebestyen et al., 2014), logistics (Da Xu et al., 2014), home automation (Miori and Russo, 2014), smart agriculture (Kamienski et al., 2019) just to name a few.

In 2009, Guinard and Trifa with their PhD theses, proposed the adoption of Web standards to achieve interoperability among heterogeneous devices. This idea brought to the birth of the Web of Things. This new paradigm pivots the concept of Thing Description, an abstraction layer to equalize all the existing devices. The Thing Description of a device (i.e., a *thing*) is a detailed description of the device's URI, actions, events and properties. The Web of Things does not necessarily replace the Internet of Things paradigm, but can be considered as an additional layer built on top of it. In fact, while IoT silos may still exists, the Web of Things could be employed to bridge them providing a standard-compliant interface to the significant resources. The importance of the Web of Things emerged years later, when the W3C started a working group and an interest group focused on it. Many key enterprises of the technological area (e.g., Samsung, Intel, Google, Panasonic and Fujitsu to name a few) are taking part to these groups to shape the future standards for the Web of Things.

The Semantic Web of Things (SWoT) is slightly different from the WoT, since it poses the accent on the adoption of Semantic Web technologies. The SWoT definition has been first proposed by Scioscia and Ruta (Scioscia & Ruta, 2009) ten years ago. Pfisterer et al. (Pfisterer & al., 2011) later on defined the SWoT as *a service infrastructure that makes the deployment and use of semantic applications involving Internet-connected sensors almost as easy as building, searching, and reading a web page.* In the rest of the chapter, we will refer to the Semantic Web of Things, as an area born from the WoT where semantics is used to represent the Thing Description and accordingly permit discovery and interaction with devices. The Semantic Web of Things may be intended as a slight variation of the Service Oriented Architecture (SOA) paradigm. The combination of loosely coupled SOAs is the key to flexibility and scalability (Barker & Van Hemert, 2007) and through the standards promoted by the SWoT, the aim is to push further on the interoperability dimension. A notable contribution in the field of the SWoT is the one provided by Serena et al. (Serena, Poveda-Villalón, García-Castro, 2017), who proposed an ontology to support device discovery in the Web of Things. This ontology, as will be better detailed later on, has been extended to grant the ability to access devices (i.e., reading their properties, subscribing to their events or invoking their actions). To the best of our knowledge, the work presented in this Chapter, is the first complete ecosystem to deal with Web Things in a Semantic Web of Things domain. In fact, we propose a layered architecture with all the necessary components to model Web Things as the above-mentioned ontology, an automation framework, a set of APIs and a semantic publish/subscribe broker acting as the core of the system.

SEPA AND THE WEB OF THINGS

The Web, and more specifically the Semantic Web, may be the key to overcome the fragmentation of the current Internet of Things. But how do Smart-M3 become part of the (Semantic) Web of Things? In this Section, we propose a novel broker inspired by the Smart-M3 platform and named SEPA (SPARQL Event Processing Architecture) (Roffia et al., 2018) on top of which a proper framework for the Web of Things has been developed. Figure 1 reports the proposed view of the system.

The overall architecture is imagined as a layered system pivoting an RDF store. On top of it, of course, runs SEPA which provides publish/subscribe functionalities to the store. Applications could not be developed without proper APIs that sit on top of the SEPA engine. These three layers are already enough to develop SEPA-based applications, but in order to be compliant to the SWoT paradigm, we envision the adoption of the Semantic Web of Things ontology that constitutes a further layer. Cocktail allows to face the steep learning curve of semantic technologies with a simple framework that

Figure 1. SEPA Framework for the Web of Things (Viola, 2019)

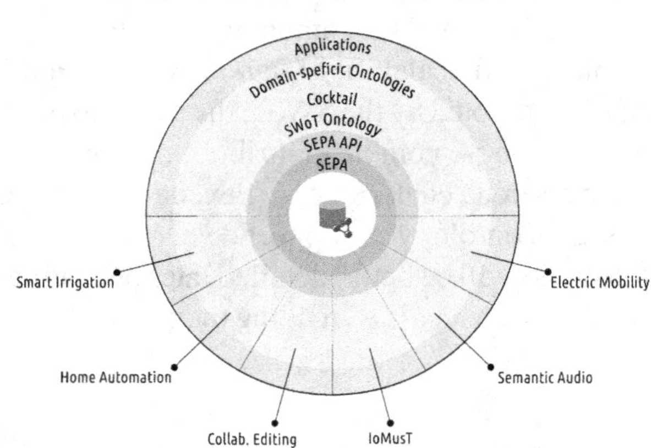

Figure 2. Web of things integration patterns. First row: the direct integration pattern. Second row: on the left the gateway integration pattern, on the right the cloud one

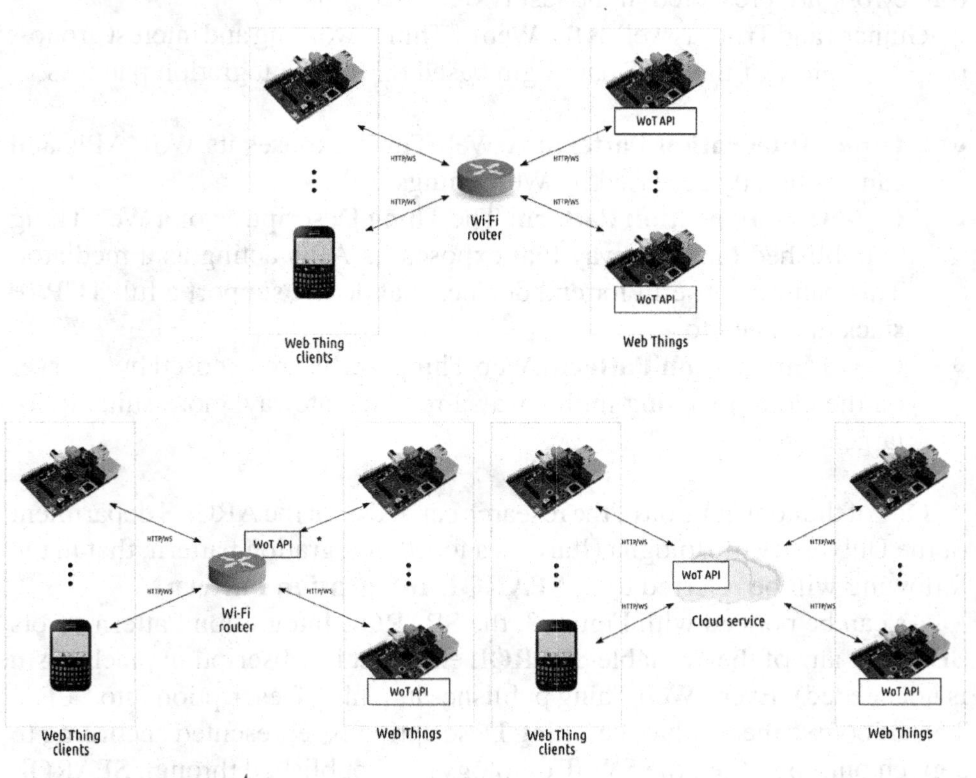

automates all the most frequent operations (e.g., creation/publication of a Web Thing, request of actions and so on). While the SWoT ontology permits the creation of Web Things, therefore allows wrapping every software agent with a common envelope based on the Thing Description, domain-specific ontologies are employed to represent the knowledge base related to the specific application (e.g., home automation, electric mobility, etc). Adopting the SWoT ontology among different applications allows achieving a high level of interoperability, since every (physical or virtual) device can be discovered/ accessed in the same way, regardless of its application domain.

The main issues faced in will be addressed in the rest of the Chapter. In particular, the next Subsection will be focused on SEPA, while the subsequent Subsection proposes an analysis of the possible algorithms to process subscriptions in the SWoT. Then, the following Subsection presents the SWoT ontology. The Semantic Application Profile (SAP) and the Cocktail framework are presented in the last two Subsections.

Guinard and Trifa, as well as the Web of Things working and interest groups, propose a view of the WoT paradigm based on three integration patterns:

- **Direct Integration Pattern**: A Web Thing exposes its WoT APIs and can be directly accessed by Web Things.
- **Gateway Integration Pattern:** The Thing Description of a Web Thing is published on a gateway that exposes its APIs acting as a mediator. This pattern is useful for end devices that do not support a full TCP/IP stack and need to
- **Cloud Integration Pattern:** Web Things APIs are exposed by a server on the cloud realizing in this way a remote gateway, more suitable for large scenarios.

One of the contribution of the research carried on at the ARCES department of the University of Bologna (Italy) is a fourth integration pattern, that in the following will be referred to as **SPARQL Integration Pattern**.

As can be noticed with Figure 3, the SPARQL Integration Pattern pivots SEPA (or any of the available SPARQL endpoint if subscription mechanism is not needed). Every Web Thing publishes its Thing Description into SEPA. This of course means that the Thing Description is represented according to a given ontology (i.e., the SWoT ontology) and published through SPARQL Update requests. In this way, differently from the previous integration patterns, the Thing Description is fully semantic. Web Things do not need to run any server instance, since action requests can be delivered to the Thing as SPARQL notification via Web sockets while properties and events are published by the things on the SEPA store through SPARQL Update requests.

SEPA: The Core of the Framework

The Web, and more specifically the Semantic Web, may be the key to overcome fragmentation. But how do Smart-M3 become part of the (Semantic) Web of Things? First of all, the Smart-M3 broker (i.e. the Semantic Information Broker or SIB) should be a transparent overlay on a SPARQL Endpoint. Rather than embedding an RDF store, a broker for the Web of Things should be able to attach to whatever SPARQL Endpoint, being it a local one or a remote one, allowing the access to the world of Linked Data. Then, a first novelty of the last evolution of the Smart-M3 platform towards SEPA is the

Figure 3. SEPA -based integration pattern for the web of things

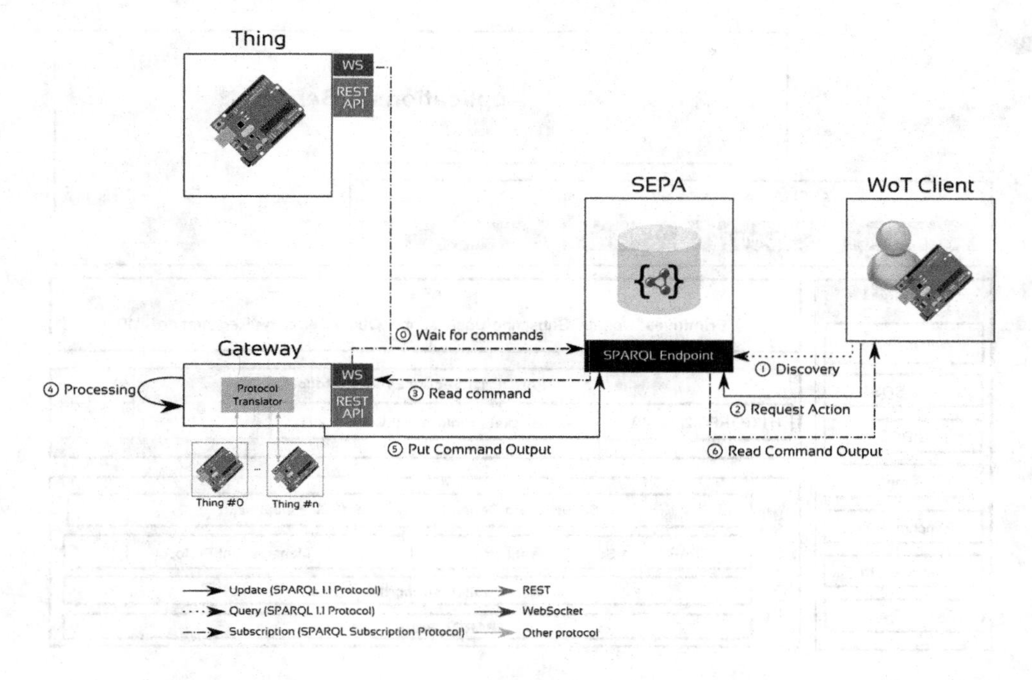

ability to attach to an instance of Blazegraph, Fuseki, Virtuoso and so on. SEPA is then also able to connect, for example, to DBpedia thus allowing the access to a worldwide knowledge base. To act as a transparent overlay, SEPA must expose a standard interface compliant with the SPARQL 1.1 Protocol. Then, the SSAP protocol has been replaced by HTTP to perform SPARQL updates and queries. The SPARQL 1.1 Secure Event Protocol proposed by SEPA embraces HTTP and Websockets; the latter are used to deal with subscriptions. The newly designed broker could then be employed to interact with a set of SPARQL endpoints to grant the aggregation of data from multiple knowledge bases. Moreover, a fundamental requirement of a platform for the Web of Things is the presence of a security infrastructure that allows for the secure communication of clients with the broker. SEPA grants security and dependability through a proper layer based on SSL and OAuth2. An high-level view of the architecture of the new broker is proposed in Figure 4.

Figure 4. High-level view of the SEPA architecture (Roffia et al., 2018)

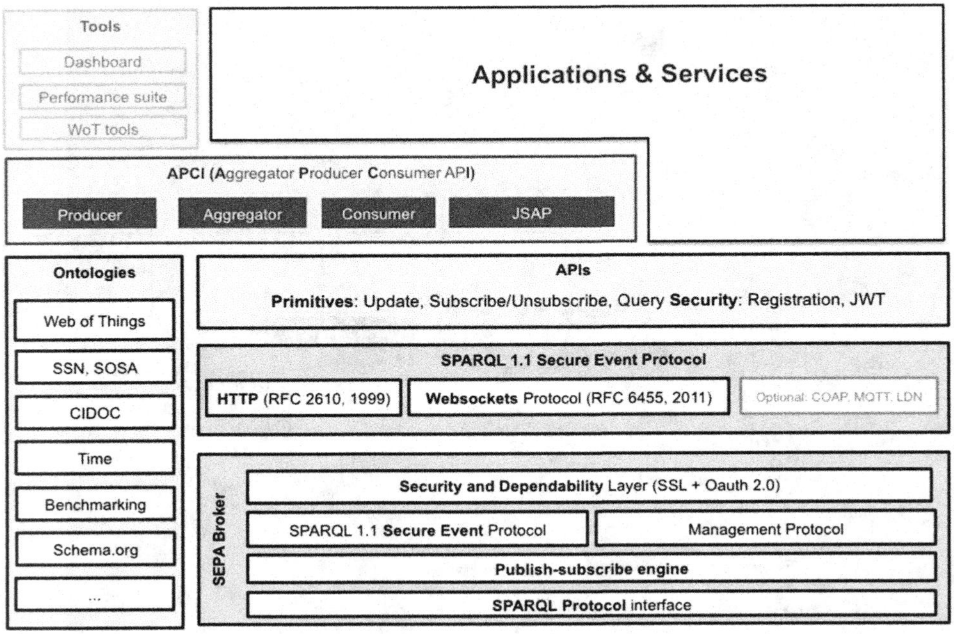

More in detail, the internal architecture of the publish-subscribe engine features a set of processors to deal with query and update requests and especially with subscription requests. Subscriptions deserve a special mention, since they represent the key difference between a SEPA and a standard SPARQL Endpoint, the key element that motivates the adoption of a SEPA for a Web of Things environment. Subscriptions in fact, allows for real-time notification of changes in a graph, avoiding polling mechanisms that would stress the system and result in worse performance. SEPA should then be able to timely process subscriptions and dispatch notifications regardless the scale of the scenario. A low-level view of the internal architecture is proposed by Figure 5, showing the presence of the multiple processors for queries, updates and subscriptions, while a detailed description of the possible algorithms is proposed in the next Subsection.

As highlighted by Figure 1, a SEPA infrastructure is domain agnostic and permits working with data represented according to very different ontologies. To address the needs of a Web of Things application, a proper vocabulary to deal with a SWoT scenarios should be developed. This requirement is

Figure 5. Low-level view of the SEPA Architecture (Roffia et al., 2018)

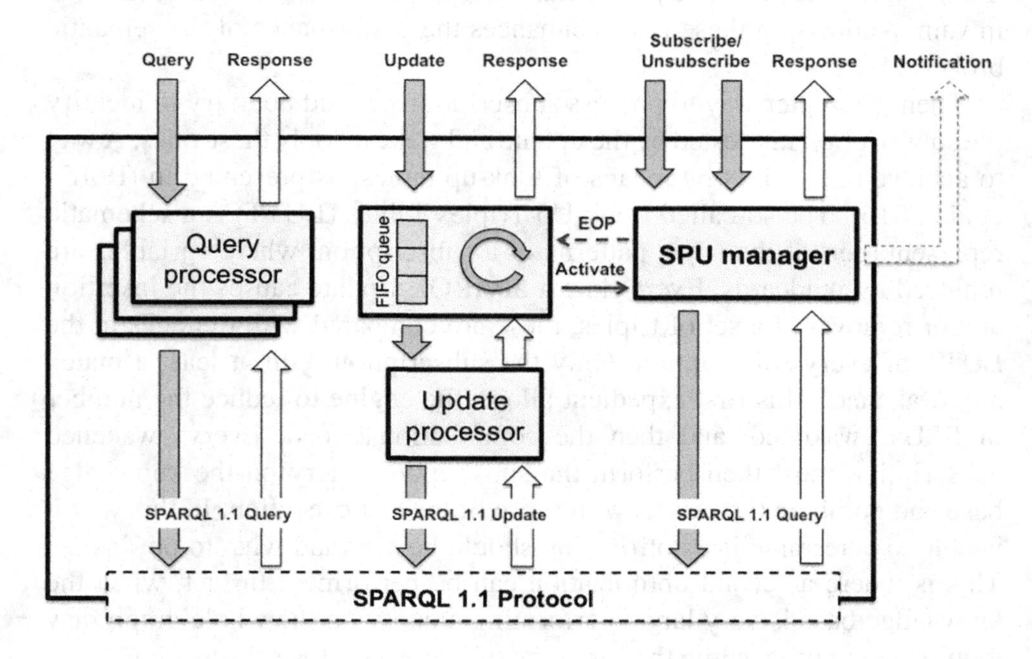

addressed later on, in a dedicated Subsection that introduces the above-mentioned SWoT ontology.

Processing Subscriptions in a SEPA

Subscriptions provide a way to timely react to changes in the knowledge base. But how timely depends on the specific subscription processing policy. Let's name Subscription Processing Unit (SPU) every process or thread demanded to monitor a single subscription and determine when to send a notification and its content. Regardless the adopted subscription policy, every SPU must be able to detect changes in the knowledge base that affect the results of the query specified as a subscription. That said, the most basic subscription processing algorithm we could think of, simply wakes up all the SPUs when a SPARQL Update request occurs; SPUs will then query the knowledge base and compare the results before and after the update to detect if something has changed and eventually build and send a notification. Even if we think of SPUs as threads working in parallel, this very simple algorithm presents at least two criticalities: the first related to the potentially high number of triples in the graph (that implies longer times for the algorithm to converge), the second to the potentially high number of subscriptions that are awakened in vain. Addressing these issues enhances the performance of the semantic broker.

Then, a smarter way to process subscriptions would be to try to identify the subscription interested by the update and wake up only these ones. A way to achieve this task is by means of look-up tables, as presented in (Roffia et al., 2016). The so-called Look-Up Triples Tables (LUTT) is a schematic representation of the triple patterns of a subscription, where variables are replaced by wildcards. Every time a SPARQL Update causes the insertion and/or removal of a set of triples, these are compared with the ones in the LUTT of every subscription. Only the subscription with at least a match are awakened. This first expedient allows the engine to reduce the number of SPUs awakened, and then the computational load. Every awakened subscription must then perform the subscription query on the knowledge base and compare the results with those of the last execution. In this way it is able to determine if a notification should be sent and what to put inside. This is where a second optimization can be performed. In fact, when the knowledge base is very large, performing a query on the whole graph may require a long time, while the subgraph of interest for the subscription is just a small portion of it. The way to speed up the processing is then adding a local context store for every subscription, containing only the subgraph of interest. The triples put in the context store (and also those removed from it) derive from the triples matching the LUTT. All of these triples affect the content of the local store, that we name Context Triple Store (CTS). Then, every time a subscription is triggered, it updates the CTS according to the LUTT, and determines if and what to return as a notification with a more efficient query performed on the local graph. LUTTs and CTSs require, of course, a higher amount of memory but permit better performance of the engine. Performances are in fact a trade-off between time and space. A third optimization is the so-called *booster*. This component takes as input the added and removed triple matching a LUTT and tries to bind as many variables as possible in the SPARQL query. This allows reducing the uncertainty of the query and thus reducing the time required to perform it. This complex subscription algorithm results then more scaleable than the first one, since it prevents waking up all the subscriptions, but focuses only on those that may produce a notification.

The Web of Things can be successfully employed to solve the discoverability problem (Guinard and Trifa, 2016), by means of a semantic broker (like SEPA) where the Thing Description of every device is published. The discovery consists in looking for new devices matching a set of criteria. Then, in an ecosystem made up of many devices, it is likely that there are equivalent subscriptions running to detect Web Things joining/leaving the smart space. What happen if *n* equivalent subscription are running? Then, *n* copies of the same LUTT and of the same CTS will be employed by the engine. This is where a further optimization can be performed. According to the Amdahl's Law, the common cases should be made fast, and we know that the presence of many equivalent subscriptions is a very common case in the Web of Things. A way to optimize LUTTs is to have a centralized structure, shared by all the subscriptions. The centralized LUTT (CLUTT from now on) is then a table with four columns, one more than the standard LUTTs. This columns allows to specify the subscription interested by the triple pattern defined in the first three cells of the same row. Advantages of the centralized LUTT are twofold: one one hand it allows reducing the amount of memory required to store the look-up tables avoiding duplication of information; on the other hand it permits a reduction of the operations performed by the engine, since multiple subscriptions can be awakened with the same analysis of the LUTT. Finally, a centralized set of CTSs referenced by the proper SPUs can be employed to reduce the duplication of CTSs. The CLUTT algorithm considerably improves the scalability of the platform allowing a higher set of subscriptions with the same memory. Moreover, the reduction of the required memory is also important for fog computing scenarios, where computation takes place on the edge of the network, often on small devices with low resources. Figure 6 shows the relation between LUTTs and a CLUTT.

To conclude, a last optimization can be applied to the CLUTT to reduce its size. It consists in a hierarchical approach that we name Centralized Hierarchical LUTT (CHLUTT) that envisions a four-layered tree where the first layer contains all the subject. Then, they are linked to the second layer containing all the predicates such that subject and predicate appear together in a triple pattern of the look up tables. Every predicate, is then linked to the third level containing all the related objects. The fourth and last layer contains the ID of all the SPUs interested by that triple pattern.

Figure 7 proposes an example to better understand how the introduction of CLUTT and CHLUTT results in a lower space occupation. Three different SPARQL subscriptions types (sub_i, sub_j, sub_k) are reported in white boxes on the left. Considering m, n and p subscriptions, respectively of type sub_i, sub_j and sub_k, with the mechanism proposed in (Roffia et al., 2016) the system creates $m+n+p$ LUTTs (depicted with the pink color), resulting in $6 \cdot m + 2 \cdot n + 6 \cdot p$ entries. Grouping at least the equivalent subscriptions would allow to

Figure 6. From LUTTs to Centralized LUTT and CHLUTT (Viola, 2019)

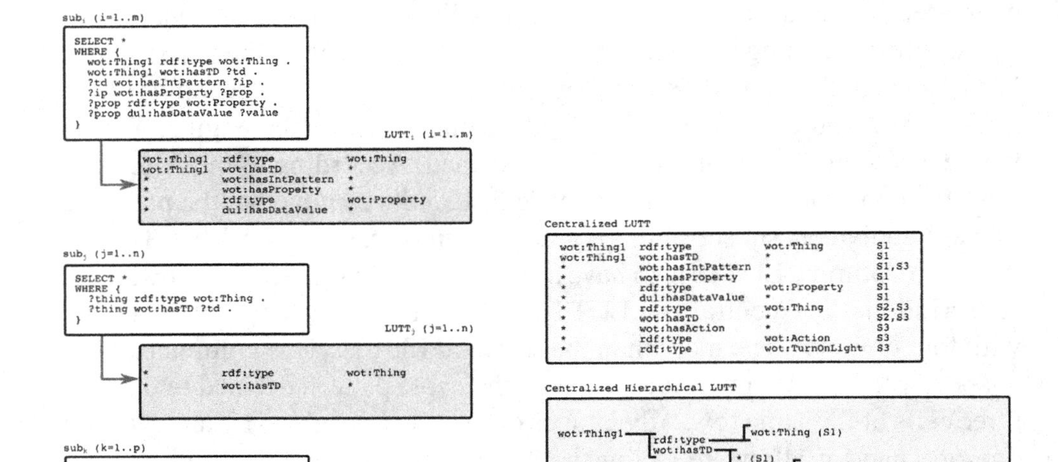

store only *6 + 2 + 6* entries. The centralized LUTT (depicted with the yellow color in Figure 7) is instead able to group all the equivalent subscriptions but also to avoid repeated entries resulting then in 11 rows. Of course, in this case, a list of the interested subscriptions must be saved. The centralized hierarchical lutt (green in Figure 7) permits a further reduction of the memory occupation, since repeated subjects can be grouped into a single field.

The new structures proposed in this Section play an important role in the Web of Things, since it is likely to have very crowded scenarios where a set of devices perform the same SPARQL subscriptions to monitor for example the appearance of new devices, or newly generated events.

The optimization of the data structures used by SEPA is still an open research task.

Figure 7. Comparison among LUTTs, Centralized LUTT and Centralized Hierarchical LUTT (Viola, 2019)

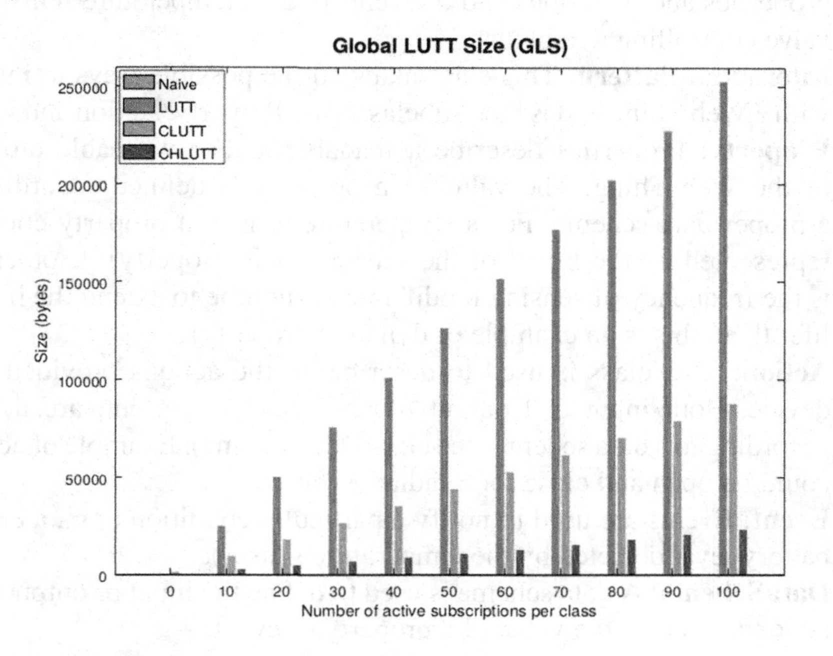

SEPA and the Web of Things: The Semantic Web of Things Ontology

In order to discover, access and control devices through a SPARQL endpoint (or an subscription-enhanced version like SEPA), a proper ontology is needed. Based on the work by (Serena, Poveda-Villalón, García-Castro, 2017), we propose an ontology for the Web of Things. It extends the previous work towards a new direction that not only considers a semantic approach to the discovery of Web Things, but also envisions a way to interact with them. This novel ontology then, paves the way towards more complex scenarios where orchestration of devices is possible by means of SEPA. This ontology, successfully used by the authors in (Antoniazzi et al., 2017) and (Viola et al., 2018) mainly pivots the Thing class and its subclasses Action, Event and Property to describe a device and its profile (i.e. *Thing Description*).

The SWoT Ontology is based on the following set of classes:

- **Thing**: Any thing which has a distinct and independent existence and can have one or more web representation. In our domain, a Thing (short name for Web Thing) is any physical or virtual device exposing a set of properties and/or actions and/or events (e.g., a temperature sensor or a valve controlling a radiator).

- **InteractionPattern**: This class maps all the possible ways to interact with a Web Thing and is then subclassed by Property, Action and Event.
- **Property**: Properties describe a readable and/or writeable attribute of the Web Thing. The value of a property is defined according to a proper data schema. For a temperature sensor, a property could be represented by the brand of the sensor (static property); another one is the frequency of sensing modifiable at runtime to extend the battery life (then, this is an example of dynamic property).
- **Action**: This class is used to describe all the actions provided by a device. Both input and output of an action, if present, are defined according to a data schema (see class DataSchema). Example of actions could be open and close for a radiator valve.
- **Event**: Events are used to notify a particular condition (e.g., a critical battery level detected by the temperature sensor).
- **DataSchema**: A data schema is used to define the input or output of an action as well as the value of a property or event.

The class tree of the SWoT ontology is depicted in Figure 8 and is rooted on owl:Thing (not to be confused with Thing, the class describing Web Things). A further subdivision is that of DataSchema into InputSchema and OutputSchema, respectively used to define the input schema for an action or for the information related to an action output/event/property.

A very basic Web Thing can then be described with the following triples (reported with the Notation3 format):

Figure 8. SWoT ontology tree

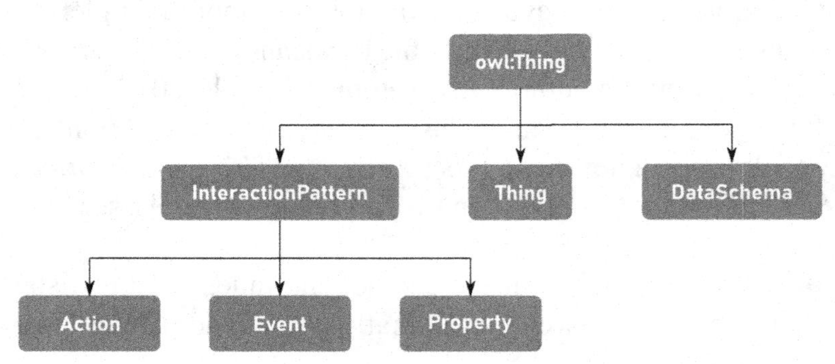

```
@prefix rdf:<http://www.w3.org/1999/02/22-rdf-syntax-ns#> .
@prefix swot:<http://wot.arces.unibo.it/ontology/web_of_
things#> .
swot:Thing1_URI rdf:type swot:Thing .
swot:Thing1_URI swot:hasName "Example of a web thing" .
```

Adding an action to the Web Thing can be achieved with the following additional triples:

```
@prefix xsd:<http://www.w3.org/2001/XMLSchema#> .
swot:Thing1_URI swot:hasInteractionPattern swot:IntPat1_URI .
swot:IntPat1_URI rdf:type swot:Action .
swot:IntPat1_URI swot:hasName swot:TurnOnLight_URI .
swot:TurnOnLight_URI swot:hasInputDataSchema swot:DS1_URI .
swot:DS1_URI rdf:type swot:DataSchema .
swot:DS1_URI swot:hasFieldSchema swot:FS1_URI .
swot:FS1_URI rdf:type xsd:decimal .
```

Such a data representation allows discovering Web Things with simple queries or subscriptions, like the following one, aimed at retrieving all the Web Things providing at least an action, their action and the optional input and output dataschema:

```
PREFIX rdf:<http://www.w3.org/1999/02/22-rdf-syntax-ns#>
PREFIX swot:<http://wot.arces.unibo.it/ontology/web_of_things#>
SELECT ?thing ?action ?ids ?idsType ?ods ?odsType
WHERE {
  ?thing rdf:type swot:Thing .
  ?thing swot:hasInteractionPattern ?action .
  ?action rdf:type swot:Action .
  OPTIONAL {
    ?action swot:hasInputDataSchema ?ids .
    ?ids rdf:type ?idsType
  }
  OPTIONAL {
    ?action swot:hasOutputDataSchema ?ods .
    ?ods rdf:type ?odsType
  }
}
```

Or the following one to discover all the web things able to generate a fire alarm event:

```
PREFIX rdf:<http://www.w3.org/1999/02/22-rdf-syntax-ns#>
PREFIX swot:<http://wot.arces.unibo.it/ontology/web_of_things#>
```

```
PREFIX ns:<http://ns#>
SELECT ?thing
WHERE {
  ?thing rdf:type swot:Thing .
  ?thing swot:hasInteractionPattern ?ip .
  ?ip rdf:type swot:Event .
  ?ip rdf:type ns:FireEvent
}
```

The SWoT ontology provides a way to invoke actions through SEPA. In fact, the class **ActionInstance** allows clients to create a request the execution of an action. Web Things providing that action are simply subscribed to their control interface and, every time they get a notification of a new action instance, they can accept or reject the request and eventually attach the result of the elaboration to the action instance. This mechanisms of course, paves the way towards the orchestration of actions, a fundamental step to achieve complex tasks in the Web of Things through very simple bricks.

The Semantic Application Profile

A fast prototyping mechanism help developers to deploy devices (i.e., Web Things) in a short time. The Semantic Application Profile, is a flexible tool oriented at speeding-up the deployment process. A Semantic Application Profile is file (serialized through JSON or YAML) containing the whole set of SPARQL Updates and Queries/Subscriptions describing the information flow involving a Web Thing as well as the connection parameters for the SPARQL Event Processing Architecture instances used. The following is an example of YAML Semantic Application Profile. The first section (key "parameters") hosts the details of the SPARQL endpoint(s) to which the Web Thing will register itself. The section with key "namespaces" is used to define prefixes used by SPARQL updates and subscriptions/queries that are respectively listed in sections "updates" and "queries". Every SPARQL listing also includes a "forcedBindings" key: through this structure, the programmer lists a set of variables that should be replaced by a concrete value at execution time.

```
parameters:
  host: "localhost"
  ports:
    http: 8000
    https: 8443
```

```
    ws: 9000
    wss: 9443
  paths:
    query: "/query"
    update: "/update"
    subscribe: "/subscribe"
    register: "/oauth/register"
    tokenRequest: "/oauth/token"
    securePath: "/secure"
namespaces:
  rdf: "http://www.w3.org/1999/02/22-rdf-syntax-ns#"
  wot: "http://wot.arces.unibo.it/sepa#"

updates:
  UPDATE_PROPERTY:
    sparql: "DELETE {
              $property dul:hasDataValue ?value
            }
            INSERT {
              $property dul:hasDataValue $newValue
            }
            WHERE {
              $thing wot:hasTD ?thingDesc .
              ?thingDesc wot:hasInteractionPattern $property
              $property dul:hasDataValue ?value
            }"
    forcedBindings:
      thing:
        type: "uri"
        value: ""
      action:
        type: "uri"
        value: ""
      newValue:
          type: "literal"
        value: ""


queries:
  DISCOVERY_BY_ACTION:
    sparql: "SELECT ?thing
            WHERE {
              ?thing wot:hasTD ?thingDesc .
              ?thingDesc wot:hasInteractionPattern $action
            }"
    forcedBindings:
      action:
        type: "uri"
        value: ""
```

Cocktail

All the steps required to build and push the representation of a Thing Description, to subscribe to the control interfaces, to invoke action and subscribe to events and properties can be highly automated by means of the Cocktail framework developed at the University of Bologna. This framework provides all the required functionalities through a Python library, simplifying the process of building and managing Web Things.

More specifically, Cocktail contains high level functions and classes to:

- Declare the Things, defining a friendly name, an URI, and a ThingDescription resource;
- Append to this resource all the needed interaction patterns needed (i.e., Actions, Events, Properties) with their friendly names, URIs;
- Define, if needed, new DataSchemas;
- Discover Things in the environment;
- Request the execution of an Action, and wait for its completion;
- Post the output of an action and handle the related timestamps;
- Subscribe to Event notifications;
- Delete all the instances of things as well as interaction patterns.

Figure 9 shows the Web Thing lifecycle that we hereby describe:

Figure 9. Web thing lifecycle

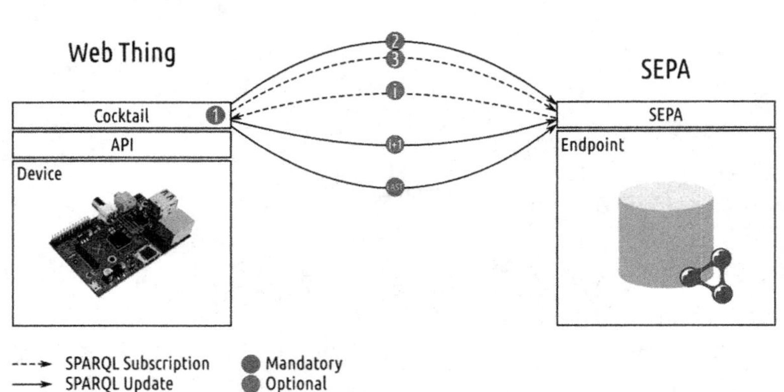

- Step 1 consists of the invocation of Cocktail to produce a Thing Description containing all the actions, events and properties of the related device.
- Step 2 consists in the publication of the Thing Description through a SPARQL Update. Both this and the previous one are mandatory steps.
- Step 3 if a Web Thing exposes an action, it must subscribe to the action requests to promptly execute them. In the same way, if the Thing is interested in events generated from other Web Things, it starts a proper subscription. This step is optional.
- Step *i* is again an optional step that depends on whether or not the Web Thing exposes one or more actions. In this case, whenever an action request is pushed into SEPA, a notification is sent to the Web Thing, then the request is handled and the output is written into the broker. This step can be of course repeated while the Web Thing is running.
- Closing the Web Thing causes the deletion of its Thing Description from the broker (the last step of this lifecycle).

SOLUTIONS AND RECOMMENDATIONS

To create interoperable applications in the Semantic Web of Things, five solutions have been identified (see Table 1).

FUTURE RESEARCH DIRECTIONS

As the (Semantic) Web of Things is in its early stages, new application scenarios may emerge and may require further analysis of the subscriptions processing policies. In particular, one interesting research direction is that of indexing the SPUs to prioritize, for example, the most frequently or the most recently awakened. Moreover, SPARQL Event Processing Architectures are still built as wrappers on top of existing SPARQL endpoints: a further enhancement of the performance of such architectures could be achieved by a native implementation of the SPARQL Subscribe Protocol in SPARQL endpoints to reduce the computational overhead.

As regards the interface towards the external world, SEPA provides an HTTP server to listen for SPARQL Update and Query requests and a Websocket interface to deal with subscriptions. However, the Internet of Things has

Table 1. How to face the IoT fragmentation through the semantic web of things paradigm

#	Solution	Comment
1	Adopt standards	First of all, to fight the fragmentation of the IoT and the isolation of applications into vertical silos, it is important to adopt standards. The solution proposed by the WoT paradigm consists in the adoption of HTTP and Websocket. SEPA fulfills this requirement.
2	Publish/subscribe	Applications in the IoT are characterized by strict requirements in terms of latency and timeliness. Subscriptions allow to be timely notified about changes in the knowledge base. SEPA fulfills this requirement by implementing the SPARQL 1.1 Subscribe protocol designed at the University of Bologna.
3	Adopt the SWoT ontology	In the Web of Things paradigm every device is described in terms of events, properties and actions. The SWoT ontology allows representing the Thing Description in a semantic way.
4	Adopt a SEPA	A SEPA permits the adoption of the SPARQL Interaction Pattern. Every Web Thing may then expose its actions/events/properties through SEPA without the need for a server process running on it.
5	Rely on automation tools	The Semantic Application Profile and the Cocktail Framework are the solutions to the complexity of this new model.

seen the proliferation of lightweight protocols for efficient communication also with constrained devices (Naik, 2017). Therefore, a further analysis to provide a communication interface based on a lightweight protocol can be considered as one of the future works. A preliminary work to start from is C Minor (Viola, Turchet, Antoniazzi and Fazekas, 2018), a semantic context broker with a CoAP interface specifically designed to bring semantics in the Internet of Musical Things (IoMusT) (Turchet, Viola, Fazekas and Barthet, 2018). The choice of CoAP is motivated by the simple mapping rules between this protocol and HTTP that would make easy to map the SPARQL 1.1 Protocol on CoAP.

A third future contribution regards instead the security infrastructure. The current SEPA framework in fact, allows for a secure communication among clients and brokers, thanks to HTTPS and Secure Websockets. This solution grants security on the communication channel among the involved entities, but is not enough to secure a subgraph from unauthorised modifications. Every triple in the graph in fact, is not bound to a specific owner, so every client authorized to interact with a SEPA is allowed to freely modify the knowledge base. This is why a deeper security layer is one of the priorities of the next releases.

To conclude, a last important future contribution of the SEPA broker will be the support for federated queries, that enables the virtual aggregation of multiple smart spaces in a wider ecosystem.

Table 2. Open problems related to the development of SEPA for the semantic web of things

#	Open problem	Comment
1	Native implementation of SPARQL 1.1 Subscribe protocol	SPARQL Event Processing Architecture are currently being developed on top of SPARQL endpoints instead inside them. Native implementations of SEPAs inside SPARQL endpoints may provide a sensible enhancement of the performances.
2	Lightweight protocols	The IoT has seen the proliferation of protocols at all the levels of the networking stack. SPARQL 1.1 protocol is based on HTTP and SPARQL 1.1 Subscribe protocol is also uses Websockets. Studying the adoption of the novel IoT protocols in place of these ones may further speed up SEPA.
3	Security infrastructure	A security infrastructure is needed to protect the information in the graphs.
4	Federated queries	Federated queries would allow to adopt multiple endpoints with a SEPA.

CONCLUSION

This chapter introduced the SEPA platform and all the necessary tools to build (Semantic) Web of Things applications through it. To solve the problem of discoverability, but also to provide a mean to interact with Web Things through a Semantic infrastructure a proper framework has been developed. The core of this framework is the SEPA broker inspired by the Smart-M3 platform and leveraging a general standard SPARQL endpoint. Several strategies to process subscriptions in the broker have been presented, with particular attention to the optimization of the engine to provide a scaleable architecture. On top of the framework a set of APIs, and an ontology to deal with Web Things were designed to permit the easy creation and management of Web Things. Moreover, to simplify the development and deployment of Web Things, two utilities have been proposed: the Semantic Application Profile and the Cocktail framework. The first allows storing and loading the full application configuration in terms of network parameters and information flow (i.e., SPARQL updates, queries and subscriptions) in a single file, to easily set up or replicate a set of Web Things. The latter instead, provides all the primitives to build and (un)publish the Thing Description and deal with properties, actions and events at a high level of abstraction.

Examples of the creation of Web Things according to the ontology have been provided in order to demonstrate how this vocabulary enables a clear and powerful semantic representation of Web Things. This complete infrastructure is, to the best of our knowledge, the first framework that fully supports not only the discovery of Web Things, but also the interaction with this kind of entities. In order to provide such a support, an ontology has been developed, based on the one proposed by Serena et al. (Serena, Poveda-Villalón, García-Castro, 2017), properly extended to go beyond the pure discovery tasks. Such approach allows developing interoperable application where, regardless of the application field, all the components are developed according to a unified model. In this way, application can interoperate instead of being isolated silos. This model can be applied not only to physical devices, but also to virtual ones as demonstrated by Viola et al. (Viola et al., 2018) in the field of Semantic Audio.

As highlighted in the previous Section, future works on this platform will be oriented at a stronger security infrastructure, as well as supporting lightweight IoT protocols (e.g., CoAP) and designing efficient indexes for a better management of subscriptions.

ACKNOWLEDGMENT

The author would like to acknowledge Francesco Antoniazzi (ARCES, University of Bologna, Italy), Cristiano Aguzzi (ARCES, University of Bologna, Italy) and Professor Tullio Salmon Cinotti (ARCES, University of Bologna, Italy) for their valuable contributions. The work presented in this chapter is being developed at the Advanced Research Center on Electronic Systems "Ercole De Castro" (ARCES), University of Bologna, 40125 Bologna, Italy.

REFERENCES

Abowd, G. D., Dey, A. K., Brown, P. J., Davies, N., Smith, M., & Steggles, P. (1999, September). Towards a better understanding of context and context-awareness. In *International symposium on handheld and ubiquitous computing* (pp. 304-307). Springer. 10.1007/3-540-48157-5_29

Antoniazzi, F., Paolini, G., Roffia, L., Masotti, D., Costanzo, A., & Cinotti, T. S. (2017, November). A web of things approach for indoor position monitoring of elderly and impaired people. In *Open Innovations Association (FRUCT), 2017 21st Conference of* (pp. 51-56). IEEE. 10.23919/FRUCT.2017.8250164

Ashton, K. (2009). That 'Internet of Things' thing, in the real world things matter more than ideas. *RFiD Journal, 22*.

Asin, A., & Gascon, D. (2012). *50 sensor applications for a smarter world.* Libelium Comunicaciones Distribuidas, Tech. Rep.

Barker, A., & Van Hemert, J. (2007, September). Scientific workflow: a survey and research directions. In *International Conference on Parallel Processing and Applied Mathematics* (pp. 746-753). Springer.

Bedogni, L., Bononi, L., Borghetti, A., Bottura, R., D'Elia, A., Di Felice, M., ... Viola, F. (2016). An integrated traffic and power grid simulator enabling the assessment of e-mobility impact on the grid: A tool for the implementation of the smart grid/city concept. *Technical Sciences*, *1*(1), 73–89.

Bedogni, L., Bononi, L., Di Felice, M., D'Elia, A., Mock, R., Montori, F., . . . Vergari, F. (2013, June). An interoperable architecture for mobile smart services over the internet of energy. In *World of Wireless, Mobile and Multimedia Networks (WoWMoM), 2013 IEEE 14th International Symposium and Workshops on a* (pp. 1-6). IEEE. 10.1109/WoWMoM.2013.6583495

Charpenay, V., Käbisch, S., & Kosch, H. (2016). Introducing Thing Descriptions and Interactions: An Ontology for the Web of Things. In SR+ SWIT@ ISWC (pp. 55-66). Academic Press.

D'Elia, A., Aguzzi, C., Viola, F., Antoniazzi, F., & Cinotti, T. S. (2017, September). Implementation and evaluation of the last will primitive in a semantic information broker for IoT applications. In *Research and Technologies for Society and Industry (RTSI), 2017 IEEE 3rd International Forum on* (pp. 1-5). IEEE. 10.1109/RTSI.2017.8065947

D'Elia, A., Viola, F., Montori, F., Di Felice, M., Bedogni, L., Bononi, L., ... Mock, R. (2015). Impact of Interdisciplinary Research on Planning, Running, and Managing Electromobility as a Smart Grid Extension. *IEEE Access: Practical Innovations, Open Solutions*, *3*, 2281–2305. doi:10.1109/ACCESS.2015.2499118

D'Elia, A., Viola, F., Roffia, L., Azzoni, P., & Cinotti, T. S. (2017). Enabling interoperability in the internet of things: A OSGi semantic information broker implementation. *International Journal on Semantic Web and Information Systems*, *13*(1), 147–167. doi:10.4018/IJSWIS.2017010109

Da Xu, L., He, W., & Li, S. (2014). Internet of things in industries: A survey. *IEEE Transactions on Industrial Informatics*, *10*(4), 2233–2243. doi:10.1109/TII.2014.2300753

Guinard, D., & Trifa, V. (2016). *Building the web of things: with examples in node. js and raspberry pi*. Manning Publications Co.

Hamza, H. S., Gamaleldin, A. M., Abdallah, M. M., Elkader, O. A., Nabih, A. K., & Ashraf, E. (2014, October). A technology transfer approach for stimulating innovation of ICT SMEs in Egypt. In *eChallenges e-2014, 2014 Conference* (pp. 1-11). IEEE.

Jara, A. J., Olivieri, A. C., Bocchi, Y., Jung, M., Kastner, W., & Skarmeta, A. F. (2014). Semantic web of things: An analysis of the application semantics for the iot moving towards the iot convergence. *International Journal of Web and Grid Services*, *10*(2-3), 244–272. doi:10.1504/IJWGS.2014.060260

Kamienski, C., Soininen, J. P., Taumberger, M., Dantas, R., Toscano, A., Salmon Cinotti, T., ... Torre Neto, A. (2019). Smart Water Management Platform: IoT-Based Precision Irrigation for Agriculture. *Sensors (Basel)*, *19*(2), 276. doi:10.339019020276 PMID:30641960

Medvedev, A., Fedchenkov, P., Zaslavsky, A., Anagnostopoulos, T., & Khoruzhnikov, S. (2015, August). Waste management as an IoT-enabled service in smart cities. In *Conference on smart spaces* (pp. 104-115). Springer. 10.1007/978-3-319-23126-6_10

Miori, V., & Russo, D. (2014, May). Domotic evolution towards the IoT. In *Advanced Information Networking and Applications Workshops (WAINA), 2014 28th International Conference on* (pp. 809-814). IEEE. 10.1109/WAINA.2014.128

Naik, N. (2017, October). Choice of effective messaging protocols for IoT systems: MQTT, CoAP, AMQP and HTTP. In *Systems Engineering Symposium (ISSE), 2017 IEEE International* (pp. 1-7). IEEE.

Pfisterer, D., Romer, K., Bimschas, D., Kleine, O., Mietz, R., Truong, C., ... Karnstedt, M. (2011). SPITFIRE: Toward a semantic web of things. *IEEE Communications Magazine*, *49*(11), 40–48. doi:10.1109/MCOM.2011.6069708

Rao, Y. R. (2017). Automatic smart parking system using Internet of Things (IOT). *Int. J. Eng. Tech. Sci. Res*, *4*, 2394–3386.

Roffia, L., Azzoni, P., Aguzzi, C., Viola, F., Antoniazzi, F., & Salmon Cinotti, T. (2018). Dynamic Linked Data: A SPARQL Event Processing Architecture. *Future Internet, 10*(4), 36. doi:10.3390/fi10040036

Roffia, L., Morandi, F., Kiljander, J., D'Elia, A., Vergari, F., Viola, F., ... Cinotti, T. S. (2016). A semantic publish-subscribe architecture for the Internet of Things. *IEEE Internet of Things Journal*, *3*(6), 1274–1296. doi:10.1109/JIOT.2016.2587380

Scioscia, F., & Ruta, M. (2009, September). Building a Semantic Web of Things: issues and perspectives in information compression. In *Semantic Computing, 2009. ICSC'09. IEEE International Conference on* (pp. 589-594). IEEE. 10.1109/ICSC.2009.75

Sebestyen, G., Hangan, A., Oniga, S., & Gál, Z. (2014, May). eHealth solutions in the context of Internet of Things. In *Automation, Quality and Testing, Robotics, 2014 IEEE International Conference on* (pp. 1-6). IEEE.

Serena, F., Poveda-Villalón, M., & García-Castro, R. (2017, June). Semantic Discovery in the Web of Things. In *International Conference on Web Engineering* (pp. 19-31). Springer.

Talari, S., Shafie-Khah, M., Siano, P., Loia, V., Tommasetti, A., & Catalão, J. (2017). A review of smart cities based on the internet of things concept. *Energies*, *10*(4), 421. doi:10.3390/en10040421

Turchet, L., Viola, F., Fazekas, G., & Barthet, M. (2018). Towards a Semantic Architecture for the Internet of Musical Things. In *Proceedings of the 23rd FRUCT Conference*. IEEE. 10.23919/FRUCT.2018.8587917

Vergari, F., Cinotti, T. S., D'Elia, A., Roffia, L., Zamagni, G., & Lamberti, C. (2011). An integrated framework to achieve interoperability in person-centric health management. *International Journal of Telemedicine and Applications*, *2011*, 5. doi:10.1155/2011/549282 PMID:21811499

Viola, F. (2019, April). *Semantic Web and the Web of Things: concept, platform and applications* (PhD Thesis). Advanced Research Center on Electronic Systems (ARCES), University of Bologna, Italy.

Viola, F., D'Elia, A., Korzun, D., Galov, I., Kashevnik, A., & Balandin, S. (2016, November). The M3 architecture for smart spaces: Overview of semantic information broker implementations. In *Open Innovations Association (FRUCT), 2016 19th Conference of* (pp. 264-272). IEEE.

Viola, F., D'Elia, A., Roffia, L., & Cinotti, T. (2016, November). Performance Evaluation Suite for Semantic Publish-Subscribe Message-oriented Middlewares. *Proceedings of the UBICOMM*.

Viola, F., D'Elia, A., Roffia, L., & Salmon Cinotti, T. (2016, April). A modular lightweight implementation of the Smart-M3 semantic information broker. In *Proceedings of the 18th Conference of Open Innovations Association FRUCT* (pp. 370-377). FRUCT Oy. 10.1109/FRUCT-ISPIT.2016.7561552

Viola, F., Stolfi, A., Milo, A., Ceriani, M., Barthet, M., & Fazekas, G. (2018, October). Playsound. space: enhancing a live music performance tool with semantic recommendations. In *Proceedings of the 1st International Workshop on Semantic Applications for Audio and Music* (pp. 46-53). ACM.

Viola, F., Turchet, L., Antoniazzi, F., & Fazekas, G. (2018). C Minor: a Semantic Publish/Subscribe Broker for the Internet of Musical Things. In *Proceedings of the 23rd FRUCT Conference*. IEEE.

Weiser, M. (1991). The Computer for the 21 st Century. *Scientific American*, *265*(3), 94–105. doi:10.1038cientificamerican0991-94 PMID:1675486

KEY TERMS AND DEFINITIONS

Centralized Hierarchical LUTT (CHLUTT): The third step of the evolution of the LUTT data structure to deal with subscriptions. Differently from LUTT, this is a centralized structure containing all the triple patterns of every running subscriptions. Differently from CLUTT, this is organized in a hierarchical way to reduce the space occupation.

Centralized LUTT (CLUTT): The second step of the evolution of the LUTT data structure to deal with subscriptions. Differently from LUTT, this is a centralized structure containing all the triple patterns of every running subscriptions.

Cocktail: Framework designed to simplify the creation, publication, deletion and management of a Web Thing through a set of primitives.

Context Triple Store (CTS): A CTS is one of the possible mechanisms to optimize the processing of subscriptions. If the system is using this optimization, then every SPU manages one CTS. It is a subset of the global knowledge base hosted by the broker and contains only the triples (potentially) of interest for the related subscription.

Interaction Pattern: One of the ways to interact with a Web Thing. An interaction pattern can be an action, a property or an event exposed by the Web Thing.

Internet of Things (IoT): The internetworking of physical entities represented by devices that enable these entities to collect and exchange data for a achieving a common goal.

Look-Up Triples Table (LUTT): A data structure employed by some of the Smart-M3 brokers and by SEPA to speed-up the processing of the running subscriptions after a SPARQL update.

Semantic Web of Things (SWoT): The new paradigm involving Semantic Web technologies to control devices in IoT applications.

SEPA: SPARQL Event Processing Architecture. A publish-subscribe architecture built on top of a standard SPARQL endpoint.

Smart Space: A set of communicating nodes and information storages, which has embedded logic to acquire and apply knowledge about its environment and adapt to its inhabitants in order to improve their experience in the environment.

Smart-M3: An open-source software platform that aims to provide a smart spaces infrastructure. It combines the ideas of distributed, networked systems and semantic web. The ultimate goal is to enable smart environments and linking of real and virtual worlds.

SPARQL Endpoint: A semantic database hosting an RDF knowledge base and providing read/write access through the SPARQL 1.1 protocol with SPARQL Query and SPARQL Update languages.

Subscription Processing Unit (SPU): An SPU is a process or thread devoted to the management of subscriptions in a Smart-M3 or SEPA broker.

Thing Description (TD): The profile of a Web Thing containing its description in terms of properties, events and actions.

Web of Things (WoT): The new evolution of the IoT toward the adoption of the standards that made the web popular.

Related Readings

To continue IGI Global's long-standing tradition of advancing innovation through emerging research, please find below a compiled list of recommended IGI Global book chapters and journal articles in the areas of internet of things, fog computer, and ambient intelligence. These related readings will provide additional information and guidance to further enrich your knowledge and assist you with your own research.

A., S., & Thampi, S. M. (2018). Voice Biometrics: The Promising Future of Authentication in the Internet of Things. In P. Raj, & A. Raman (Eds.), *Handbook of Research on Cloud and Fog Computing Infrastructures for Data Science* (pp. 360-389). Hershey, PA: IGI Global. doi:10.4018/978-1-5225-5972-6.ch017

Alageswaran, R., & Amali, S. M. (2018). Evolution of Fog Computing and Its Role in IoT Applications. In P. Raj & A. Raman (Eds.), *Handbook of Research on Cloud and Fog Computing Infrastructures for Data Science* (pp. 33–52). Hershey, PA: IGI Global. doi:10.4018/978-1-5225-5972-6.ch002

Almeida, F., & Monteiro, J. A. (2018). UX Challenges and Best Practices in Designing Web and Mobile Solutions. In A. Elçi (Ed.), *Handbook of Research on Contemporary Perspectives on Web-Based Systems* (pp. 68–89). Hershey, PA: IGI Global. doi:10.4018/978-1-5225-5384-7.ch004

Awad, A. Y., & Mohan, S. (2019). Internet of Things for a Smart Transportation System. *International Journal of Interdisciplinary Telecommunications and Networking*, *11*(1), 57–70. doi:10.4018/IJITN.2019010105

Balaji, V. S. (2019). Fog Computing and Its Challenges. In K. Srinivasa, P. Lathar, & G. Siddesh (Eds.), *The Rise of Fog Computing in the Digital Era* (pp. 36–52). Hershey, PA: IGI Global. doi:10.4018/978-1-5225-6070-8.ch002

Balakrishnan, P., Venkatesh, V., & Raj, P. (2018). Fog Computing: Introduction, Architecture, Analytics, and Platforms. In P. Raj & A. Raman (Eds.), *Handbook of Research on Cloud and Fog Computing Infrastructures for Data Science* (pp. 68–84). Hershey, PA: IGI Global. doi:10.4018/978-1-5225-5972-6.ch004

Bansal, A., Ahirwar, M. K., & Shukla, P. K. (2019). Assessment on Different Classification Algorithms Used in Internet of Things Applications. *International Journal of Organizational and Collective Intelligence*, *9*(1), 1–11. doi:10.4018/IJOCI.2019010101

Baranidharan, B. (2018). Internet of Things (IoT) Technologies, Architecture, Protocols, Security, and Applications: A Survey. In P. Raj & A. Raman (Eds.), *Handbook of Research on Cloud and Fog Computing Infrastructures for Data Science* (pp. 149–174). Hershey, PA: IGI Global. doi:10.4018/978-1-5225-5972-6.ch008

Behara, G. K. (2019). Big-Data-Based Architectures and Techniques: Big Data Reference Architecture. In P. Gupta, T. Ören, & M. Singh (Eds.), *Predictive Intelligence Using Big Data and the Internet of Things* (pp. 19–50). Hershey, PA: IGI Global. doi:10.4018/978-1-5225-6210-8.ch002

Ben Seghir, N., Kazar, O., & Rezeg, K. (2018). A Personalized Approach for Web Service Discovery in Distributed Environments. In A. Elçi (Ed.), *Handbook of Research on Contemporary Perspectives on Web-Based Systems* (pp. 308–339). Hershey, PA: IGI Global. doi:10.4018/978-1-5225-5384-7.ch014

Bencherif, K., Bensaber, D. A., & Malki, M. (2018). Integrating Heterogeneous Services for Semantic Mashup Construction. In A. Elçi (Ed.), *Handbook of Research on Contemporary Perspectives on Web-Based Systems* (pp. 362–386). Hershey, PA: IGI Global. doi:10.4018/978-1-5225-5384-7.ch016

Bhandari, G. P., & Gupta, R. (2019). An Overview of Cloud and Edge Computing Architecture and Its Current Issues and Challenges. In K. Munir (Ed.), *Advancing Consumer-Centric Fog Computing Architectures* (pp. 1–37). Hershey, PA: IGI Global. doi:10.4018/978-1-5225-7149-0.ch001

Bhardwaj, A., & Goundar, S. (2019). Unique Fog Computing Taxonomy for Evaluating Cloud Services. In K. Munir (Ed.), *Advancing Consumer-Centric Fog Computing Architectures* (pp. 145–162). Hershey, PA: IGI Global. doi:10.4018/978-1-5225-7149-0.ch008

Bhavsar, S. A., & Modi, K. J. (2019). Design and Development of Framework for Platform Level Issues in Fog Computing. *International Journal of Electronics, Communications, and Measurement Engineering*, *8*(1), 1–20. doi:10.4018/IJECME.2019010101

Bisht, A. K., Singh, R., Bhutiani, R., & Bhatt, A. (2019). Application of Predictive Intelligence in Water Quality Forecasting of the River Ganga Using Support Vector Machines. In P. Gupta, T. Ören, & M. Singh (Eds.), *Predictive Intelligence Using Big Data and the Internet of Things* (pp. 206–218). Hershey, PA: IGI Global. doi:10.4018/978-1-5225-6210-8.ch009

Borah, J., Sarma, K. K., & Gohain, P. J. (2019). Learning-Aided IoT Set-Up for Home Surveillance Applications. In P. Gupta, T. Ören, & M. Singh (Eds.), *Predictive Intelligence Using Big Data and the Internet of Things* (pp. 180–205). Hershey, PA: IGI Global. doi:10.4018/978-1-5225-6210-8.ch008

Brahmia, Z., Grandi, F., Oliboni, B., & Bouaziz, R. (2018). Supporting Structural Evolution of Data in Web-Based Systems via Schema Versioning in the tXSchema Framework. In A. Elçi (Ed.), *Handbook of Research on Contemporary Perspectives on Web-Based Systems* (pp. 271–307). Hershey, PA: IGI Global. doi:10.4018/978-1-5225-5384-7.ch013

Caeiro, J. J., & Martins, J. C. (2019). Water Management for Rural Environments and IoT. In P. Cardoso, J. Monteiro, J. Semião, & J. Rodrigues (Eds.), *Harnessing the Internet of Everything (IoE) for Accelerated Innovation Opportunities* (pp. 83–99). Hershey, PA: IGI Global. doi:10.4018/978-1-5225-7332-6.ch004

Cardoso, P. J., Monteiro, J., Pinto, N., Cruz, D., & Rodrigues, J. M. (2019). Application of Machine Learning Algorithms to the IoE: A Survey. In P. Cardoso, J. Monteiro, J. Semião, & J. Rodrigues (Eds.), *Harnessing the Internet of Everything (IoE) for Accelerated Innovation Opportunities* (pp. 31–56). Hershey, PA: IGI Global. doi:10.4018/978-1-5225-7332-6.ch002

Casas, S., Portalés, C., García-Pereira, I., & Gimeno, J. (2019). Mixing Different Realities in a Single Shared Space: Analysis of Mixed-Platform Collaborative Shared Spaces. In P. Cardoso, J. Monteiro, J. Semião, & J. Rodrigues (Eds.), *Harnessing the Internet of Everything (IoE) for Accelerated Innovation Opportunities* (pp. 175–192). Hershey, PA: IGI Global. doi:10.4018/978-1-5225-7332-6.ch008

Çelenk, U., Ertuğrul, D. Ç., Zontul, M., Elçi, A., & Uçan, O. N. (2018). Dynamic Quota Calculation System (DQCS): Pricing and Quota Allocation of Telecom Customers via Data Mining Approaches. In A. Elçi (Ed.), *Handbook of Research on Contemporary Perspectives on Web-Based Systems* (pp. 434–459). Hershey, PA: IGI Global. doi:10.4018/978-1-5225-5384-7.ch019

Choudhary, S., & Kesswani, N. (2019). A Survey: Intrusion Detection Techniques for Internet of Things. *International Journal of Information Security and Privacy*, *13*(1), 86–105. doi:10.4018/IJISP.2019010107

Dhanda, N., Datta, S. S., & Dhanda, M. (2019). Machine Learning Algorithms. In H. Purnomo (Ed.), *Computational Intelligence in the Internet of Things* (pp. 210–233). Hershey, PA: IGI Global. doi:10.4018/978-1-5225-7955-7.ch009

Dillon, S., Rastrick, K., Stahl, F., & Vossen, G. (2018). Using the Web While Offline: A Case Comparison. In A. Elçi (Ed.), *Handbook of Research on Contemporary Perspectives on Web-Based Systems* (pp. 108–124). Hershey, PA: IGI Global. doi:10.4018/978-1-5225-5384-7.ch006

Dinc, E., Kuscu, M., Bilgin, B. A., & Akan, O. B. (2019). Internet of Everything: A Unifying Framework Beyond Internet of Things. In P. Cardoso, J. Monteiro, J. Semião, & J. Rodrigues (Eds.), *Harnessing the Internet of Everything (IoE) for Accelerated Innovation Opportunities* (pp. 1–30). Hershey, PA: IGI Global. doi:10.4018/978-1-5225-7332-6.ch001

Duggirala, S. (2018). Fog Computing and Virtualization. In P. Raj & A. Raman (Eds.), *Handbook of Research on Cloud and Fog Computing Infrastructures for Data Science* (pp. 53–67). Hershey, PA: IGI Global. doi:10.4018/978-1-5225-5972-6.ch003

El Kassmi, I., & Jarir, Z. (2018). Measurable and Behavioral Non-Functional Requirements in Web Service Composition. In A. Elçi (Ed.), *Handbook of Research on Contemporary Perspectives on Web-Based Systems* (pp. 340–361). Hershey, PA: IGI Global. doi:10.4018/978-1-5225-5384-7.ch015

Ertuğrul, D. Ç., & Elçi, A. (2018). Educational Activity Suggestion System of Children With Pervasive Developmental Disorder for Guiding Education and Training Staff Activities. In A. Elçi (Ed.), *Handbook of Research on Contemporary Perspectives on Web-Based Systems* (pp. 142–165). Hershey, PA: IGI Global. doi:10.4018/978-1-5225-5384-7.ch008

G., R., Lathar, P., & Siddesh, G. M. (2019). Fog Computing Application Deployment and Management. In K. Srinivasa, P. Lathar, & G. Siddesh (Eds.), *The Rise of Fog Computing in the Digital Era* (pp. 68-83). Hershey, PA: IGI Global. doi:10.4018/978-1-5225-6070-8.ch004

Guleria, P., & Sood, M. (2019). Big Data Analytics: Educational Data Classification Using Hadoop-Inspired MapReduce Framework. In P. Gupta, T. Ören, & M. Singh (Eds.), *Predictive Intelligence Using Big Data and the Internet of Things* (pp. 77–108). Hershey, PA: IGI Global. doi:10.4018/978-1-5225-6210-8.ch004

Gupta, K., & Goel, A. (2018). Integrating Tagging Software in Web Application. In A. Elçi (Ed.), *Handbook of Research on Contemporary Perspectives on Web-Based Systems* (pp. 46–67). Hershey, PA: IGI Global. doi:10.4018/978-1-5225-5384-7.ch003

Gupta, R. (2019). Resource Provisioning and Scheduling Techniques of IoT Based Applications in Fog Computing. *International Journal of Fog Computing*, *2*(2), 57–70. doi:10.4018/IJFC.2019070104

Hartomo, K. D., Prasetyo, S. Y., Anwar, M. T., & Purnomo, H. D. (2019). Rainfall Prediction Model Using Exponential Smoothing Seasonal Planting Index (ESSPI) For Determination of Crop Planting Pattern. In H. Purnomo (Ed.), *Computational Intelligence in the Internet of Things* (pp. 234–255). Hershey, PA: IGI Global. doi:10.4018/978-1-5225-7955-7.ch010

Holland, J. L., & Lee, S. (2019). Internet of Everything (IoE): Eye Tracking Data Analysis. In P. Cardoso, J. Monteiro, J. Semião, & J. Rodrigues (Eds.), *Harnessing the Internet of Everything (IoE) for Accelerated Innovation Opportunities* (pp. 215–245). Hershey, PA: IGI Global. doi:10.4018/978-1-5225-7332-6.ch010

Honarvar, A. R., & Sami, A. (2018). Improve Home Energy Management System by Extracting Usage Patterns From Power Usage Big Data of Homes' Appliances. In A. Elçi (Ed.), *Handbook of Research on Contemporary Perspectives on Web-Based Systems* (pp. 126–141). Hershey, PA: IGI Global. doi:10.4018/978-1-5225-5384-7.ch007

Hossain, K., Rahman, M., & Roy, S. (2019). IoT Data Compression and Optimization Techniques in Cloud Storage: Current Prospects and Future Directions. *International Journal of Cloud Applications and Computing*, *9*(2), 43–59. doi:10.4018/IJCAC.2019040103

Hudaib, A., & Albdour, L. (2019). Fog Computing to Serve the Internet of Things Applications: A Patient Monitoring System. *International Journal of Fog Computing*, *2*(2), 44–56. doi:10.4018/IJFC.2019070103

Hussain, M. M., & Beg, M. S. (2019). Using Vehicles as Fog Infrastructures for Transportation Cyber-Physical Systems (T-CPS): Fog Computing for Vehicular Networks. *International Journal of Software Science and Computational Intelligence*, *11*(1), 47–69. doi:10.4018/IJSSCI.2019010104

Hussain, M. M., Beg, M. S., Alam, M. S., & Laskar, S. H. (2019). Big Data Analytics Platforms for Electric Vehicle Integration in Transport Oriented Smart Cities: Computing Platforms for Platforms for Electric Vehicle Integration in Smart Cities. *International Journal of Digital Crime and Forensics*, *11*(3), 23–42. doi:10.4018/IJDCF.2019070102

Izosimov, V., & Törngren, M. (2019). Security Awareness in the Internet of Everything. In P. Cardoso, J. Monteiro, J. Semião, & J. Rodrigues (Eds.), *Harnessing the Internet of Everything (IoE) for Accelerated Innovation Opportunities* (pp. 272–301). Hershey, PA: IGI Global. doi:10.4018/978-1-5225-7332-6.ch012

Jamal, D. N., Rajkumar, S., & Ameen, N. (2018). Remote Elderly Health Monitoring System Using Cloud-Based WBANs. In P. Raj & A. Raman (Eds.), *Handbook of Research on Cloud and Fog Computing Infrastructures for Data Science* (pp. 265–288). Hershey, PA: IGI Global. doi:10.4018/978-1-5225-5972-6.ch013

Jayanthiladevi, A., Surendararavindhan, & Sakthivel, (2018). Fast Data vs. Big Data With IoT Streaming Analytics and the Future Applications. In P. Raj, & A. Raman (Eds.), Handbook of Research on Cloud and Fog Computing Infrastructures for Data Science (pp. 344-359). Hershey, PA: IGI Global. doi:10.4018/978-1-5225-5972-6.ch016

Jayanthiladevi, A., Murugan, S., & Manivel, K. (2018). Text, Images, and Video Analytics for Fog Computing. In P. Raj & A. Raman (Eds.), *Handbook of Research on Cloud and Fog Computing Infrastructures for Data Science* (pp. 390–410). Hershey, PA: IGI Global. doi:10.4018/978-1-5225-5972-6.ch018

Jeba, J. A., Roy, S., Rashid, M. O., Atik, S. T., & Whaiduzzaman, M. (2019). Towards Green Cloud Computing an Algorithmic Approach for Energy Minimization in Cloud Data Centers. *International Journal of Cloud Applications and Computing*, *9*(1), 59–81. doi:10.4018/IJCAC.2019010105

Kakulapati, V., & Mahender Reddy, S. (2019). Improved Usability of IOT Devices in Healthcare Using Big Data Analysis. In P. Gupta, T. Ören, & M. Singh (Eds.), *Predictive Intelligence Using Big Data and the Internet of Things* (pp. 110–127). Hershey, PA: IGI Global. doi:10.4018/978-1-5225-6210-8.ch005

Kashyap, R. (2019). Deep Learning: An Application in Internet of Things. In H. Purnomo (Ed.), *Computational Intelligence in the Internet of Things* (pp. 130–158). Hershey, PA: IGI Global. doi:10.4018/978-1-5225-7955-7.ch006

Kasnesis, P., Kogias, D. G., Toumanidis, L., Xevgenis, M. G., Patrikakis, C. Z., Giunta, G., & Calsi, G. L. (2019). An IoE Architecture for the Preservation of the Cultural Heritage: The STORM Use Case. In P. Cardoso, J. Monteiro, J. Semião, & J. Rodrigues (Eds.), *Harnessing the Internet of Everything (IoE) for Accelerated Innovation Opportunities* (pp. 193–214). Hershey, PA: IGI Global. doi:10.4018/978-1-5225-7332-6.ch009

Kaur, R., Verma, K., Jain, S. K., & Kesswani, N. (2019). Efficient Routing Protocol for Location Privacy Preserving in Internet of Things. *International Journal of Information Security and Privacy*, *13*(1), 70–85. doi:10.4018/IJISP.2019010106

Kaushik, S., & Gandhi, C. (2019). Fog vs. Cloud Computing Architecture. In K. Munir (Ed.), *Advancing Consumer-Centric Fog Computing Architectures* (pp. 87–110). Hershey, PA: IGI Global. doi:10.4018/978-1-5225-7149-0.ch005

Kaushik, S., & Gandhi, C. (2019). Fog/Cloud Service Scalability, Composition, Security, Privacy, and SLA Management. In K. Munir (Ed.), *Advancing Consumer-Centric Fog Computing Architectures* (pp. 38–62). Hershey, PA: IGI Global. doi:10.4018/978-1-5225-7149-0.ch002

Khanum, N. K., Lathar, P., & Siddesh, G. M. (2019). Confidentiality and Safekeeping Problems and Techniques in Fog Computing. In K. Srinivasa, P. Lathar, & G. Siddesh (Eds.), *The Rise of Fog Computing in the Digital Era* (pp. 84–107). Hershey, PA: IGI Global. doi:10.4018/978-1-5225-6070-8.ch005

Kitanov, S., & Janevski, T. (2019). Introduction to Fog Computing. In K. Srinivasa, P. Lathar, & G. Siddesh (Eds.), *The Rise of Fog Computing in the Digital Era* (pp. 1–35). Hershey, PA: IGI Global. doi:10.4018/978-1-5225-6070-8.ch001

Lamia, M., & Mohamed, H. (2018). Development of Adaptive Social Network Based on Learners' Thinking and Learning Styles. In A. Elçi (Ed.), *Handbook of Research on Contemporary Perspectives on Web-Based Systems* (pp. 90–107). Hershey, PA: IGI Global. doi:10.4018/978-1-5225-5384-7.ch005

Lathar, P., Srinivasa, K. G., Kumar, A., & Siddiqui, N. (2018). Comparison Study of Different NoSQL and Cloud Paradigm for Better Data Storage Technology. In P. Raj & A. Raman (Eds.), *Handbook of Research on Cloud and Fog Computing Infrastructures for Data Science* (pp. 312–343). Hershey, PA: IGI Global. doi:10.4018/978-1-5225-5972-6.ch015

M., D. N., Kousalya, G., P., B., & Raj, P. (2018). Fuzzy-Logic-Based Decision Engine for Offloading IoT Application Using Fog Computing. In P. Raj, & A. Raman (Eds.), *Handbook of Research on Cloud and Fog Computing Infrastructures for Data Science* (pp. 175-194). Hershey, PA: IGI Global. doi:10.4018/978-1-5225-5972-6.ch009

Marques, G. (2019). Ambient Assisted Living and Internet of Things. In P. Cardoso, J. Monteiro, J. Semião, & J. Rodrigues (Eds.), *Harnessing the Internet of Everything (IoE) for Accelerated Innovation Opportunities* (pp. 100–115). Hershey, PA: IGI Global. doi:10.4018/978-1-5225-7332-6.ch005

McKenna, H. P. (2019). *Ambient Urbanities as the Intersection Between the IoT and the IoP in Smart Cities* (pp. 1–333). Hershey, PA: IGI Global. doi:10.4018/978-1-5225-7882-6

Megdadi, K., Akkaya, M., & Sari, A. (2018). Internet of Things and Smart City Initiatives in Middle Eastern Countries. In P. Raj & A. Raman (Eds.), *Handbook of Research on Cloud and Fog Computing Infrastructures for Data Science* (pp. 289–311). Hershey, PA: IGI Global. doi:10.4018/978-1-5225-5972-6.ch014

Meigal, A. Y., Korzun, D. G., Gerasimova-Meigal, L. I., Borodin, A. V., & Zavyalova, Y. V. (2019). Ambient Intelligence At-Home Laboratory for Human Everyday Life. *International Journal of Embedded and Real-Time Communication Systems*, *10*(2), 117–134. doi:10.4018/IJERTCS.2019040108

Mekouar, S. (2018). Social Network Analysis: Basic Concepts, Tools, and Applications. In A. Elçi (Ed.), *Handbook of Research on Contemporary Perspectives on Web-Based Systems* (pp. 388–415). Hershey, PA: IGI Global. doi:10.4018/978-1-5225-5384-7.ch017

Mohanasundaram, R., Jayanthiladevi, A., & G., K. (2018). Software-Defined Cloud Infrastructure. In P. Raj, & A. Raman (Eds.), *Handbook of Research on Cloud and Fog Computing Infrastructures for Data Science* (pp. 108-123). Hershey, PA: IGI Global. doi:10.4018/978-1-5225-5972-6.ch006

Moharir, M., & Patil, B. R. (2019). Fog Computing and Networking Architectures. In K. Srinivasa, P. Lathar, & G. Siddesh (Eds.), *The Rise of Fog Computing in the Digital Era* (pp. 53–67). Hershey, PA: IGI Global. doi:10.4018/978-1-5225-6070-8.ch003

Mohsin, A., & Yellampalli, S. S. (2019). IoT-Based Cold Chain Logistics Monitoring. In P. Gupta, T. Ören, & M. Singh (Eds.), *Predictive Intelligence Using Big Data and the Internet of Things* (pp. 144–179). Hershey, PA: IGI Global. doi:10.4018/978-1-5225-6210-8.ch007

Mounir, A., Adel, A., Makhlouf, D., Sébastien, L., & Philippe, R. (2019). A New Two-Level Clustering Approach for Situations Management in Distributed Smart Environments. *International Journal of Ambient Computing and Intelligence*, *10*(2), 91–111. doi:10.4018/IJACI.2019040107

Mukherjee, S., Bhattacharjee, A. K., Bhattacharya, D., & Ghosal, M. (2019). Analysis of Industrial and Household IoT Data Using Computationally Intelligent Algorithm. In H. Purnomo (Ed.), *Computational Intelligence in the Internet of Things* (pp. 25–48). Hershey, PA: IGI Global. doi:10.4018/978-1-5225-7955-7.ch002

Munir, K., & Mohammed, L. A. (2019). Comparing User Authentication Techniques for Fog Computing. In K. Munir (Ed.), *Advancing Consumer-Centric Fog Computing Architectures* (pp. 111–125). Hershey, PA: IGI Global. doi:10.4018/978-1-5225-7149-0.ch006

Munir, K., & Mohammed, L. A. (2019). Secure Data Integrity Protocol for Fog Computing Environment. In K. Munir (Ed.), *Advancing Consumer-Centric Fog Computing Architectures* (pp. 126–144). Hershey, PA: IGI Global. doi:10.4018/978-1-5225-7149-0.ch007

Murthy, J. S. (2019). EdgeCloud: A Distributed Management System for Resource Continuity in Edge to Cloud Computing Environment. In K. Srinivasa, P. Lathar, & G. Siddesh (Eds.), *The Rise of Fog Computing in the Digital Era* (pp. 108–128). Hershey, PA: IGI Global. doi:10.4018/978-1-5225-6070-8.ch006

Muthusamy, M., & Periasamy, K. (2019). A Comprehensive Study on Internet of Things Security: Challenges and Recommendations. In K. Munir (Ed.), *Advancing Consumer-Centric Fog Computing Architectures* (pp. 72–86). Hershey, PA: IGI Global. doi:10.4018/978-1-5225-7149-0.ch004

Mwashita, W., & Odhiambo, M. O. (2019). Interference Management Techniques for Device-to-Device Communications. In P. Gupta, T. Ören, & M. Singh (Eds.), *Predictive Intelligence Using Big Data and the Internet of Things* (pp. 219–245). Hershey, PA: IGI Global. doi:10.4018/978-1-5225-6210-8.ch010

Narayanasamy, S. K., & Muruganantham, D. (2018). Effective Entity Linking and Disambiguation Algorithms for User-Generated Content (UGC). In A. Elçi (Ed.), *Handbook of Research on Contemporary Perspectives on Web-Based Systems* (pp. 416–433). Hershey, PA: IGI Global. doi:10.4018/978-1-5225-5384-7.ch018

Naresh, E., Vijaya Kumar, B. P., Hampiholi, A., & Jeevan, B. (2019). Software Engineering in Internet of Things. In K. Srinivasa, P. Lathar, & G. Siddesh (Eds.), *The Rise of Fog Computing in the Digital Era* (pp. 157–176). Hershey, PA: IGI Global. doi:10.4018/978-1-5225-6070-8.ch008

Nisha Angeline, C. V., & Lavanya, R. (2019). Fog Computing and Its Role in the Internet of Things. In K. Munir (Ed.), *Advancing Consumer-Centric Fog Computing Architectures* (pp. 63–71). Hershey, PA: IGI Global. doi:10.4018/978-1-5225-7149-0.ch003

Ougouti, N. S., Belbachir, H., & Amghar, Y. (2018). Proposition of a New Ontology-Based P2P System for Semantic Integration of Heterogeneous Data Sources. In A. Elçi (Ed.), Handbook of Research on Contemporary Perspectives on Web-Based Systems (pp. 240-270). Hershey, PA: IGI Global. doi:10.4018/978-1-5225-5384-7.ch012

P., A. (2018). Data Mining Algorithms and Techniques. In P. Raj, & A. Raman (Eds.), *Handbook of Research on Cloud and Fog Computing Infrastructures for Data Science* (pp. 195-208). Hershey, PA: IGI Global. doi:10.4018/978-1-5225-5972-6.ch010

P., A. (2018). Machine Learning. In P. Raj, & A. Raman (Eds.), *Handbook of Research on Cloud and Fog Computing Infrastructures for Data Science* (pp. 209-230). Hershey, PA: IGI Global. doi:10.4018/978-1-5225-5972-6.ch011

Pal, K. (2019). Quality Assurance Issues for Big Data Applications in Supply Chain Management. In P. Gupta, T. Ören, & M. Singh (Eds.), *Predictive Intelligence Using Big Data and the Internet of Things* (pp. 51–76). Hershey, PA: IGI Global. doi:10.4018/978-1-5225-6210-8.ch003

Papadopoulou, P., Kolomvatsos, K., & Hadjiefthymiades, S. (2019). Enhancing E-Government With Internet of Things. In H. Purnomo (Ed.), *Computational Intelligence in the Internet of Things* (pp. 110–129). Hershey, PA: IGI Global. doi:10.4018/978-1-5225-7955-7.ch005

Patel, D. T. (2019). Distributed Computing for Internet of Things (IoT). In H. Purnomo (Ed.), *Computational Intelligence in the Internet of Things* (pp. 84–109). Hershey, PA: IGI Global. doi:10.4018/978-1-5225-7955-7.ch004

Phu, V. N., & Tran, V. T. (2019). Neural Network for Big Data Sets. In H. Purnomo (Ed.), *Computational Intelligence in the Internet of Things* (pp. 271–303). Hershey, PA: IGI Global. doi:10.4018/978-1-5225-7955-7.ch012

Pinto, N., Cruz, D., Monteiro, J., Cabrita, C., Semião, J., Cardoso, P. J., ... Rodrigues, J. M. (2019). IoE-Based Control and Monitoring of Electrical Grids: A Smart Grid's Perspective. In P. Cardoso, J. Monteiro, J. Semião, & J. Rodrigues (Eds.), *Harnessing the Internet of Everything (IoE) for Accelerated Innovation Opportunities* (pp. 57–82). Hershey, PA: IGI Global. doi:10.4018/978-1-5225-7332-6.ch003

Portalés, C., Casas, S., & Kreuzer, K. (2019). Challenges and Trends in Home Automation: Addressing the Interoperability Problem With the Open-Source Platform OpenHAB. In P. Cardoso, J. Monteiro, J. Semião, & J. Rodrigues (Eds.), *Harnessing the Internet of Everything (IoE) for Accelerated Innovation Opportunities* (pp. 148–174). Hershey, PA: IGI Global. doi:10.4018/978-1-5225-7332-6.ch007

Pradhan, R., & Sharma, D. K. (2018). TempClass: Implicit Temporal Queries Classifier. In A. Elçi (Ed.), *Handbook of Research on Contemporary Perspectives on Web-Based Systems* (pp. 188–212). Hershey, PA: IGI Global. doi:10.4018/978-1-5225-5384-7.ch010

R., M., R., D., Sulthana, R., & N., K. (2018). A Comprehensive Survey of IoT Edge/Fog Computing Protocols. In P. Raj, & A. Raman (Eds.), *Handbook of Research on Cloud and Fog Computing Infrastructures for Data Science* (pp. 85-107). Hershey, PA: IGI Global. doi:10.4018/978-1-5225-5972-6.ch005

Raj, P., & J., P. (2018). Expounding the Edge/Fog Computing Infrastructures for Data Science. In P. Raj, & A. Raman (Eds.), *Handbook of Research on Cloud and Fog Computing Infrastructures for Data Science* (pp. 1-32). Hershey, PA: IGI Global. doi:10.4018/978-1-5225-5972-6.ch001

Rodge, J., & Jaiswal, S. (2019). Comprehensive Overview of Neural Networks and Its Applications in Autonomous Vehicles. In H. Purnomo (Ed.), *Computational Intelligence in the Internet of Things* (pp. 159–173). Hershey, PA: IGI Global. doi:10.4018/978-1-5225-7955-7.ch007

Sah, A., Bhadula, S. J., Dumka, A., & Rawat, S. (2018). A Software Engineering Perspective for Development of Enterprise Applications. In A. Elçi (Ed.), *Handbook of Research on Contemporary Perspectives on Web-Based Systems* (pp. 1–23). Hershey, PA: IGI Global. doi:10.4018/978-1-5225-5384-7.ch001

Sah, A., Dumka, A., & Rawat, S. (2018). Web Technology Systems Integration Using SOA and Web Services. In A. Elçi (Ed.), *Handbook of Research on Contemporary Perspectives on Web-Based Systems* (pp. 24–45). Hershey, PA: IGI Global. doi:10.4018/978-1-5225-5384-7.ch002

Sarhan, A. (2019). Cloud-Based IoT Platform: Challenges and Applied Solutions. In P. Cardoso, J. Monteiro, J. Semião, & J. Rodrigues (Eds.), *Harnessing the Internet of Everything (IoE) for Accelerated Innovation Opportunities* (pp. 116–147). Hershey, PA: IGI Global. doi:10.4018/978-1-5225-7332-6.ch006

Savin, S. (2019). Motion Planning Method for In-Pipe Walking Robots Using Height Maps and CNN-Based Pipe Branches Detector. In H. Purnomo (Ed.), *Computational Intelligence in the Internet of Things* (pp. 1–24). Hershey, PA: IGI Global. doi:10.4018/978-1-5225-7955-7.ch001

Segall, R. S., Cook, J. S., & Niu, G. (2019). Overview of Big Data-Intensive Storage and its Technologies for Cloud and Fog Computing. *International Journal of Fog Computing*, *2*(1), 74–113. doi:10.4018/IJFC.2019010104

Sekhar, S. R., Bysani, S. S., & Kiranmai, V. P. (2019). Security and Privacy Issues in IoT: A Platform for Fog Computing. In K. Srinivasa, P. Lathar, & G. Siddesh (Eds.), *The Rise of Fog Computing in the Digital Era* (pp. 129–156). Hershey, PA: IGI Global. doi:10.4018/978-1-5225-6070-8.ch007

Semião, J., Cabral, R., Cavalaria, H., Santos, M., Teixeira, I. C., & Teixeira, J. P. (2019). Ultra-Low-Power Strategy for Reliable IoE Nanoscale Integrated Circuits. In P. Cardoso, J. Monteiro, J. Semião, & J. Rodrigues (Eds.), *Harnessing the Internet of Everything (IoE) for Accelerated Innovation Opportunities* (pp. 246–271). Hershey, PA: IGI Global. doi:10.4018/978-1-5225-7332-6.ch011

Shah, J. L., Bhat, H. F., & Khan, A. I. (2019). CloudIoT: Towards Seamless and Secure Integration of Cloud Computing With Internet of Things. *International Journal of Digital Crime and Forensics*, *11*(3), 1–22. doi:10.4018/IJDCF.2019070101

Shetty, C., Sowmya, B. J., Anemish, S., & Seema, S. (2019). IOT and Data Analytics Solution for Reducing Pollution, Accidents, and Its Impact on Environment. In K. Srinivasa, P. Lathar, & G. Siddesh (Eds.), *The Rise of Fog Computing in the Digital Era* (pp. 177–209). Hershey, PA: IGI Global. doi:10.4018/978-1-5225-6070-8.ch009

Singh, D., Mishra, M., & Sahana, S. (2019). Big-Data-Based Techniques for Predictive Intelligence. In P. Gupta, T. Ören, & M. Singh (Eds.), *Predictive Intelligence Using Big Data and the Internet of Things* (pp. 1–18). Hershey, PA: IGI Global. doi:10.4018/978-1-5225-6210-8.ch001

Singh, M., Kant, U., Gupta, P. K., & Srivastava, V. M. (2019). Cloud-Based Predictive Intelligence and Its Security Model. In P. Gupta, T. Ören, & M. Singh (Eds.), *Predictive Intelligence Using Big Data and the Internet of Things* (pp. 128–143). Hershey, PA: IGI Global. doi:10.4018/978-1-5225-6210-8.ch006

Sinha, K., Paul, P., & Amritanjali. (2019). Network Security Approaches in Distributed Environment. In H. Purnomo (Ed.), *Computational Intelligence in the Internet of Things* (pp. 174-209). Hershey, PA: IGI Global. doi:10.4018/978-1-5225-7955-7.ch008

Sowmya, B. J., Shetty, C., Cholappagol, N. V., & Seema, S. (2019). IOT and Data Analytics Solution for Smart Agriculture. In K. Srinivasa, P. Lathar, & G. Siddesh (Eds.), *The Rise of Fog Computing in the Digital Era* (pp. 210–237). Hershey, PA: IGI Global. doi:10.4018/978-1-5225-6070-8.ch010

Surendar, A. (2019). Computer Forensic Investigation in Cloud of Things. In H. Purnomo (Ed.), *Computational Intelligence in the Internet of Things* (pp. 256–270). Hershey, PA: IGI Global. doi:10.4018/978-1-5225-7955-7.ch011

Suresh, P., Koteeswaran, S., Malarvizhi, N., & Aswathy, R. H. (2018). Internet of Things (IoT): A Study on Key Elements, Protocols, Application, Research Challenges, and Fog Computing. In P. Raj & A. Raman (Eds.), *Handbook of Research on Cloud and Fog Computing Infrastructures for Data Science* (pp. 124–148). Hershey, PA: IGI Global. doi:10.4018/978-1-5225-5972-6.ch007

Thilagamani, S., Jayanthiladevi, A., & Arunkumar, N. (2018). Data Mining Algorithms, Fog Computing. In P. Raj & A. Raman (Eds.), *Handbook of Research on Cloud and Fog Computing Infrastructures for Data Science* (pp. 231–264). Hershey, PA: IGI Global. doi:10.4018/978-1-5225-5972-6.ch012

Tiwari, A., & Sharma, R. M. (2019). Realm Towards Service Optimization in Fog Computing. *International Journal of Fog Computing*, *2*(2), 13–43. doi:10.4018/IJFC.2019070102

Turcu, C. E., & Turcu, C. O. (2018). New Perspectives on Sustainable Healthcare Delivery Through Web of Things. In A. Elçi (Ed.), *Handbook of Research on Contemporary Perspectives on Web-Based Systems* (pp. 166–187). Hershey, PA: IGI Global. doi:10.4018/978-1-5225-5384-7.ch009

Vourgidis, I. S., Carter, J., Maglaras, L., Janicke, H., Folia, Z., & Fragkou, P. (2018). A Novel Method for Calculating Customer Reviews Ratings. In A. Elçi (Ed.), *Handbook of Research on Contemporary Perspectives on Web-Based Systems* (pp. 460–478). Hershey, PA: IGI Global. doi:10.4018/978-1-5225-5384-7.ch020

Wahyono, T., & Heryadi, Y. (2019). Machine Learning Applications for Anomaly Detection. In H. Purnomo (Ed.), *Computational Intelligence in the Internet of Things* (pp. 49–83). Hershey, PA: IGI Global. doi:10.4018/978-1-5225-7955-7.ch003

Wang, T. (2019). Key Technology for Intelligent Interaction Based on Internet of Things. *International Journal of Distributed Systems and Technologies, 10*(1), 25–36. doi:10.4018/IJDST.2019010103

Wittke, C., Lehniger, K., Weidling, S., & Schoelzel, M. (2019). Securing Over-the-Air Code Updates in Wireless Sensor Networks. In P. Cardoso, J. Monteiro, J. Semião, & J. Rodrigues (Eds.), *Harnessing the Internet of Everything (IoE) for Accelerated Innovation Opportunities* (pp. 302–328). Hershey, PA: IGI Global. doi:10.4018/978-1-5225-7332-6.ch013

Zahaf, A., & Malki, M. (2018). Methods for Ontology Alignment Change. In A. Elçi (Ed.), *Handbook of Research on Contemporary Perspectives on Web-Based Systems* (pp. 214–239). Hershey, PA: IGI Global. doi:10.4018/978-1-5225-5384-7.ch011

About the Authors

Dmitry Korzun received his B.Sc. (1997) and M.Sc. (1999) degrees in Applied Mathematics and Computer Science from the Petrozavodsk State University (PetrSU, Russia). He received a Ph.D. degree in Physics and Mathematics from the St.-Petersburg State University (Russia) in 2002. He is an Associate Professor at Department of Computer Science of PetrSU (since 2003 and ongoing). He was Visiting Research Scientist at the Helsinki Institute for Information Technology HIIT, Aalto University, Finland (2005-2014). In 2014-2016 he performed the duties of Vice-dean for Research at Faculty of Mathematics and Information Technology of PetrSU. Since 2014 he has acted as Leading Research Scientist at PetrSU, originating research and development activity within fundamental and applied research projects on emerging topics in ubiquitous computing, smart spaces, and Internet technology. Dmitry Korzun serves on technical program committees and editorial boards of a number of international conferences and journals. His research interests include modeling and evaluation of distributed systems, mathematical modeling and concept engineering of cyber-physical systems, ubiquitous computing and smart spaces, Internet of Things and its applications, software engineering and programming methods, algorithm design and complexity, linear Diophantine analysis and its applications, theory of formal languages and parsing. His educational activity started in 1997 at the Faculty of Mathematics of PetrSU (now Institute of Mathematics and Information Technology). Since that time he has taught more than 25 study courses on hot topics in Computer Science, Applied Mathematics, Information and Communication Technology, and Software Engineering. He is an author and co-author of more than 150 research and educational publications.

Ekaterina Balandina received her Dipl.-Ing. (2011) and M.Sc. (2013) degrees in Mathematical Provision and Administration of Information Systems. In 2010 Ekaterina won personal Presidential scholar for studies abroad and started her PhD studies at University of Oulu. Later she moved to the Tampere University of Technology, where she is currently finalizing the dissertation. Her research interests include intelligent networks, smart spaces, Internet of Things, location-aware solutions, and protocol design. She is an author of over 25 research publications.

Alexey Kashevnik received his B.Sc. (2003) and M.Sc (2005) degrees in Automated Systems for Information Processing and Control from the Peter the Great St.Petersburg Polytechnic University (POLYTECH, Russia). He received a Ph.D. degree in Technical Science from the St.Petersburg Institute for Informatics and Automation of the Russian Academy of Sciences (SPIIRAS, Russia) in 2008. He is a Senior Researcher at the Laboratory of Computer Aided Integrated Systems (since 2003) and an Associate Professor (since 2014) at the Saint Petersburg National Research University of Information Technologies, Mechanics and Optics (ITMO University, Russia). He is part-time Associate Professor at the Department of Computer Science of PetrSU (since 2012). Alexey Kashevnik is an associate editor of the International Journal of Embedded and Real-Time Communication Systems (IJERTCS); advisory board member in Association of Open Innovations FRUCT; Expert of Russian Science Foundation; Expert of National Center of Science and Technology Evaluation JSC, Republic of Kazakhstan, and serves on technical program committees and editorial boards of a number of international conferences. His research interests include smart spaces, Internet of Things, service-based systems, knowledge and context management, ontologies, user profiling, competency management, robotics systems. He is an author and co-author of more than 200 research and educational publications.

Sergey Balandin received his M.Sc. degrees in Computer Science from St.-Petersburg Electro-Technical University "LETI" (Russia, 1999) and in Telecommunications from Lappeenranta University of Technology (Finland, 2000). In 2003 graduated from PhD School of Nokia Research Center and got PhD degree in Telecommunications and Control Theory from St.-Petersburg Electro Technical University "LETI". In 2012 Sergey got MBA degree in Finland. He is a founder and president of FRUCT Association and Adjunct Professor at the Tampere University of Technology. In 1999-2011 Sergey Balandin worked for Nokia Research Center, his last position was Principal Scientist of Ubiquities Architectures team. Sergey is IARIA Fellow, Editor-in-Chief of International Journal of Embedded and Real-Time Communication Systems (IJERTCS), invited Professor at ITMO University, and author of over 100 papers and 29 international patents. He also holds expert position in various organizations and international programs, including, EURIPIDES[2], Skolkovo Foundation, Russian Academy of Science, National State Scientific Center of Kazakhstan, etc. He co-edited several books published in LNCS, IEEE Xplore and IGI. His current research interests include various aspects of Smart Spaces, network and services performance evaluation, and Internet of Things.

Fabio Viola was born in Lecce, Italy, in 1986. He received the Bachelor's degree in Information Engineering from the University of Salento, Lecce, Italy, in 2011, and the Master's degree and a PhD in Computer Science Engineering from the University of Bologna, Bologna, Italy, respectively in 2014 and 2019. His current research interests include semantic technologies for the Internet and Web of Things, Dynamic Linked Data and Big Data architectures.

Index